D1274660

ENERGY AND
THE IMAGINATION

ENERGY AND THE IMAGINATION

A Study of the Development of Blake's Thought

BY

MORTON D. PALEY

OXFORD
AT THE CLARENDON PRESS
1970

Oxford University Press, Ely House, London W. 1

GLASGOW NEW YORK TORONTO MELBOURNE WELLINGTON
CAPE TOWN SALISBURY IBADAN NAIROBI DAR ES SALAAM LUSAKA ADDIS ABABA
BOMBAY CALCUTTA MADRAS KARACHI LAHORE DACCA
KUALA LUMPUR SINGAPORE HONG KONG TOKYO

PRINTED IN GREAT BRITAIN
AT THE UNIVERSITY PRESS, OXFORD
BY VIVIAN RIDLER
PRINTER TO THE UNIVERSITY

FOR MY PARENTS

GEORGE AND AUGUSTA PALEY

AND MY BROTHER ALAN

Preface

THIS book proposes to study the thought of William Blake as it developed from the works of his early maturity through his great culminating statement, *Jerusalem*. I have tried to see Blake in his time, and as having a deliberately chosen relationship to certain intellectual and literary traditions of the past. The principal aim is not the tracing of specific sources, but the provision of a background against which the unique figure of Blake stands more clearly outlined. For reasons that will, I hope, become evident in the course of exposition, I have focused on two concepts, Energy and the Imagination, and have tried to show how these were defined in the several phases of Blake's thought. Too often Blake's 'system' has been taken as consistent throughout his works, evolving with teleological certainty from the early lyrics through the late epics. I have not made such an assumption but have tried to show how the development of Blake's thought is embodied in the symbolism of his poetry and painting. I do not wish, however, to suggest that there were two or more distinctly different Blakes or that the later Blake is in every way opposite to the earlier one. William Blake lived a long and mentally vigorous life; it would indeed be strange if his ideas had not developed and changed in response to experience.

In writing this book, I have incurred obligations which it is a pleasure to acknowledge: the greatest of these are to Professor S. Foster Damon, under whom I was lucky enough to study Blake at Brown University; Professor Lionel Trilling, who supervised my Columbia University dissertation on Blake with patience and rigour; and Professor David V. Erdman, who has generously shared some of his knowledge of Blake with me over the past few years. The errors and inadequacies of this book are entirely my own, but without such help there would have been many more of them. I am also grateful for information or criticism

Preface

received from Gerald E. Bentley, Jr., Carl Ray Woodring, Josephine Miles, Anne T. Kostelanetz, Barbara LeBihan, Suzanne R. Hoover, Ulrich C. Knoepflmacher, Geoffrey Carnall, Michael Nagler, and Joel Miles Porte.

I am also indebted to the librarians of the University of California, Columbia University, Brown University, the City University of New York, the Pierpont Morgan Library, the Houghton Library, the Henry E. Huntington Library, and the New York Public Library; to William Van Devanter, Curator of the Paul Mellon Collection; to the British Museum Library, Department of Manuscripts, and Department of Prints and Drawings; and to Martin Butlin of the Tate Gallery. I wish to thank Amy Tsuji for bibliographic assistance and Roger Carson Price for typing the manuscript.

While working on this book, I have had the advantage of annual research grants, a Summer Faculty Fellowship, and a Humanities Research appointment from the University of California, Berkeley. For this generous assistance, I am grateful to the Committee on Research and the Chancellor of the Berkeley campus, and to the Regents of the University.

Parts of this book incorporate material revised from three published articles: 'The Female Babe and "The Mental Traveller"', *Studies in Romanticism*, i (1962), 97–104; 'Method and Meaning in Blake's *Book of Ahania*', *BNYPL*, lxx (1966), 27–33; and 'Tyger of Wrath', *PMLA*, lxxxi (1966), 540–51. My thanks to the editors of these journals for permission to include versions of these articles.

Berkeley, California   M.D.P.

January 1968

Textual Note

THE editions of Blake most frequently cited in this study are abbreviated as follows:

E = David V. Erdman, ed. *The Poetry and Prose of William Blake*. Commentary by Harold Bloom. Garden City, N.Y.: Doubleday, 1965.

K = Geoffrey Keynes, ed. *The Complete Writings of William Blake*, with Variant Readings. London: Oxford University Press, 1966.

M = H. M. Margoliouth, ed. *William Blake's Vala*, Blake's Numbered Text. Oxford: Clarendon Press, 1956.

B = Gerald E. Bentley, Jr., ed. *Vala or The Four Zoas*, A Facsimile of the Manuscript, a Transcript of the Poem, and a Study of Its Growth and Significance. Oxford: Clarendon Press, 1963.

The Keynes and Erdman editions each present certain advantages and certain disadvantages, depending on one's purposes. Mine required having the texts of Blake's poems in exactly the form in which he wrote them or etched them, rather than a normalized version; therefore I have generally used E. However, as E does not include all the letters and it seemed needlessly complicated to quote different letters from different texts, I have drawn on K for these. M has been used for *Vala* in Chapter 5 for the reason indicated there. B was consulted frequently for *The Four Zoas*, but owing to its variety of type faces, it is difficult to use it for citations, and therefore E is the cited text there also, with variations in B indicated. For Blake's longer poems the method of citation is: plate or manuscript page number, followed by line number, and then by page number in the edition used. For example, '*Jerusalem*, 96 : 1–10, E 253' refers to Plate 96, lines 1–10, on page 253 of the Erdman edition. In quoted passages, I have used the editorial symbols of E: italics within square brackets indicate words deleted or erased; words within angle brackets are additions; words or letters in roman type within square brackets indicate editorial insertions.

The two Nights VII of *The Four Zoas* are indicated differently in the several editions. The Night that I call 'VIIa' is VII[a] in E; VII in K, VII in M, VIIa in B. My 'VIIb' is VII[b] in E and in K VII *bis* in M, and VIIb in B.

For quotations from Shakespeare, I have used *The Complete Works of Shakespeare*, ed. Hardin Craig (Chicago: Scott, Foresman, 1951). For quotations from Milton, the text is *The Works of John Milton*, ed. Frank Allen Patterson, 18 vols. (New York: Columbia, 1931–8). The periodical abbreviations follow the *MLA Style Sheet*.

Contents

List of Plates

1

The Sublime of Energy

It was disgusting to Keck to see a strip of a fellow, with
light curls round his head, get up and speechify by the hour
against institutions 'which had existed when he was in his
cradle.' And in a leading article of the 'Trumpet,' Keck
characterised Ladislaw's speech at a Reform meeting as
'the violence of an energumen. . . .'

'That was a rattling article yesterday, Keck,' said Dr.
Sprague, with satirical intentions. 'But what is an energumen?'

'Oh, a term that came up in the French Revolution,'
said Keck.

GEORGE ELIOT: *Middlemarch*

THE study of Blake's thought begins with *The Marriage of
Heaven and Hell*. Before 1790, the year in which work on
this book of twenty-seven etched plates was begun, Blake had
made several fragmentary statements about the nature of his
beliefs—in passages of *Tiriel* (1789), which remained in
manuscript; in marginalia to books by Johann Caspar
Lavater and Emmanuel Swedenborg; and in the three short
tractates *There Is No Natural Religion* and *All Religions Are
One* (1788). It is in *The Marriage*, however, that we find a
fully developed presentation of Blake's ethic of liberation.
The redemptive force is to be Energy—which is 'the only
life and is from the Body' and which is 'Eternal Delight'.[1]
The Marriage is a devil's hornbook in the service of revolutionary energy: by means of aphorism, parable, and emblem
Blake argues that the regeneration of human society will
follow the breaking of the chains of 'the Governor or Reason',
chains which are 'the cunning of weak and tame minds which

---

[1] *The Poetry and Prose of William Blake*, ed. David V. Erdman, with a
commentary by Harold Bloom (Garden City, N.Y., 1965), p. 34. This edition
hereafter cited as E.

have the power to resist energy'. The Devils and Giants of *The Marriage*, its eagles, lions, and tigers, its Leviathan and its Christ, all are embodiments of such liberation. Blake thus anticipates the concerns, if not always the conclusions of later writers such as Stendhal, Matthew Arnold, George Eliot, and John Stuart Mill. Eliot asked for 'no light, great Heaven, but such as turns / To energy of human fellowship'. Mill asserted that 'Whoever thinks that individuality of desires and impulses should not be encouraged to unfold itself, must maintain that society has no need of strong natures . . . and that a high general average of energy is not desirable.'

> Genius [wrote Arnold] is mainly an affair of energy, and poetry is mainly an affair of genius; therefore, a nation whose spirit is characterised by energy may well be eminent in poetry;—and we have Shakespeare. Again, the highest reach of science is, one may say, an inventive power, a faculty of divination, akin to the highest power exercised in poetry; therefore, a nation whose spirit is characterised by energy may well be eminent in science;—and we have Newton. Shakespeare and Newton: in the intellectual sphere there can be no higher names. And what that energy, which is the life of genius, above everything demands and insists upon is freedom; entire independence of all authority, prescription and routine,—the fullest room to expand as it will.[1]

Arnold, of course, differs from Blake in balancing the advantages of institutions against the claims of energy;[2] but he does recognize and articulate the largeness of those claims,

---

[1] Motto to 'The Lifted Veil', *The Works of George Eliot* (Edinburgh and London, 1878), ii. 276; *On Liberty* (Boston, 1864), pp. 116–17; 'The Literary Influence of Academies', *Essays in Criticism*, 1st ser. (New York, 1883), pp. 50–1.

[2] '. . . A nation whose chief spiritual characteristic is energy, will not be very apt to set up, in intellectual matters, a fixed standard, an authority, like an academy. By this it certainly escapes certain real inconveniences and dangers, and it can, at the same time, as we have seen, reach undeniably splendid heights in poetry and science. On the other hand, some of the requisites of intellectual work are specially the affair of quickness of mind and flexibility of intelligence' (p. 51). Lionel Trilling in *Matthew Arnold* (New York, 1949), remarks that 'Nothing in the literature of the time—especially in France—is more striking than the sense of frustrated energy and talent which haunts its pages. . . . *Energy*, Stendhal's magic word, is frustrated by modern society and that is what he means by tragedy. For Balzac, on the other hand, energy itself is the evil; for it is perverted to bad ends by "the decay of religion and the preeminence of finance, which is simply solidified selfishness"' (pp. 115–16).

which Blake was the first to urge. Beyond this, Blake was the first critic of civilization to endorse the *subversive* nature of the claims of energy, prefiguring the views of such modern apocalyptists as Nietzsche, Lawrence, Camus, and Norman O. Brown. Yet Blake did not so much invent a conception of energy as extend and enlarge existing ones. In order to understand *The Marriage* in its particularity, we must know what these previous conceptions were, for Blake assumes such knowledge as a target point for his polemical assault.

1

'Energy' was a fashionable word in the eighteenth century. It was employed with an aura of positiveness and varying degrees of precision. Gray praised 'the energy of Pope'; Dr. Johnson's *Dictionary* quoted Roscommon's lines 'Who did ever, in French authours see, / The comprehensive, English *energy*?' According to Cowper, God's works were 'the visible display / Of all-creating energy and might', while the early Coleridge refers to God Himself as 'Nature's essence, mind, and energy.'[1] In addition to literary and religious usage, the word was current in morals, science, and psychology. In a passage of the *Covent-Garden Journal* which Martin Price has discussed, Henry Fielding traces the pleasures of both virtue and passion to energy:

> Let us leave the Merit of good Actions to others, let us enjoy the Pleasure of them. *In the Energy itself of Virtue* (says Aristotle) *there is great Pleasure.* . . . If we examine the Matter abstractedly, and with due Attention, we may extend the Observation of Aristotle to every human Passion: For in what, but in the Energies themselves, can the Pleasures of Ambition, Avarice, Pride, Hatred, and Revenge, be conceived to lie?[2]

[1] Thomas Gray, 'Stanzas to Mr. Richard Bentley' (1752), *The Works of Thomas Gray*, ed. Edmund Gosse (London, 1884), i. 122. Samuel Johnson, *A Dictionary of the English Language* (London, 1785), i. n.p. William Cowper, *The Task, Poetical Works*, ed. H. S. Milford (London, 1963), p. 212. Samuel Taylor Coleridge, 'Religious Musings' (1794), *Complete Poetical Works*, ed. Ernest Hartley Coleridge (Oxford, 1912), i. 111.

[2] Henry Fielding, *The Covent-Garden Journal* (11 April 1752), ed. Gerard Edward Jensen (New Haven, 1915), i. 308; Martin Price, *To the Palace of Wisdom* (Garden City, New York, 1964), p. 288.

In an article on sun-spots in the Royal Society's *Philosophical Transactions* for 1783, we find the statement that 'Nature unquestionably abounds with numberless unthought-of energies . . .'[1] The scientist is characterized by Wordsworth as one 'To whom a burning energy has given / That other eye which darts thro' earth and heaven'; and in a notebook fragment of 1798–9, Wordsworth traces the creative power of the mind to the energy of the senses:

> There is creation in the eye,
> Nor less in all the other senses; powers
> They are that colour, model, and combine
> The things perceived with such an absolute
> Essential energy that we may say
> That those most godlike faculties of ours
> At one and the same moment are the mind
> And the mind's minister.[2]

By the end of the century, energy could be considered a fashionable cult-word, as we see in Elizabeth Hamilton's satirical novel *Memoirs of Modern Philosophers* (London, 1800), where the anti-heroine is found 'renovating my energies by the impressive eloquence of Rousseau', and in which the following conversation takes place:

'Happy had it been for the world, if not only your arm, but every bone in your body had been broken, so that it had been the means of furnishing mankind with a proof of the perfectibility of philosophical energy!'

. . . . .

'It most unfortunately happens, though, (replied Vallaton, writhing in great agony, from an attempt to move) it unfortunately happens, that one's energies are apt to desert one, at the very time they are most wanted. . . .'

'I grant you,' returned Myope, 'that even a philosopher may sometimes be taken by surprise. Besides, in a corrupt state of society, where many people believe in a God, the existence of laws and government generates weakness, which no one can entirely escape; the energies cannot arrive at that state of perfection to which

---

[1] Alexander Wilson, 'An Answer to the Objections Stated by M. De la Lande', lxxiii. 160.

[2] *Poetical Works*, ed. E. de Selincourt (Oxford, 1940), i. 13 n. ('An Evening Walk', manuscript addition dated 1794), v. 343; see Geoffrey H. Hartman, *Wordsworth's Poetry 1787–1814* (New Haven and London, 1964), pp. 180, 194.

they will be found to approximate, as soon as these existing causes of depravity have been entirely removed.'

'All removed among the Hottentots!' cried Glib. 'No obstacles to perfectibility among the Gonoquais. No priests! No physicians! All exert their energies.'[1]

Energy, as we see, could have numerous meanings. In Johnson's *Dictionary*, these are divided into four groups. One— 'strength of expression; force of signification; spirit; life'— is rhetorical; the Roscommon couplet above is an example of this meaning. Energy in this sense was frequently associated with the Longinian sublime, particularly with the language of the Old Testament. Another meaning, 'faculty; operation', is the early scientific one, illustrated by John Ray's statement that 'Matter, though divided into the subtilest parts, moved swiftly, is senseless and stupid, and makes no approach to vital *energy*.' Still another meaning, 'power not exerted in action', may be considered a negative aspect of the definition closest to Blake's own usage: 'force; vigour; efficacy; influence'. In this sense, as these two examples (from Dryden and Thomson) indicate, energy is considered a divine, non-material phenomenon:

> Whether with particles of heavenly fire
> The God of nature did his soul inspire;
> Or earth, but new divided from the sky,
> And pliant still, retain'd th' ethereal *energy*.

> What but God!
> Inspiring God! who, boundless spirit all,
> And unremitting *energy*, pervades,
> Adjusts, sustains, and agitates the whole.

This theological usage of the term derives, of course, from Greek philosophy, and most particularly from the language

---

[1] i. 190, ii. 19–20. Moses may be dismissed, according to Miss Bridgeticia, because 'His energies were cramped by superstition' (i. 4). She looks forward to the day 'when mankind are sufficiently enlightened to cure all diseases by the exertion of their energies' (i. 101). 'In a reasonable state of society women will not restrain their powers, they will then display their energies' (i. 195). According to Mr. Glib, 'Energies would make a man of the monkey himself in a fortnight' (i. 35). Julia consents to a tryst with Mr. Vallaton in the garden because 'I could not bear the thought of appearing despicable in his eyes by my *want of energy*.' (i. 92). The novel purports to be anti-Godwinian.

of Neoplatonism, where it is frequently encountered. Blake
was almost certainly familiar with its meaning in the works
of the Cambridge Platonist Henry More and in those of his
own contemporary Thomas Taylor.[1] More defines energy as
'Operation, Efflux, Activity', giving as examples 'the light of
the Sun, the phantasmes of the soul'. Citing the use of the
term by Plotinus, he concludes: 'I cannot better explain this
Platonick term, *Energie*, then by calling it the rayes of an
essence, or the beams of a vitall Centre. For essence is the
Centre as it were, of that which is truly called *Energie*, and
Energie the beams and rayes of an essence. . . .'[2] Blake follows More in conceiving of energy as vital and in representing it as flowing from the centre of a circle. They also share
the notion of God's being manifest in the created universe
through energy. 'The production of the World being by
way of energy, or emanation,' More comments, 'hath drawn
strange expression from some of the Ancients.' He gives
an example from Trismegistus: 'For God being the sole
Artificer, is alwayes in his work, being indeed that which he
maketh.' More calls this 'Hyperbolicall' but adds that 'It
is not at all strange that all things are the mere energie of
God . . .' (p. 142). All the same, this divine, vital, and active
energy was *not* considered by the Neoplatonists to be a
property of the body. This is especially evident in the writings
of Blake's contemporary Thomas Taylor. Taylor was peculiarly fond of the terms 'energy' and 'energizing'—so much
so that in his translation of the *Timaeus*, according to R.
Catesby Taliaferro, he frequently uses it when it is not in the
Greek text[3]—but for Taylor, energy was a property only of

---

[1] For parallels between More and Blake, see S. Foster Damon, *William Blake: His Philosophy and Symbols* (Gloucester, Mass., 1958; Boston, 1924), pp. 37 n., 167, 328, 341, 367, 384, 467. On Taylor and Blake, see Frederick E. Pierce, 'Blake and Thomas Taylor', *PMLA*, xliii (1928), 1121–41; George Mills Harper, *The Neoplatonism of William Blake* (Chapel Hill, N.C., 1961); Kathleen Raine, 'Blake's Debt to Antiquity', *Sewanee Review*, lxxi (1963), 352–450.

[2] 'The Interpretation Generall', *The Complete Poems of Henry More*, ed. Alexander B. Grosart (Edinburgh, 1878), p. 161; cf. More's paraphrase of Plotinus, pp. 141–2.

[3] Foreword to *The Timaeus and the Critias or Atlanticus* (New York, 1944), p. 10.

the soul and of the intellect which pertained to it. 'All bodies', he wrote, 'therefore belong to those natures which are moved only, and are naturally passive; since they are destitute of all inherent energy, on account of their sluggish nature. . . .'[1] Blake's opposed view is that 'Energy is the only life and is from the body.' Taylor (p. 19) speaks of 'the passivity and imperfection of bodies', Blake of 'the active springing from Energy'. 'Soul', Taylor declares, 'must be more ancient than body; and all corporeal motion must be the progeny of soul, and of her inherent energy' (pp. 19–20). Blake, as it were, replies: 'Man has no Body distinct from his Soul for that calld Body is a portion of Soul discernd by the five Senses, the chief inlets of Soul in this age' (E 34).

The Marriage of Heaven and Hell is directed against the very dualism of Body and Soul that 'Angels' like Taylor and Swedenborg promulgated. This did not prevent Blake from borrowing and inverting the sense of Angelic wisdom. For example, Taylor says that 'the mutual communications of energies among the gods was called by antient theologists ἱερὸς γάμος a sacred marriage'.[2] But for Taylor the marriage is mere allegory—there is no real consummation. The soul can only be debased by the body. 'Flying from an indivisible and Dionysiacal life, and energizing according to a titanic and revolting energy, she becomes bound in the body as in a prison.'[3] In *The Marriage*, of course, the prison is precisely this illusion. 'The Giants who formed this world into its sensual existence and now seem to live in it in chains, are in truth. the causes of its life & the sources of all activity' (E 39). Taylor regards 'adultery and rapes, as represented in the machinery of the mysteries' as 'nothing more than a communication of divine energies';[4] while Blake uses such symbolism as a vehicle for his ethic of total liberation (as, for example, in the 'Preludium' to *America*, where Orc's 'fierce embrace' invests Nature, 'the shadowy daughter of Urthona',[5]

---

[1] 'Preliminary Dissertation' to *The Hymns of Orpheus* (London, 1787), pp. 17–18.
[2] *A Dissertation on the Eleusinian and Bacchic Mysteries* (London, 1790), p. 181.
[3] Ibid., p. 150.   [4] Ibid., p. 184.
[5] See Damon, *William Blake*, p. 334.

with human energy). Blake must have read Taylor as he read the Bible and Milton: 'in the infernal or diabolical sense'.

At the time that Blake wrote *The Marriage*, 'energy' also had currency as a term in the language of scientific or pseudo-scientific speculation. It did not yet have the meaning of the power to do work; this was to be introduced by Thomas Young, in his *Lectures on Natural Philosophy* in 1807.[1] On the earlier meaning, Professor Marjorie Hope Nicolson writes:

> We read in the histories that 'Kepler replaced the notion of soul, the animism of the earlier thinkers, by the notion of physical energy.' Such was his effect, yet his passages on energy are usually embedded, as here, in others developing his belief that the world possesses both a living body with senses and a soul with memory, which, as he says here, like a pregnant woman, has the potency of producing from itself something apart from itself. . . . In the energy of the earth is the essence of the soul: 'It is the steady burning of a flame.' God himself is the 'essence of energy', and, as the 'essence of the flame is in its burning, so the essence of the image of God lies in its activity, its energy.'[2]

It is unlikely that Blake knew Kepler's *Harmonice Mundi*, the source of Professor Nicolson's quotations, but there was a source of discussion much closer to hand: Joseph Priestley's *Disquisitions Relating to Matter and Spirit*,[3] published by Joseph Johnson (who frequently employed Blake as an engraver). Blake was familiar with Priestley's phlogiston theory, which he satirized in *An Island in the Moon* (1784), and he may have known Priestley himself.[4] Priestley's denial of the dichotomy of soul and body and his claim that energy could be an attribute of body are views very close to the ones

---

[1] See J. Clerk Maxwell, *Theory of Heat* (London, 1875), pp. 90–1; Alexander Wood and Frank Oldham, *Thomas Young, Natural Philosopher* (Cambridge, 1954), p. 129; Thomas Young, *A Course of Lectures on Natural Philosophy and the Mechanic Arts* (London, 1807), i. 78–80. As Maxwell and others point out, the meaning is prefigured by Leibniz's term *vis viva*, usually translated as 'force'. See also J. M. Child, Introduction to *A Theory of Natural Philosophy* by Roger Joseph Boscovich, S.J. (Chicago and London, 1922), p. xiii.

[2] *The Breaking of the Circle* (New York, 1960), p. 150.

[3] London, 1777; a second, enlarged edition was published in 1782.

[4] See Damon, *William Blake*, pp. 32–3; David V. Erdman, *Blake: Prophet Against Empire* (Princeton, 1954), pp. 96–9.

expressed by Blake's 'voice of the Devil'. 'Like the generality
of christians in the present age,' Priestley wrote (p. xi), 'I
had always taken it for granted, that man had a soul distinct
from his body . . . and I believed this soul to be a substance
so intirely distinct from matter, as to have no property in
common with it.' This is, of course, the error that the Devil
accuses 'All Bibles or sacred codes' of promulgating, 'That
Man has two real existing principles Viz: a Body & a Soul.'
Priestley goes further in anticipating Blake's arguments:

I am rather inclined to think . . .
that man does not consist of *two principles* so essentially different from one
another as *matter* and *spirit*. . . . I
rather think . . . that the property of
perception, as well as the other powers
that are termed *mental,* is the result
(whether necessary, or not) of such
an organical structure as that of the
brain . . .   (pp. xiii–xiv)

Man has no Body dis-
tinct from his Soul for that
calld Body is a portion of
Soul discerned by the
five Senses, the chief inlets of Soul in this age.
                    (E 34)

. . . what *evidence* can there be that it
[the mind] is not dependent upon the
body for its *existence* also? that is,
what evidence can there be that the
faculty of thinking does not inhere in
the body itself, and that there is no
such thing as a *soul* separate from it?
                    (p. 124)

Energy is the only life
and is from the Body and
Reason is the bound or
outward circumference of
Energy.
                    (E 34)

We should not be misled by Priestley's professed materialism
and Blake's hostility to materialist philosophies—Priestley
himself, remarking that 'The world has been too long amused
by mere names' (1782, p. 33), recognized that one could as
well conclude that all things were spirit from what he had
written. What is important here is that Priestley attacks the
conventional view that the body 'can in no manner *aid* or
assist its [the soul's] powers or energy'.[1] The natural world,
according to Priestley, is composed of God's energy as

---

[1] p. 45; see also p. 68.

represented by the *Logos* of the fourth gospel: 'This divine power and energy was always with God, always belonged to him, and was inherent in him' (p. 291). As H. W. Piper observes of Priestley's doctrine, 'If there was no solidity in Nature, but only energy, then the barrier between the physical and the mental or the spiritual disappeared, for both were the same thing.'[1]

Yet, despite these similarities, the meaning of Energy in *The Marriage* has a dimension we do not find in Priestley: Blake conceives of energy as erotic in origin and as revolutionary in expression. The American Revolution begins when Orc rapes the shadowy daughter of Urthona, and it culminates with 'the females naked and glowing with the lusts of youth' (E 56). The liberation of energy through the interplay of contraries is seen as in itself desirable, beyond moral categories. This conception of energy first appears, though sketchily, in Blake's annotations to *Aphorisms on Man* by Johann Caspar Lavater, made a year or two before *The Marriage* was begun.[2]

In reading Fuseli's translation of *Aphorisms on Man*, Blake accepted the author's invitation to underline the aphorisms he liked and to mark those which made him uneasy; he also added comments of his own. Three of these aphorisms concern energy. Aphorism 352—'He alone has *energy that cannot be deprived of it*'—anticipates Blake's description of the Prolific: 'Thus one portion of being, is the Prolific. the other, the Devouring: to the devourer it seems as if the producer was in his chains, but it is not so, he only takes portions of existence and fancies that the whole' (E 39). Blake thought Aphorism 97 'Sterling', though it made him uneasy; 'He only, who can give durability to his exertions, has genuine power *and energy of mind*' (E 576). Most important, in his rejoinder to Aphorism 409, Blake sketched out the ironical inversion of moral values that would be so prominent in *The Marriage*. Lavater had written: 'He alone is good, who, though possessed of energy, prefers virtue, *with the appearance of weakness, to the*

---

[1] *The Active Universe* (London, 1962), p. 35.

[2] As Blake, having engraved the frontispiece for Johnson, obtained an unbound copy, he probably read the book before its publication in 1789.

invitation of acting brilliantly ill.'[1] Blake replied, 'Noble But Mark Active Evil is better than Passive Good' (E 581). In *The Marriage* he developed this idea further by making it part of his own dialectic, undercutting the dichotomies of 'the religious' to show the underlying unity of human experience.

Without Contraries is no progression. Attraction and Repulsion, Reason and Energy, Love and Hate, are necessary to Human existence.

From these contraries spring what the religious call Good & Evil. Good is the passive that obeys Reason[.] Evil is the active springing from Energy. (E 34)

2

The idea of representing human life as a marriage of heaven and hell occurred to Blake as a result of his reading of Swedenborg, with whom he at first found many affinities.[2] In his copy of Swedenborg's *Heaven and Hell* (Eng. trans. 1784), Blake wrote: '. . . hell is the outward or external of heaven. & is of the body of the lord. for nothing is destroyd' (E 591), and at the end of *Divine Love and Divine Wisdom* (1788) 'Heaven & Hell are born together' (E 598). Swedenborg described evil as man's reaction against God, saying 'so far as he believes that all his Life is from God, and every Good of Life from the Action of God, and every Evil of Life from the Reaction of Man, Reaction thus becomes correspondent with Action, and Man acts with God as for himself'. Blake's marginal comment on this contains the seed of his own book— 'Good & Evil are here both Good & the two contraries Married' (E 594). Yet we can see that here and elsewhere in the Swedenborg marginalia, Blake is carrying the meaning further than Swedenborg intends. Although Swedenborg was

---

[1] I give the page references in E for the reader's convenience, but Blake's annotations are transcribed from the original in the Huntington Library. Where Blake's intention was clearly to score under lines of text, I have italicized the whole lines, although Blake's pen frequently skipped the words at either margin. For this reason the italicization here differs from that in E.

[2] On Blake's changing view of Swedenborg, see Erdman, *Blake*, pp. 127–8 and 160–2; Martin K. Nurmi, *Blake's* 'Marriage of Heaven and Hell': *a Critical Study*, Kent State Univ. Bull., Research Ser. III (Kent, O., April 1957), pp. 25–30; Damon, *A Blake Dictionary* (Providence, 1965), pp. 392–4.

a visionary and opposed the existing institutional churches, his moral views were for the most part conventional and repressive, and his hells were conceived to be really inhabited. Blake finally had to admit this when he read *The Wisdom of Angels concerning the Divine Providence* (1790). He now condemned Swedenborg as 'A Spiritual Predestinarian' (E 600) and set about writing a satire on and corrective to Swedenborg's views.

Now hear a plain fact: Swedenborg has not written one new truth: Now hear another: he has written all the old falshoods.

And now hear the reason. He conversed with Angels who are all religious, & conversed not with Devils who all hate religion, for he was incapable thro' his conceited notions.   (E 42)

The Marriage begins, after 'The Argument', by referring to Swedenborg's announcement of a new heaven: 'it is now thirty-three years since its advent: the Eternal Hell revives'.[1] Swedenborg is merely 'the Angel sitting at the tomb; his writings are the linen clothes folded up'. The resurrected body has no need of such garments, or for life-denying Angelic wisdom. Swedenborg declared that 'As this Fire or Hell signifies every propensity to evil flowing from the love of self, so likewise it signifies it's punishment in those self-tormenting passions of hatred, revenge, and cruelty towards those who are the objects of them. . . .'[2] Blake contrarily presents himself as 'walking among the fires of hell, delighted with the enjoyments of Genius; which to Angels look like torment and insanity' (E 35). The doctrine of progression through contraries is itself a correction of Swedenborg's view.

An Equilibrium is necessary to the existence and subsistence of all things, and consists in the equality of action and re-action between two opposite powers, producing Rest or Equilibrium. . . . Thus there exists a spiritual Equilibrium or Liberty betwixt good and evil, by the action of one, and the re-action of the other. . . .[3]

[1] See Damon, *William Blake*, pp. 89, 316. Blake, of course, was born in 1757.
[2] *A Treatise Concerning Heaven and Hell and of the Wonderful Things Therein*, 2nd ed. (London, 1784), pp. 379–80.
[3] Ibid., pp. 389–90. The similarity, but not the difference, between this passage and Blake's is noted by F. W. Bateson, *Selected Poems of William Blake* (New York, 1957), p. 128.

This is a static view in which there is no 'progression' but the maintenance of an existing order. The two forces are not contraries in Blake's sense, but negations: 'Men of an enlightened understanding, moreover, see good and evil in the same fulness of contrariety and opposition that Heaven and Hell stand in to each other, and how all good comes from the former, and all evil from the latter' (546, p. 363). Blake assigns this dualism to 'the religious' and subverts it with the 'extraordinary pre-Hegelian dialectic'[1] which he learned from Jakob Boehme.

The idea of change through 'the struggl of contrarieties', as Milton calls it,[2] is at least as old as the pre-Socratic philosophers. However, there is an important particular of Blake's notion of contrariety, as a critic quite hostile to this aspect of his thought points out:

> The idea of harmony *in spite* of conflict, or simple reconciliation of apparent or superficial conflict, is a staple Greek and Roman, Medieval and Renaissance, idea. The idea of harmony, or at least of some desirable wholeness or sanity or salvation, only *because of* or *through* some kind of strife of contraries may not at first sound much different, but the difference between these ideas is actually profound—the difference, for example, between Satan and Prometheus.[3]

The distinction is well taken; the example will bear discussion later. It is true that by progression through contraries Blake means something different from the tension between Reason and Self-Love in Pope's *Essay on Man*. Here, as in Swedenborg, there is merely a compromise through opposition. For Blake, the clash of contraries is part of a process of human transformation. This is also true of Paracelsus and Boehme, from whose writings Blake says, 'Any man of mechanical talents may . . . produce ten thousand volumes of

[1] The phrase is Mark Schorer's (*William Blake: the Politics of Vision* [New York, 1946], p. 126).

[2] *Reason of Church-Government*, in *The Works of John Milton*, ed. Frank Allen Patterson (New York, 1931), iii (pt. 1), 223. On the subject of contrariety in Blake, see Martin K. Nurmi, 'Blake's Doctrine of Contraries: a Study in Visionary Metaphysics' (Univ. of Minn. diss. 1954).

[3] W. K. Wimsatt, Jr., 'Horses of Wrath: Recent Critical Lessons', *Essays in Criticism*, xii (1962), 8.

equal value with Swedenborg's' (E 42). Boehme uses the dialectic of contraries to describe the regeneration of the soul; for Paracelsus the transmutation of metals takes place by a series of 'marriages' of contrary chemicals. The refining agent is fire, and destruction makes the perfection of the Great Work possible.

Destruction perfects that which is good; for the good cannot appear on account of that which conceals it. The good is least good whilst it is thus concealed. The concealment must be removed that so the good may be able freely to appear in its own brightness. . . . By the element of fire all that is imperfect is destroyed and taken away. . . .'[1]

In *The Marriage* Blake presents his method of etching metal plates in an acid bath as analogous to this alchemical process. 'But first the notion that man has a body distinct from his soul, is to be expunged; this I shall do, by printing in the infernal method, by corrosives, which in Hell are salutary and medicinal, melting apparent surfaces away, and displaying the infinite which was hid' (E 38). The human energies which blaze through the imagery of *The Marriage*, like the alchemists' refining fire, destroy in order to purify. The goal is the undoing of the fall of man—'the return of Adam into Paradise' (E 34). Here, too, Blake follows Paracelsus's characterization of the Great Work: '. . . When the seed of the man embraces the seed of the woman, this is the first sign and the key of this whole work and Art.'[2] As the naked figures which embrace in flame on Blake's title-page indicate, the

[1] Paracelsus, 'Coelum Philosophorum', *The Hermetic and Alchemical Writings of Paracelsus*, ed. Arthur Edward Waite (London, 1894), i. 4. On Blake's relation to the alchemists, see Gerald E. Bentley, Jr., 'William Blake and the Alchemical Philosophers' (Merton Coll., Oxford, undergraduate thesis 1954).

[2] 'Concerning the Spirits of the Planets', *Hermetic and Alchemical Writings*, i. 86. Blake may also have found a source of erotic mysticism in the Kabbala, according to which 'Every true marriage is a symbolical realization of the union of God and the Shekinah' (Gershom G. Scholem, *Major Trends in Jewish Mysticism* (New York, 1946), p. 235; see also p. 227: 'In God there is a union of the active and the passive, procreation and conception from which all mundane life and bliss are derived.'). The Shekinah, or divine radiance, would correspond to what Blake later calls the Emanation. Although there are many other parallels between Blake's thought and the Kabbala (see Denis Saurat, *Blake and Modern Thought* (London, 1929), pp. 98–106), it is not at all certain that he was directly

marriage of contraries has a literal meaning as well as a symbolic one; naked beauty and sexual desire are God's work and His joy; the fulfilment of love is in itself a return to Paradise.

Is Blake's argument, as Professor Wimsatt suggests, a form of Satanism? This would be true only if the inversion of values in *The Marriage* were literal, if Blake were saying, 'Evil, be thou my good.' In fact, the transposition is ironical. Blake views evil as negative—'Hindering Another'. At the end of his annotations to Lavater, he warns against confusing repression with virtue. 'But as I understand Vice it is a Negative—It does not signify what the laws of Kings & Priests have calld Vice we who are philosophers ought not to call the Staminal Virtues of Humanity by the same name that we call the omissions of intellect springing from poverty' (E 590). Repression is a form of murder; a morality of restraint derives from the error of believing that 'Womans Love is Sin. in consequence all the Loves & Graces . . . are Sin.' Blake sees the Satan of Christianity as a grotesque, fear-induced distortion of the true Messiah: 'Messiah or Satan or Tempter was formerly thought to be one of the Antediluvians who are our Energies' (E 39). Therefore, when by an act of 'demoniac imperialism', as Camus calls it,[1] Blake enlists Milton into the Devil's party, he turns Milton's account of the fall into an allegory of contraries opposite in meaning to what 'the Governor or Reason' intended. It is a true history, 'adopted by both parties', but the party of Energy calls Milton's Satan Christ. The real Satan is the life-denying principle which 'Hinders Another': 'in the Book of Job Miltons Messiah is call'd Satan' (E 34). This is something entirely different from the blasphemous piety of Baudelaire's 'Litanies of Satan'. Blake wants to reclaim the Loves and Graces for the divine in man and to identify God with life-giving energy: 'the Jehovah of the Bible being no other than he, who dwells in flaming fire' (E 35).

familiar with Kabbalistic thought. Many of the notions which Blake shares with the Kabbala are also to be found in the writings of Paracelsus and Boehme, and also in Hermetic and Neoplatonic literature. (There is, however, a reference to a specifically Kabbalistic doctrine in 'To the Jews', *Jerusalem*, 27, E 170.)

[1] *The Rebel*, trans. Anthony Bower (New York, 1954), p. 44.

Blake's doctrine of liberation is at the same time individual and social, for at this point in his thought, the two cannot be separated. For society, as for the individual, the agent of regeneration is Energy. In 'A Song of Liberty', appended to *The Marriage*, Blake celebrates the triumph of Energy with his first revolutionary myth, in which a 'new born fire' overthrows a 'starry king'. These figures, soon to become Orc and Urizen in the Lambeth books, represent the new and the old world orders; the 'jealous king' becomes the real fallen Satan and, at the same time, Moses promulgating his ten commands in the wilderness. The divine child returns as the Christ of the Parousia—'the son of fire in his eastern cloud'—and proclaims the end of empire. A final chorus commands an end to sexual repression 'that wishes but acts not!' (E 44). Blake envisions, not revolution *and* sexual freedom, but a revolution which is libidinal in nature. This is what he refers to as the return to Paradise which will come to pass by 'an improvement of sensual enjoyment'. As Norman O. Brown remarks,

Freud and Blake are asserting that the ultimate essence of our being remains in our unconscious secretly faithful to the principle of pleasure, or, as Blake calls it, delight. To say this is to call in question the psychological assumptions upon which our Western morality has been built. For two thousand years or more man has been subjected to a systematic effort to transform him into an ascetic animal. He remains a pleasure-seeking animal. Parental discipline, religious denunciation of bodily pleasure, and philosophic exaltation of the life of reason have all left man overtly docile, but secretly in his unconscious unconvinced, and therefore neurotic. Man remains unconvinced because in infancy he tasted the fruit of the tree of life, and knows that it is good, and never forgets.[1]

Angels fear revolution because they fear themselves: this is what the fourth 'Memorable Fancy' of *The Marriage* satirically demonstrates. Blake's Angel takes him on a journey in which the history of the Christian Church is represented: 'thro' a stable [the Nativity] & thro' a church [the apostolic

---

[1] *Life Against Death: the Psychoanalytical Meaning of History* (Middletown, Conn., 1959), p. 31.

church] & down into the church vault [the institutional church] at the end of which was a mill [Deism]: thro' the mill we went, and came to a cave' (E 40). We are now back to the situation of Plate 3, where Swedenborg is the Angel sitting at the tomb with the body of Christ gone. The Angel continues to lead Blake 'down the winding cavern', further into error, until the abyss appears below them. Now Blake parodies Swedenborg's *Divine Providence*, proposing to the Angel, 'if you please we will commit ourselves to this void, and see whether providence is here also. . . .' In the void appear 'vast spiders, crawling after their prey . . . these are Devils'. (Swedenborg: 'But infernal Love, with it's Affections of Evil and of what is False, which are Concupiscences . . . may be compared to a Spider and the Web which encompasseth it . . . the Love itself is the Spider . . . and the Delights of these Concupiscences with deceitful Machinations are the more remote Threads, where Flies are caught, entangled, and devoured.')[1] Next there appears Leviathan, in a purposely over-written description—'his forehead was divided into streaks of green & purple like those on a tygers forehead'. He comes, as Martin K. Nurmi points out,[2] from the direction of Paris, 'to the east, distant about three degrees'. The Angel, terrified by this vision of revolutionary energy 'advancing toward us with all the fury of a spiritual existence', retreats into his mill of reason. But a fool sees not the same Leviathan as a wise man sees: 'I remain'd alone, & then this appearance was no more, but I found myself sitting on a pleasant bank beside a river by moon light hearing a harper who sung to the harp. . . .'

Next Blake, Swedenborg's volumes in hand, shows the Angel his own 'eternal lot' or hidden, underlying attitude. Opening the Bible, which becomes 'a deep pit' (its 'infernal or diabolical sense', E 43), he reveals a society of Yahoos living in a Hobbesian state of nature.

. . . soon we saw seven houses of brick, one we enterd; in it were a number of monkeys, baboons, & all of that species chaind by the middle, grinning and snatching at one another, but witheld by the

---

[1] *The Wisdom of Angels Concerning the Divine Providence* (London, 1790), pp. 137–8.
[2] *Blake's* Marriage, p. 51.

shortness of their chains: however I saw that they sometimes grew numerous, and then the weak were caught by the strong and with a grinning aspect, first coupled with & then devourd, by plucking off first one limb and then another till the body was left a helpless trunk. this after grinning & kissing it with seeming fondness they devourd too; and here & there I saw one savourily picking the flesh off of his own tail; as the stench terribly annoyd us both we went into the mill, & I in my hand brought the skeleton of a body, which in the mill was Aristotles Analytics.   (E 41)

This is the Angel's and Swedenborg's real view of man. 'As this Fire of Hell signifies every propensity to evil flowing from the love of self, as likewise it signifies it's punishment in those self-tormenting passions of hatred, revenge, and cruelty towards those who are the objects of them; for this kind of love is the root of all tyranny and arbitrary power, and the enemy of God and man. . . .'[1] Such a view of life makes one prefer horses to human beings, like Gulliver; authority to freedom, like Hobbes; repression to Eros, like Swedenborg. Because they fear Energy, Angels try to contain it within their moral categories. 'Has not Jesus Christ given his sanction to the law of ten commandments . . .?' (E 42). But Energy bursts the bounds of such categories—'Jesus was all virtue, and acted from impulse. not from rules.' Even the destructive aspects of Energy are 'portions of eternity too great for the eye of man' (E 36). That is to say, in the terms of Blake's time, that Energy is a manifestation of the sublime.

3

There have been admirable discussions of sublimity in Blake's art and in the style of his poetry,[2] but the place of the sublime in his thought has been rather overlooked. This may be because of Blake's vehement rejection of Burke's theories.

Burke's Treatise on the Sublime & Beautiful is founded on the Opinions of Newton & Locke on this Treatise Reynolds has grounded many of his assertions. in all his Discourses I read Burkes

---

[1] *Heaven and Hell*, pp. 379–80.
[2] Sir Anthony Blunt, *The Art of William Blake* (New York, 1959), pp. 13–21; Josephine Miles, *Eras and Modes in English Poetry* (Berkeley and Los Angeles, 1957), pp. 78–99.

Treatise when very Young at the same time I read Locke on
Human Understanding & Bacons Advancement of Learning on
Every one of these Books I wrote my Opinions & on looking them
over find that my Notes on Reynolds in this Book are exactly
Similar. I felt the Same Contempt & Abhorrence then; that I do
now. They mock Inspiration & Vision Inspiration & Vision was
then & now is & I hope will always Remain my Element my
Eternal Dwelling place. how can I then hear it Contemnd without
returning Scorn for Scorn—[1]

Blake's contempt and abhorrence were excited by Burke's
pseudo-physiological explanation, which, he believed, denigra-
ted the truth of 'Inspiration & Vision'. It is Burke's reductive
theory, not the concept of the sublime itself, to which Blake is
hostile. In fact, in his view of the nature and function of
poetry, Blake has much in common with a number of other
poets, critics, and literary theorists who wrote about the
sublime in the eighteenth century. Writers as diverse
as John Dennis, Edward Young, Robert Lowth, Burke,
and Blake shared certain assumptions about sublimity.
It is intense, suggestive of infinity, and productive of enthusiasm; it is associated with energy and is produced by
contraries; it is, in its most powerful form, terrifying; and
the chief source of it in literature is the Old Testament.[2]
All these qualities are displayed in *The Marriage*, though
once more with a difference that only Blake supplied.

'I saw no God, nor heard any', says Blake's Isaiah, 'in a
finite organical perception; but my senses discover'd the infinite in every thing . . .' (E 38). This is virtually a formula
for the sublime in the Longinian tradition. In discussing
'Visions, which by some are called Images', Longinus describes them as arising 'When the Imagination is so warm'd
and affected, that you seem to behold yourself the very things
you are describing, and to display them to the life before the
Eyes of an Audience.'[3] A vision is an imaginative perception,

---

[1] Annotations to *The Works of Sir Joshua Reynolds*, E 650. These are usually
dated *c.* 1808, but see E 801 for the argument that some may have been written
as early as 1798.

[2] On the subject of the sublime in general, see Samuel Holt Monk, *The
Sublime* (Ann Arbor, Mich., 1960 (New York, 1935)).

[3] *Dionysius Longinus on the Sublime*, trans. William Smith (London, 1739),
pp. 39–40.

not an hallucination. The prophet's 'desire of raising other men into a perception of the infinite' is as well the desire of the sublime poet. The choice of Hebrew prophets as spokesmen for the Poetic Genius, Ezekiel's statement that 'we of Israel taught that the Poetic Genius (as you now call it) was the first principle' and his reference to 'our great poet King David'—all these are in accordance with the belief that 'Sublimity', as Coleridge later said, 'is Hebrew by birth.'[1] Longinus' choice of an illustration of the sublime from the Old Testament (Gen. 1:3) was followed and amplified by the English sublime critics. William Smith, in his much-reprinted translation of *Peri Hupsous*, noted examples of sublimity in the Psalms and in Habbakuk (pp. 127–8). For Burke, the single most important source of the sublime was Job. Robert Lowth declared of Psalm 50:

> That high degree of sublimity, to which the Psalmist rises upon such occasions, is only to be attained by the Hebrew Muse; for, it is a truth universally acknowledged, that no religion whatever, no poetic history is provided with a store of imagery so striking and so magnificent, so capable of embellishing a scene which may be justly accounted the most sublime that the human imagination is able to comprehend.[2]

This eighteenth-century view of the sublimity of the Old Testament merges with an older tradition in medieval and Renaissance critical theory, according to which the prophets were poets.[3] Milton, drawing upon this tradition, provides Blake with a powerful example, in speaking of

a work not to be rays'd from the heat of youth, or the vapours of wine, like that which flows at wast from the pen of some vulgar

---

[1] Quoted by Monk, op. cit., p. 79 n., from Coleridge's *Table Talk and Omniana* (London, 1884), p. 174.

[2] *Lectures on the Sacred Poetry of the Hebrews* (London, 1787), ii. 237–8. Lowth's lectures originally appeared in Latin in 1759; Joseph Johnson published the English translation. On the importance of Lowth, see Monk, op. cit., pp. 79–83; M. H. Abrams, *The Mirror and the Lamp* (New York, 1953 (1958)), pp. 76–8; and Murray Roston, *Prophet and Poet* (London, 1965), pp. 71–2, 133–8.

[3] See Ernst Robert Curtius, *European Literature and the Latin Middle Ages* (New York, 1953), pp. 216–26; J. E. Spingarn, *A History of Literary Criticism in the Renaissance* (New York, 1954), pp. 9–11, 188–94, 265–9; Roston, op. cit, passim.

Amorist, or the trencher fury of a riming parasite, nor to be obtain'd by the invocation of Dame Memory and her Siren daughters, but by devout prayer to that eternall Spirit who can enrich with all utterance and knowledge, and sends out his Seraphim with the hallow'd fire of his Altar to touch and purify the lips of whom he pleases. . . .

Prophetic inspiration is, then, available to a modern poet:

But those frequent songs throughout the law and prophets beyond all these, not in their divine argument alone, but in the very critical art of composition may be easily made appear over all the kinds of Lyrick poesy, to be incomparable. These abilities, wheresoever they be found, are the inspired guift of God rarely bestow'd, but yet to some (though most abuse) in every Nation. . . .[1]

In the eighteenth century the Prophets are frequently declared to be sublime poets. The Muse 'turn'd to pious Notes the Psalmists's Lyre, / And fill'd Isaiah's Breast with more than Pindar's Fire!'[2] 'The Prophets were Poets by the Institution of their Order, and Poetry was one of the Prophetick Functions.'[3] 'The prophetic office had a most strict connexion with the poetic art. They had one common name, one common origin, one common author, the Holy Spirit.'[4] Blake is very much of his age in defending and imitating what he would later call 'the Sublime of the Bible' (*Milton*, E 94).

Blake and the sublime critics also agree in associating the

---

[1] Op. cit., (above, p. 13 n. 2), pp. 241, 238 resp.

[2] John Hughes (1677–1720), *On Divine Poetry*, quoted by Hoxie Neale Fairchild, *Religious Trends in English Poetry* (New York, 1939), i. 251.

[3] John Dennis, *The Grounds of Criticism in Poetry* (1704), in *Critical Works of John Dennis*, ed. Edward Niles Hooker (Baltimore, 1939), i. 370.

[4] Lowth, *Lectures*, ii. 18. Deists, Anglicans, and dissenters could agree on this, though each might draw different conclusions from it. Damon, *William Blake*, p. 61, points out that Paine wrote, in *The Age of Reason*, 'The word *prophet*, to which later times have affixed a new idea, was the Bible word for poet, and the word *prophesying* meant the art of making poetry.' Cf. Spinoza, *Tractatus Theologico-Politicus*: 'As the prophets perceived the revelations of God by the aid of imagination, they could indisputably perceive much that is beyond the boundary of the intellect, for many more ideas can be constructed from words and figures than from the principles and notions on which the whole fabric of reasoned knowledge is reared. Thus we have a clue to the fact that the prophets perceived nearly everything in parables and allegories ... for such is the usual method of imagination' (*The Chief Works of Benedict De Spinoza* (New York, 1951), i. 25).

sublime with a certain kind of obscurity. John Hughes refers
to the writings of the 'Jewish Prophets, in which we find a
Spirit of Poetry surprizingly sublime' as 'figurative and
emblematical.'[1] Dennis says of Christ, 'The Method of his
Instruction was intirely Poetical: that is, by Fables or
Parables, contriv'd, and plac'd, and adapted to work very
strongly upon human Passions.'[2] The obscurity is apparent
rather than real, and it has a purpose. In defence of the Old
Testament Proverbs, Lowth (II, 168) writes:

> Some degree of obscurity is generally an attendant upon excessive
> brevity; and the parabolic style is so far from being abhorrent of
> this quality, that it seems frequently to affect it, and to regard it
> as a perfection. This obscurity is not indeed altogether without its
> uses: it whets the understanding, excites an appetite for knowledge,
> keeps alive the attention, and exercises the genius by the labor of
> the investigation.

This statement is both pertinent to Blake's method in the
'Proverbs of Hell' and similar to his own defence against
the charge of obscurity:

> . . . What is Grand is necessarily obscure to Weak men. That
> which can be made Explicit to the Idiot is not worth my care. The
> wisest of the Ancients consider'd what is not too Explicit as the
> fittest for Instruction, because it rouzes the faculties to act. I name
> Moses, Solomon, Esop, Homer, Plato.[3]

Rousing the faculties to act results in the liberation of energy,
another characteristic of the sublime. Lowth says of Genesis
1 : 3:

> The more words you would accumulate upon this thought, the
> more you would detract from the sublimity of it: for the under-
> standing quickly comprehends the Divine power from the effect,
> and perhaps most completely, when it is not attempted to be ex-
> plained; the perception in that case is the more vivid, inasmuch as
> it seems to proceed from the proper action and energy of the mind
> itself.   (i. 350)

[1] *Essay on Allegorical Poetry*, quoted by Fairchild, op. cit. i. 251.
[2] *Grounds of Criticism*, in *Critical Works*, i. 371.
[3] Letter to Dr. Trusler, 23 August 1799, *The Complete Writings of William Blake*, ed. Geoffrey Keynes (London, 1966), p. 793. This edition is hereafter cited as K.

Of Psalm 29 Lowth declares, 'The sublimity of the matter is perfectly equalled by the unaffected energy of the style' (ii. 251). Edward Young, in his *Conjectures on Original Composition*, also associates energy with the sublime.

Who would expect to find *Pindar* and *Scotus*, *Shakespear* and *Aquinas*, of the same Party? Both equally shew an *original*, unindebted, energy; the *Vigor igneus*, and *Coelestis origo* burns in both; and leaves us in doubt if Genius is more evident in the sublime flights and beauteous flowers of poetry, or in the . . . Thorns of the schools.[1]

A principal source of the energy of the sublime is terror. According to Burke, 'Whatever is fitted in any sort to excite the ideas of pain, and danger, that is to say, whatever is in any sort terrible, or is conversant about terrible objects, or operates in a manner analogous to terror, is a source of the *sublime*; that is, it is productive of the strongest emotion which the mind is capable of feeling.' Power and terror are, to Burke, inseparable companions, the one increasing with the other. 'Now as power is undoubtedly a capital source of the sublime, this will point out evidently from whence its energy is derived, and to what class of ideas we ought to unite it.'[2] The common eighteenth-century explanation of the effect of the sublime of terror is that the mind perceives an object so great or intense that its capacity is overwhelmed; the imagination is enlarged in an effort to comprehend the object, but is unable to do so.[3] 'The burst of thunder or of cannon,' according to Hugh Blair, 'the roaring of winds, the shouting of multitudes, the sound of vast cataracts of water, are all incontestably grand objects.'[4] Dennis includes 'Tempests, raging Seas . . . Monsters, Serpents, Lions, Tygers,

[1] London, 1759, p. 35. A few years after Blake wrote *The Marriage*, Nathan Drake said of the sublime ode, 'A lighting of phrase should pervade the more impassioned parts, and an awful and even dreadful obscurity, from prophetic, or superhuman energy, diffuse its influence over the whole' (quoted by Monk, op. cit., p. 137, from *Literary Hours* (London, 1798), p. 379).
[2] *A Philosophical Enquiry into the Origin of Our Ideas of the Sublime and Beautiful*, ed. J. T. Boulton (London, 1958), pp. 39, 70.
[3] See Monk, op. cit., pp. 58, 118, 162.
[4] Quoted by Boulton, op. cit., p. lxxxviii, from *Lectures on Rhetoric and Belles Lettres* (1783). 'Grand' is here virtually synonymous with 'sublime', as in Blake's 'What is Grand is necessarily obscure to Weak men.'

Fire, War, Pestilence, Famine, etc.'[1] among objects producing 'Enthusiastick Terror', terror joined with wonder. In Blake's 'Proverbs of Hell' we find a list of sublime phenomena similar to these: 'The roaring of lions, the howling of wolves, the raging of the stormy sea, and the destructive sword. are portions of eternity too great for the eye of man' (E 36). Where Blake differs from these other writers is in locating the sublime in the energies of humanity itself, and so making it part of his dialectic of liberation. The sublimity of the human body is a major theme of *The Marriage* as of Blake's later works: 'The head Sublime, the heart Pathos, the genitals Beauty, the hands & feet Proportion' (E 37).[2] Regenerated by energy, life becomes a mode of art, an idea which Blake later reiterates in calling the Strong Man of his *Descriptive Catalogue* (1809) 'a sublime energizer' (E 535).

4

Man apprehends the sublime through his Poetic Genius, that 'true faculty of knowing' (E 2) which is the subject of *All Religions Are One*, etched by Blake in 1788 along with the two tractates called *There Is No Natural Religion*. These three texts, and the exposition by Isaiah and Ezekiel in *The Marriage*, put forward Blake's early view of the imagination. The term itself is seldom used, however: it occurs only once in *The Marriage* (twice if we count 'imagin'd'), and only once elsewhere in all Blake's writings up to 1799.[3] Poetic Genius is a somewhat looser, more inclusive, and less structured concept than what Blake later calls Imagination. It is 'the faculty which experiences', 'the first principle' of human perception. Blake anticipates Coleridge in regarding perception as an imaginative act, 'a repetition in the finite mind of

---

[1] Op. cit. (above, p. 21, n. 3), p. 361.

[2] Lavater, *Aphorisms on Man* (London, 1788), wrote: '. . . the *extraordinary* is distinguished by copiousness, and a wide range of energy' (p. 206) and 'Distinguish with exactness, if you mean to know yourself and others, what is so often mistaken—the singular, the original, the *extraordinary, the great, and the sublime man: the sublime alone unites the singular, original, extraordinary, and great, with his own uniformity and simplicity* (p. 205, underlining by Blake). For Lavater the sublime human qualities are abstract and intangible, for Blake they are concrete and physical.

[3] See below, Ch. 6, p. 147, n. 2.

the eternal act of creation in the infinite I AM'.[1] Of the chaos
of sensory data, the Poetic Genius or primary imagination
creates an order, an act parallel with—not merely analogous
to—God's creation of the universe, and to the artist's creation
of the work of art. For the process of artistic creation, Coleridge uses the term 'secondary imagination', but emphasizes
that the difference is one of mode and degree, not of kind.
Blake is unwilling to make even this distinction. All knowledge is unitive; art, religion, philosophy all derive from 'the
Poetic Genius which is every where call'd the Spirit of Prophecy' (E 2).

Then I asked: does a firm perswasion that a thing is so, make it
so?

He replied. All poets believe that it does, & in ages of imagination this firm perswasion removed mountains; but many are not
capable of a firm perswasion of any thing.   (E 38)

Blake's idea of the Poetic Genius as the first principle of
perception, actively building a reality from the materials of
sensation, has an antecedent in the philosophy of David Hume.
Of course Blake liked Hume as little as he did Burke—in the
Descriptive Catalogue Hume furnishes an example of 'the
reasoning historian, turner and twister of causes and consequences' (E 534)—but we should remember that Blake is even
willing to quote that 'contemptible Fool' Bacon when it suits
his purposes. (He directs the unimaginative Dr. Trusler to
The Advancement of Learning for 'Sense sends over to
Imagination before Reason have judged, & Reason sends over
to Imagination before the Decree can be acted' (K 794).
Hume argues that belief is not produced by abstract reason
but by the imagination acting upon either memory or sensation: 'Whenever any object is presented to the memory or
senses, it immediately, by the force of custom, carries the
imagination to conceive that object, which is usually conjoined to it; and this conception is attended with a feeling or
sentiment, different from the loose reveries of the fancy. In
this consists the whole nature of belief.' As the imagination
is a producer of fictions, a distinction must be made between
modes of belief. 'The sentiment of belief is nothing but a

---

[1] See S. T. Coleridge, *Biographia Literaria* (Oxford, 1907), i. 202.

conception more intense and steady than what attends the mere fictions of the imagination . . . this *manner* of conception arises from a customary conjunction of the object with something present to the memory or senses. . . .' This conjunction is effected according to the principles of Resemblance, Contiguity, and Causation, all of which depend upon belief in their operation. Relational knowledge of the phenomenal world, then, 'proceeds not from reason' but 'derives its origin altogether from custom and experience'.[1] 'As the true method of knowledge is experiment the true faculty of knowing must be the faculty which experiences. This faculty I treat of' (*All Religions Are One*, E 2).

In his brilliant study of Blake, *The Valley of Vision* (Toronto, 1961), the late Peter F. Fisher remarks:

> The psychological insight of Hume, who had stated that reason had usurped the rule which sensation in fact exercised in the formation of ideas, reduced the earlier rationalistic unities of experience—soul and substance—to speculative assumptions with no foundation in the nature of things. Dominated by a renewed search for some inner connection which would unite one sense with another, eighteenth-century epistemology and psychology followed a course which was, so to speak, the natural parallel of Blake's own visionary development of the concept of imagination.   (p. 237)

The term 'natural parallel' is a good one. Hume is not, of course, saying the same thing that Blake is saying. For him imaginative beliefs remain mere fiction; he is concerned to show that all belief involves an imaginative act, not with the intuitions of the poetic or prophetic character. For Blake the relation of Hume's thought to eighteenth-century rationalism would be what he later calls 'piercing Apollyon with his own bow': faith in abstract Reason is undermined by the operation of analytical reason. Blake himself employs this method in the first *There Is No Natural Religion*:

> Mans desires are limited by his perceptions. none can desire what he has not perciev'd
> The desires & perceptions of man untaught by any thing but organs of sense, must be limited to objects of sense.

[1] *An Enquiry Concerning Human Understanding* (Illinois, 1949), pp. 51, 53, 57, 58–9.

. . . If it were not for the Poetic or Prophetic character the Philosophic & Experimental would soon be at the ratio of all things, & stand still unable to do other than repeat the same dull round over again.   (E 1)

This conclusion once more has its natural parallel in Hume's *Enquiry*:

Had not the presence of an object, instantly excited the idea of those objects, commonly conjoined with it, all our knowledge must have been limited to the narrow sphere of our memory and senses; and we should never have been able to adjust means to ends, or employ our natural powers, either to the producing of good, or avoiding of evil.   (pp. 58–9)

Hume is even willing to entertain the analogy of imagination as 'this creative power, by which it [the will] raises from nothing a new idea, and with a kind of *Fiat*, imitates the omnipotence of its Maker . . . who called forth into existence all the various scenes of Nature' (p. 74). But he attacks the notion that 'Our mental vision or conception of ideas is nothing but a revelation made to us by our Maker' and that 'When we voluntarily turn our thoughts to any object, and raise up its image in the fancy, it is not the will which creates that idea: It is the universal Creator, who discovers it to the mind, and renders it present to us' (pp. 76–7). This is, of course, precisely Blake's view. All knowledge has its source in the Poetic Genius, which is 'The true Man', and of which 'The Jewish & Christian Testaments are An original derivation' (E 3).

As all religions are derived from the Poetic Genius, all are symbolic constructs with the same underlying truth and the same claim to the Spirit of Prophecy. However, the original meanings of myths become displaced by literal belief:

The ancient Poets animated all sensible objects with Gods or Geniuses, calling them by the names and adorning them with the properties of woods, rivers, mountains, lakes, cities, nations, and whatever their enlarged & numerous senses could percieve.

And particularly they studied the genius of each city & country. placing it under its mental deity.

Till a system was formed, which some took advantage of &

enslav'd the vulgar by attempting to realize or abstract the mental
deities from their objects; thus began Priesthood.

Choosing forms of worship from poetic tales.

And at length they pronouncd that the Gods had orderd such
things.

Thus men forgot that All deities reside in the human breast. (E 37)

This view of the development of religion has much in common with those widely held in the eighteenth century, both
by the Deists and by 'speculative mythologists' such as Jacob
Bryant and Paul Henri Mallet.[1] Bryant wrote:

> I must continually put the reader in mind, how common it was
> among the Greeks, not only out of the titles of the Deities, but out of
> the names of towers, and other edifices, to form personages, and
> then to invent histories, to support what they had done. When they
> had created a number of such ideal beings, they tried to find out
> some relation: and thence proceeded to determine the parentage,
> and filiation of each, just as fancy directed.[2]

Mallet's explanation is similar and even closer to Blake's:

> Perhaps no religion ever attributed so much to a divine provi-
> dence as that of the northern nations. This doctrine served them
> for a key, as commodious, as it was universal, to unlock all the
> phaenomena of nature without exception. The intelligencies united
> to different bodies, penetrated and moved them; and men needed
> not to look any further than to them, to find the cause of every
> thing they observed in them. Thus entire nature animated and
> always moved immediately by one or more intelligent causes, was
> in their system nothing more than the organ or instrument of the
> divinity, and became a kind of book in which they thought they
> could read his will, inclinations and designs. Hence that weakness
> formerly common to so many nations, and of which the traces still
> subsist in many places, that makes them regard a thousand in-
> different phaenomena, such as the quivering of leaves, the crackling
> and colour of flames, the fall of thunderbolts, the flight or singing

---

[1] On the deist view, see Albert J. Kuhn, 'English Deism and the Development of Romantic Mythological Syncretism', *PMLA*, lxxi (1956), 1094–116.
On the speculative mythologists, a term coined by Edward B. Hungerford, see
his *Shores of Darkness* (New York, 1941); and Ruthven Todd, *Tracks in the
Snow* (London, 1946).

[2] *A New System, or, An Analysis of Ancient Mythology* (London, 1774–6),
ii, 1–2.

of a bird, mens involuntary motions, their dreams and visions, the movements of the pulse, &c. as intimations which God gives to wise men, of his will. Hence came oracles, divinations, auspices, presages, and lots; in a word all that rubbish of dark superstitions, called at one time religion. . . .[1]

Implicit in Blake's own account of the genealogy of the gods is his desire to reclaim 'the mental deities' for the human breast, to break down the barrier between man and the gods he has created. This is the polemic function of *The Marriage*, to rouse the faculties to act by means of aphorism, emblem, and parable, making man aware of the energies within him. It ends appropriately with 'A Song of Liberty', a new life-affirming myth derived from the Poetic Genius.

The Marriage of Heaven and Hell was begun within a year of the fall of the Bastille. Its tone is exuberant and confident, anticipatory of the new earth and new heaven which Blake, like Wordsworth and Coleridge, expected the French Revolution to create. Only occasionally are there references to the destructive sword which the Revolution also brought. The most notable of these is 'The Argument', where war lours over Europe:

> Rintrah roars & shakes his fires in the burdend air;
> Hungry clouds swag on the deep[2]

'The Argument' leads up to the apocalyptic moment at which Energy will enter history, discharged by the wrath of the just man, who 'rages in the wilds / Where lions roam'. That moment itself is the subject of Blake's most famous single poem, in which the ominous and threatening aspect of Energy is perceived by the prophetic imagination as a sublime phenomenon.

---

[1] *Northern Antiquities* (London, 1770), i. 109–10.
[2] E 33. On interpretation of 'The Argument', see Appendix A, below.

2

Tyger of Wrath

> It is one of the great romantic visions, clearly formulated
> by Schiller and Herder as early as 1793 and still vital in
> the systems of Hegel and Marx, that the history of mankind
> consists in a departure from a condition of undifferen-
> tiated primal unity with himself and with nature, an inter-
> mediate period in which man's powers are developed
> through differentiation and antagonism (alienation) with
> himself and with nature, and a final return to a unity on a
> higher level or harmony.
>
> NORMAN O. BROWN: *Life Against Death*

IN the years immediately preceding the composition of *The Marriage* and of his first two longer poems, *Thel* and *Tiriel*, Blake had been at work on a series of lyrics. He published these as *Songs of Innocence* in 1789. By this time he had arrived at his doctrine of contraries, and both the title of the book and some of the poems in it imply a sequel about a contrary state. The *Songs of Experience* were etched in 1793, and in the following year Blake issued a combined edition with the subtitle 'Shewing the Two Contrary States of the Human Soul'. In discussing these poems, we must avoid two errors about the relation between the two groups. The first of these would be to assume that each set represents Blake's actual view of the subject at the time of composition; that after writing the *Songs of Innocence*, he went through a dark period and reversed his previous views as a result. We would then have to imagine that Blake was 'innocent' at the age of thirty-two but somehow came to be 'experienced' two or three years later, when he began to write the *Songs of Experience* in his Notebook. We would also be unable to explain how Blake could have included versions of four Songs of Innocence in his anything-but-innocent satire *An Island In the Moon* (1784).

Clearly, the innocence of these poems lies in the speakers and their attitudes, not necessarily in the subjects themselves. This, however, should not lead us to an opposite error: to regard both sets of poems as Songs of Experience, back-reading the ironies of the second group into the first. This would reduce Innocence to an illusion, not a State, and would take Experience as the ultimate reality, dissipating the complex awareness which Blake's double perspective creates.

1

> The innocent are overtaken,
> They are not innocent.
>
> DELMORE SCHWARTZ: 'The Ballad
of the Children of the Czar'

There is much to indicate that the *Songs* of 1794 constitutes a single work. The *Songs of Experience* were never issued separately from the *Songs of Innocence*. The 'Motto to the Songs of Innocence & of Experience', which Blake wrote in his Notebook in 1792 but did not publish, expounds a universal process whereby

> The Good are attracted by Mens perceptions
> And Think not for themselves
> Till Experience teaches them to catch
> And to cage the Fairies & Elves   (E 490)

—i.e., the Innocent judge the world according to their own spontaneity and openness, but after they begin to protect themselves by repressing their intuitive responses, they gain a bitter insight into the natures of others who have done so. This necessary relation of the Contrary States is more than a backward view, as is evident from the *Songs of Innocence* itself. As Erdman observes, 'Even while making his "1789" collection Blake was accumulating contrary songs, including perhaps some not fit even temporarily for Innocence' (E 714). Among these are four poems which originally appeared in *Innocence* but were transferred to *Experience* in 1794: 'The School Boy', 'The Voice of the Ancient Bard', 'The Little Girl Lost', and 'The Little Girl Found'. All four go beyond the confines of the state of Innocence. School Boy and Bard describe, respectively, the constraints and the illusions of Experience. The 'desarts' through which lovely Lyca and her parents wander likewise belong to Experience, while the theme of the harmonizing of instinctual life ('their sleeping child / Among tygers wild') goes beyond Experience to a new state which *Songs of Experience* anticipates but does not otherwise describe. Other *Songs of Innocence* demand counterparts in *Experience*. In 'The Chimney Sweeper', we are not led to endorse the child's conclusion 'So if all do their duty they need not fear harm.' The innocence of the *speaker* is affirmed, but the poet makes the reader feel what the speaker does not: outrage at a condition in which children sleep in soot and get up before dawn in order to work. Similarly, in 'Holy Thursday' the innocent speaker does not see the pathos of the charity school-children, but the reader must. These are plain ironies and should not be made over-subtle. They do not reject the vision of Innocence; they do make us aware of its limitations. Even the title *Songs of Innocence* implies, especially for a Christian poet, a temporary state—as Dryden implied in calling his version of *Paradise Lost*, *The State of Innocence*.

The necessity of Experience is also a theme in *Tiriel*, which Blake probably wrote in 1789. Part of this poem takes place in the vales of Har, a pastoral world which Blake will later call Beulah, the external equivalent to the inner world of Innocence. Here dwell Har and Heva, an aged couple who are grotesque caricatures of Innocence.

> But they were as the shadow of Har. & as the years forgotten
> Playing with flowers. & running after birds they spent the day
> And in the night like infants slept delighted with infant dreams
>
> (E 274)

Har is a debased Poetic Genius who can only 'sing in the great cage'; he and his consort have preserved a kind of pseudo-Innocence which, like that of Mr. Skimpole in *Bleak House*, is actually a form of parasitism. It is an evasion of, not an alternative to, the vicissitudes of Experience, which are evoked by Tiriel at the end of the poem:

The child springs from the womb. the father ready stands to form
The infant head while the mother idle plays with her dog on her
  couch
The young bosom is cold for lack of mothers nourishment & milk
Is cut off from the weeping mouth with difficulty & pain
The little lids are lifted & the little nostrils opend
The father forms a whip to rouze the sluggish senses to act
And scourges off all youthful fancies from the new-born man
Then walks the weak infant in sorrow compelld to number footsteps
Upon the sand. &c.
And when the drone has reachd his crawling length
Black berries appear that poison all around him.   (E 281–2)

This account of childhood in the world of Experience is very
similar to that of 'Infant Sorrow', where

> Struggling in my fathers hands:
> Striving against my swadling bands:
> Bound and weary I thought best
> To sulk upon my mothers breast.   (E 28)

The Notebook version of this poem carries the similarities
further: the child encounters 'Clusters of the wandring vine'
and is cursed by his father (E 720). In both cases the theme
is the corruption of the senses by repressive morality, and
the anguish of deprivation which results from this. Yet the
Innocent cannot remain so by circumventing the demands of
Experience. Blake never makes the error that Coleridge does
in *Christabel*, of equating goodness with inexperience and
evil with its opposite. Those who remain in the vales of Har
will never become fully human, as we are again made aware
in *The Book of Thel*.

  Thel, whose name is derived from the Greek root for
'will', is 'the mistress of the vales of Har' (2:1, E 4). She is
a virgin whose time has come to enter a new phase of her
existence, one which is unknown and terrifying to her. She
is troubled by premonitions of death and a conviction of the
futility of life. 'And all shall say, without a use this shining
woman liv'd, / Or did she only live. to be at death the food
of worms' (E 5). She is comforted by four embodiments of
universal life—the Lilly, the Cloud, the Worm, and the Clod
of Clay—each of which tells her that it lives only for and by

the love of others, and that individual death is a prelude to a larger life. As this knowledge can only be gained by the soul's descent into Generation,[1] Thel must enter the house of the matron Clay. However, she is allowed to have a preliminary glimpse of life in the lower world by going through the 'northern bar', which is the gateway of imagination.[2] She finds herself in 'A land of sorrows & of tears where never smile was seen' (E 6) and hears a voice from 'her own grave plot' (her own life in this lower world) lamenting the corruption of the senses there:

> Why cannot the Ear be closed to its own destruction?
> Or the glistning Eye to the poison of a smile!
> Why are Eyelids stord with arrows ready drawn,
> Where a thousand fighting men in ambush lie?
> Or an Eye of gifts & graces, show'ring fruits & coined gold!
> Why a Tongue impress'd with honey from every wind?
> Why an Ear, a whirlpool fierce to draw creations in?
> Why a Nostril wide inhaling terror trembling & affright
> Why a tender curb upon the youthful burning boy!
> Why a little curtain of flesh on the bed of our desire?   (E 6)

This passage is reminiscent of the one we have discussed in *Tiriel*, and it is also similar to such Songs of Experience as 'The Angel', 'The Human Abstract', 'The Garden of Love', and 'A Poison Tree', all of which describe a life of vicious, frustrating, and self-destructive egoism. Thel is unable to endure such a nightmarish vision. She flees back into the vales of Har, attempting to protract an untimely Innocence like Har himself. Her error is ironically underscored by Blake's last illustration to the poem, which shows three naked children riding the serpent of sexuality.[3]

---

[1] There is a parallel between the pre-existent soul and the innocent child, with the 'fall' into Experience analogous to the descent of the soul into its earthly body. See Damon, *William Blake*, pp. 74–6, 310–13; and also his essay 'Blake and Milton', in *The Divine Vision*, ed. V. De Sola Pinto (London, 1957), pp. 91–6, suggesting that *Thel* is Blake's reply to the Puritanism of *Comus*. George Mills Harper discusses *Thel* in the light of Thomas Taylor (*The Neoplatonism of William Blake*, pp. 246–56).

[2] See Damon, *William Blake*, p. 312.

[3] Ibid., p. 313. We should also note that while Thel is feeling sorry for herself, her older sisters are busy leading round their sunny flocks. Robert F.

The sequel to *Thel*, *Visions of the Daughters of Albion*, affirms the power of Innocence to conquer the world of Experience. Oothoon has endured the limitations of bodily existence that Thel feared:

They told me that the night & day were all that I could see;
They told me that I had five senses to inclose me up.
And they inclos'd my infinite brain into a narrow circle.
And sunk my heart into the Abyss, a red round globe hot burning
Till all from life I was obliterated and erased.
Instead of morn arises a bright shadow, like an eye
In the eastern cloud: instead of night a sickly charnel house . . .
                                                        (E 46)

But Oothoon does not shrink from the senses; she follows the dictum of *The Marriage* that the return to Paradise will come about by an improvement of sensual enjoyment, and her perceptions are transformed.

Open to joy and to delight where ever beauty appears
If in the morning sun I find it: there my eyes are fix'd
In happy copulation; if in evening mild. wearied with work;
Sit on a bank and draw the pleasures of this free born joy. (E 49)

Oothoon is an exemplar of liberation, showing that the life of Energy is the way out of the divided existence of Experience. Her story, set against the background of *Thel*, comprehends the three phases of progression implicit in all Blake's works we have so far discussed. In her state of higher innocence, Oothoon perceives the erotic nature of Innocence itself:

Infancy, fearless, lustful, happy! nestling for delight
In laps of pleasure; Innocence! honest, open, seeking
The vigorous joys of morning light . . . (E 48)

She calls upon Man to become as a little child in regaining libidinal freedom—'sweet shall be thy taste & sweet thy infant joys renew!' In the eyes of her prudish, self-tormenting lover, she is 'a whore indeed! and all the virgin joys / Of life are harlots'; but in reality she is 'a virgin fill'd with

Gleckner suggests plausibly that they are 'higher innocents, who have gone through the state of experience to achieve eternal delight' (*The Piper & the Bard* (Detroit, 1959), p. 163).

virgin fancies'. Her exuberant unity of existence, deriving from the free play of erotic energy, is a manifestation of what Norman O. Brown calls 'the dialectical metaphysic of hope': it can be achieved only through a phase of 'differentiation and antagonism'.[1] The Little Girl Lost is found when her parents lose their fear of the instincts and emotions, symbolized by beasts of prey; and Blake's most famous beast of prey shows the way out of Experience to a higher level of harmony.

2

> In peace there's nothing so becomes a man
> As modest stillness and humility,
> But when the blast of war blows in our ears,
> Then imitate the action of the tiger:
> Stiffen the sinews, summon up the blood,
> Disguise fair nature with hard-favored rage;
> Then lend the eye a terrible aspect:
> Let it pry through the portage of the head
> Like the brass cannon; let the brow o'erwhelm it
> As fearfully as doth a galled rock
> O'erhang and jutty his confounded base,
> Swilled with the wild and wasteful ocean.
>
> (*Henry V*, III. i. 3–14)

'The Tyger' has always been one of Blake's most admired poems, and it was one of the few to gain even moderate notice in his lifetime. It was one of four Blake lyrics which were copied into Wordsworth's Commonplace Book in 1803 or 1804;[2] it gave Coleridge great pleasure;[3] Lamb thought it 'glorious'.[4] In 1806 it was printed along with a few of Blake's other lyrics in *A Father's Memoir of His Child* by Benjamin Heath Malkin.[5] It was one of five poems to appear in a German periodical in 1811, along with an article on

---

[1] *Life Against Death*, (Middletown Conn. 1959). pp. 84, 86.

[2] See F. W. Bateson, *Wordsworth, A Re-Interpretation* (London, 1954), p. 133; and *Selected Poems of William Blake*, p. 116. Professor Bateson has informed me that the handwriting may be Dorothy Wordsworth's.

[3] See letter of 12 February 1818, *Collected Letters*, ed. Earl Leslie Griggs (Oxford, 1959), iv. 836–8.

[4] Letter of 15 May 1824, *The Letters of Charles Lamb & Mary Lamb*, ed. E. V. Lucas (New Haven, 1935), ii. 424–7. For Blake's reputation among his contemporaries, see Geoffrey Keynes, 'Blake with Lamb and His Circle', *Blake Studies* (London, 1949), pp. 84–104.

[5] London, 1806. The child, who died young, had been a drawing pupil of Blake's. Malkin's comment on 'The Tyger' (see below) is slight, but his

Blake by Henry Crabb Robinson.[1]   Allan Cunningham, in
his *Lives of the Most Eminent British Painters, Sculptors, and
Architects* (1830), said, 'The little poem called "The Tiger"
has been admired for the force and vigour of its thoughts by
poets of high name.'[2] Transcripts must have been circulated
privately: Damon says that 'when the authentic text was
published, protests appeared in various magazines, giving
the lines "to which we are accustomed"' (*William Blake*,
p. 276).

The poem must have continued to pass from one friend to
another after Blake's death (it was, of course, included in
J. J. Garth Wilkinson's edition of the *Songs*, published in
London in 1839), for Alexander Gilchrist, whose *Life of
William Blake* appeared in 1863, wrote: 'One poem in the
Songs of Experience happens to have been quoted often enough
. . . to have made its strange old Hebrew-like grandeur, its
Oriental latitude yet force of eloquence, comparatively
familiar:—*The Tiger*.'[3] The latter part of Gilchrist's statement echoes what Malkin had previously said: 'It wears that
garb of grandeur, which the idea of creation communi-
cates to a mind of the higher order. Our bard, having brought
the topic he descants on from warmer latitudes than his own,
is justified in adopting an imagery, of almost oriental feature
and complection' (p. xxxvii). By 'Oriental' these writers
mean Middle Eastern, Semitic; they recognize, however
vaguely, that the poem has an Old Testament model, a fact
of some importance to us here.

But none of this so far amounts to interpretation, which
begins with the first long critical essay devoted to Blake,
Algernon Charles Swinburne's *William Blake*, first published
in 1868. Although Swinburne's comments on 'The Tyger' are
scant, he does begin the long history of critics' attempts to
determine its implications. I shall try to indicate what the
important representative views have been.

judicious remarks on some of the other poems entitle him to be considered the
first Blake critic.
    [1] See K. A. Esdaile, 'An Early Appreciation of William Blake', *The Library*, v
(1914), 229–56.
    [2] See Arthur Symons, *William Blake* (London, 1907), p. 393.
    [3] London, i. 119.

Swinburne reads the poem as a piece of Romantic Satanism. Making use of Blake's Notebook, then in the possession of Dante Gabriel Rossetti, Swinburne prints an earlier version of the second stanza, then paraphrases it and some of the rest of the poem as follows:

> Burnt in distant deeps or skies
> The cruel fire of thine eyes?
> Could heart descend or wings aspire?
> What the hand dare seize the fire?

Could God bring down his heart to the making of a thing so deadly and strong? or could any lesser daemonic force of nature take to itself wings and fly high enough to assume power equal to such a creation? Could spiritual force so far descend or material force so far aspire? Or, when the very stars, and all the armed children of heaven, the "helmed cherubim" that guide and the "sworded seraphim" that guard their several planets, wept for pity and fear at sight of this new force of monstrous matter seen in the deepest night as a fire of menace to man—

> Did he smile his work to see?
> Did he who made the lamb make thee?[1]

By calling the Tyger a 'new force of monstrous matter' and 'a fire of menace to man', Swinburne distorts the question. He also ignores the typical meaning of stars in Blake's symbolism as well as the significance of a cancelled stanza's being a cancelled stanza. Yeats and Ellis, editors of the first collection of Blake's complete works, take a different view in their brief comment: 'The "Tiger" is, of course, the tiger of wrath, wiser in his own way than the horse of instruction, but always, like the roaring of lions and the destructive sword, so terrible as to be a "portion of eternity too great for the eye of man"'.[2] S. Foster Damon, in his monumental *William Blake: His Philosophy and Symbols*, finds the question of the poem to be 'how to reconcile the Forgiveness of Sins (The

---

[1] London, p. 120. For Blake's actual spelling and punctuation, see E 24–5, 717.

[2] Edwin John Ellis and William Butler Yeats, eds., *The Works of William Blake* (London, 1893), ii. 14.

Lamb) with the Punishment of Sins (The Tyger)'. The Wrath of the Tyger had to be of divine origin ('His God was essentially personal; therefore Evil must be his Wrath'). The purpose of Wrath is 'to consume Error, to annihilate those stubborn beliefs which cannot be removed by the tame "horses of instruction"'. Yet Damon also thinks that 'Did he who made the Lamb make thee?' is 'not an exclamation of wonder, but a very real question, whose answer Blake was not sure of' (pp. 277–8).

For Joseph H. Wicksteed, author of the most detailed commentary on the *Songs*, the poem's questions do seem to have a definite answer. 'The whole thesis of "The Tyger"', he writes, 'is that he is a spiritual expression of the Creator himself. . . . "The Tyger" is a tremendous treatise enunciating the nature of the God that *does* exist—the God that is mightily and terribly visible in his manifestations.' Attempting to discover the history of Blake's inner life through the visions and revisions of the Notebook, Wicksteed decides that 'the composition of this great poem registers (perhaps effects) a change in Blake's mind', carrying him beyond the world view of the *Songs of Experience* to that of the prophecies.[1]

Since the time of these pioneer critics, writers on the poem have continued to disagree about whether the Tyger is 'good', created by the Lamb's creator; ambiguous, its creator unknown and the question of the poem unanswerable; or 'evil', created by some maleficent force.[2] Our understanding of the

---

[1] *Blake's Innocence and Experience* (London, 1928), pp. 196, 212.

[2] The first of these views has been expressed succinctly by Mark Schorer: 'The juxtaposition of lamb and tiger points not merely to the opposition of innocence and experience, but to the resolution of the paradox they present. The innocent impulses of the lamb have been curbed by restraints, and the lamb has turned into something else, indeed into the tiger. Innocence is converted to experience. It does not rest there. Energy can be curbed but it cannot be destroyed, and when it reaches the limits of its endurance, it bursts forth in revolutionary wrath.' (pp. 250–1)
    Similar to Schorer's interpretation in this respect are those of David V. Erdman (*Blake*, pp. 179–80); Stanley Gardner (*Infinity on the Anvil* (Oxford, 1954), pp. 123–30); Martin K. Nurmi ('Blake's Revisions of *The Tyger*', *PMLA*, lxxi (1956), 669–85); F. W. Bateson (*Selected Poems of William Blake*, pp. 117–19); and Martin Price (*To the Palace of Wisdom* (Garden City, N.Y., 1964), pp. 398–400).
    Among those who have seen the Tyger as either ambiguous or ambivalent are Northrop Frye ('Blake After Two Centuries', *Univ. of Toronoto*

poem and of its place in Blake's thought can be deepened if we imagine how it would have been read by a responsive con-

Quarterly, xxvii (1957), 12); Hazard Adams (*William Blake: A Reading of the Shorter Poems* (Seattle, 1963), p. 73); Robert F. Gleckner (*The Piper & the Bard*, pp. 275–90); John E. Grant ('The Art and Argument of "The Tyger"', *Discussions of William Blake*, ed. John E. Grant (Boston, 1961), pp. 64–82); Paul Miner ('"The Tyger": Genesis and Evolution in the Poetry of William Blake', *Criticism*, iv (1962), 59–73); E. D. Hirsch, Jr. (*Innocence and Experience: An Introduction to Blake* (New Haven, 1964), pp. 244–52); and Philip Hobsbaum ('A Rhetorical Question Answered: Blake's Tyger and Its Critics', *Neophilologus*, xlviii (1964), 151–5). Frye advises the reader of the poem to 'leave it a question'. Adams, in his generally valuable essay on 'The Tyger', finds two views within the poem; however, he emphasizes the 'visionary' one, according to which 'the tiger symbolizes the primal spiritual energy which may bring form out of chaos and unite man with that part of his own being which he has allowed somehow to sleepwalk into the dreadful forests of material darkness'. Gleckner, setting 'The Tyger' against some passages in *The Four Zoas*, also finds two views. Grant, in his finely considered discussion, 'The Art and Argument of "The Tyger"', indicates agreement with Wicksteed but, unlike Wicksteed, finds only conditional answers.

> If he who made the Lamb also made the Tyger, it is because the two beasts are contraries . . . If the creator smiles because he sees that in the end the Tyger will leave the forest along with man, a man may feel justified in asking why it is his lot now to be cast among savage beasts. This question cannot be removed from 'The Tyger', and, in spite of assertions to the contrary, it was one of the questions which continued to concern Blake throughout his life.

Both Miner and Hirsch find two different perspectives maintained throughout the poem, though they see its final answer as affirmative. Hobsbaum cautions readers against answering the questions, as he regards Blake himself as being in doubt about them.

Two recent commentators on the poem consider the Tyger to be perceived as evil. Harold Bloom regards this perception as the error of the 'speaker' of the poem, which he thinks of as a monologue delivered by a Bard in the fallen state of Experience. 'The Bard of Experience is in mental darkness . . . The Bard is one of the Redeemed, capable of imaginative salvation, but before the poem ends he has worked his frenzy into the self-enclosure of the Elect Angels, prostrate before a mystery entirely of his own creation' (*Blake's Apocalypse* (Garden City, N.Y., 1963), pp. 137–8). This Bard, whom I cannot help regarding as entirely read into the poem, would resemble Adams's shadowy first speaker, for whom the creator of the Tyger must be a Urizenic God, a 'devil-maker' (*William Blake*, p. 65). Miss Kathleen Raine, pursuing a different method, comes to a parallel conclusion: that the creator of the Tyger *is* such a devil-maker. She suggests sources in Gnostic and Hermetic mysticism as proof that 'the Lamb was made by the son of God, the second person of the Trinity . . . the Tiger was made by the demiurge, the third person of the (Gnostic and Cabbalistic) trinity. Lamb and Tiger inhabit different worlds, and are the work of different creators.' To Miss Raine the Tyger seems 'a symbol of competitive, predacious selfhood' ('Who Made the Tyger?', *Encounter*, ii (1954), 48, 43 resp.).

temporary reader, one who was, moreover, aware of the traditions in which Blake placed himself. Such a reader would have recognized 'The Tyger' as an apostrophe to the Wrath of God as a sublime phenomenon; to the Wrath which Boehme calls the First Principle, which the Prophets saw released in history, and which Blake perceived in the tremendous energies of the French Revolution. We will see that the imagery and the rhetoric of the poem support such an interpretation.

3

In the Old Testament Prophets, divine wrath is often associated with a Day of Yahweh which will accomplish the destruction of evil and establish a community of the righteous. In the later Prophets, 'that day' brings about a new earth and a new heaven, sometimes ruled by the Messiah. Similarly, the manifestation of wrath in Revelation destroys Babylon and is followed by the Parousia and the building of the new Jerusalem. This eschatological wrath, in both the Old and the New Testaments, frequently appears in the images of fire and of beasts of prey; sometimes it is represented by both together. Elsewhere, as the echoes of Isaiah in *The Marriage* and in *America* indicate, Blake portrayed the revolutionary events of his day as a fulfilment of this Prophetic vision. A few of many possible examples will suggest that he also did so in 'The Tyger'.

In the Prophets' depictions of the Day of Yahweh, the Wrath which brings on the establishment of the Kingdom is commonly depicted, as in Blake's poem, as fire:

For, behold, the LORD will come with fire, and with his chariots like a whirlwind, to render his anger with fury, and his rebuke with flames of fire. (Isa. 66 : 15)

But who may abide the day of his coming? and who shall stand when he appeareth? for he is like a refiner's fire, and like fullers' soap. (Mal. 3 : 2)

Sometimes, once more as in Blake's poem, the image of a forest is introduced:

Therefore thus saith the Lord GOD; As the vine tree among the trees of the forest, which I have given to the fire for fuel, so will I give the inhabitants of Jerusalem. And I will set my face against them; they shall go out from one fire, and another fire shall devour them . . . (Ezek. 15 : 6–7)

But I will punish you according to the fruit of your doings, saith the LORD; and I will kindle a fire in the forest thereof, and it shall devour all things round about it. (Jer. 21 : 14)[1]

In Amos, we find both the images of the beast of prey and the fire as symbols of God's wrath and coming Judgement:

Will a lion roar in the forest, when he hath no prey? (3 : 4)

The lion hath roared, who will not fear? the Lord GOD hath spoken, who can but prophesy? (3 : 8)

Seek the LORD, and ye shall live; lest he break out like fire in the house of Joseph, and devour it. . . . (5 : 6)

In beginning his poem with the Tyger burning bright in the night forests, Blake was using a figurative conception familiar to him in the writing of the Prophets. The allusion is to the Wrath of the Lord burning through the forests of a corrupt social order. To this eschatological conception Blake brings his own doctrine of contraries, partly derived from Boehme.

We have already touched on Blake's debt to Paracelsus and Boehme in connection with *The Marriage*, where they are ranked below the greatest poets but far above Swedenborg. In the little intellectual biography which Blake sent to John Flaxman in 1800, 'Paracelsus & Behmen' are two of the six influences mentioned, and they keep august company: Milton, Ezra, Isaiah, and Shakespeare (K 799). Twenty-five years later, Blake told Henry Crabb Robinson that Boehme was 'a divinely inspired man'. 'Bl praised too the figures in Law's transln. as being very beautiful. Mich. Angelo cod. not have done better.'[2] One of the seminal ideas that Blake derived

---

[1] This passage from Jeremiah is cited in connection with 'The Tyger' by Erdman, *Blake*, p. 181 n. A. J. Heschel writes in *The Prophets* (New York and Evanston, 1962): 'The divine word moved in Jeremiah as fire because he lived through the experience of divine wrath. Just as the pathetic wrath of God could become a physical fire of destruction, so the wrathful word of the prophet could work itself out as a destructive fiery element' (p. 116).

[2] *Blake, Coleridge, Wordsworth, Lamb, Etc.*, ed. Edith J. Morley (Manchester and London, 1922), p. 6.

from Boehme is that God manifests Himself in two contrary
principles: Wrath and Love, Fire and Light, Father and Son.
These principles are not dualistically opposed: they are
contraries in an unending dialectic whose synthesis is the
Godhead. As this conception is of great importance to an
understanding of Blake's thought, I shall quote at some length
from Boehme. Reference is to the 'Law translation', which is
really an edition made up by Law and his followers.

As God the Father himself is *All*; he is the Number Three of the
Deity; he is the Majesty; he is the still Eternity; he is the Nature,
and in it he is the Love and the Anger: the Anger is a cause of his
Strength and Might; as also a cause of Life, and of all Mobility, as
the Poison [or Gall] in Man is: and the Love is a cause of the
Heart of his Majesty, and a cause of the Number Three, and of the
Three Principles.
. . . the Fire is a cause of the Light, for without fire there would
be no Light, so there would be no *Love* without Light; the Light
is Love . . . and we see that the Light and the fire have *two several*
[properties or] sources; the *fire* is biting, wrathful, devouring and
consuming; and the *Light* is pleasant, sweet, and desirous of a Body;
the Love desireth a Body; and the fire also desireth a Body for its
nourishment, but devoureth it quite; and the Light raiseth it up,
and desireth to fill it; it taketh nothing away from the Body, but
quickens it, and makes it friendly.
Thus we may consider with ourselves, *whence* it ariseth that there
is a wrathful and a good will: For you see the Fire hath *two* Spirits,
one is that which proceedeth from the Heat, and the other that
which proceedeth from the Light: Now the Heat is Nature, and the
Light is the Eternal Liberty without [or beyond] Nature: for Nature
comprehendeth not the Light.
And so you must understand us concerning the *two* sorts of wills
in God, the *one* is Nature, and is not called God, and yet is God's,
for he is angry, severe, sharp as a sting, consuming, attracting all
things to himself, and devouring them, always striving, to fly up
above the Light, [whch is the *other* will,] and yet cannot . . .[1]

A flame represents the interaction and interdependence of the
two wills, its light corresponding to God's Love, its heat to
His Wrath.

[1] *The Threefold Life of Man*, ch. 7, secs. 62, 63, 65, 66, in *The Works of
Jacob Behmen, the Teutonic Theosopher* (London, 1764–81), ii. 76.

And yet the Fire gives or represents to us a *Mystery* of the eternal Nature, and of the Deity also, wherein a Man is to understand two Principles of a twofold Source, *viz.* I. a hot, fierce, astringent, bitter, anxious, consuming One in the Fire-source. And out of the Fire comes the II. *viz.* the Light, which dwells in the Fire, but is not apprehended or laid hold on by the Fire; also it has another Source then [*sic*] the Fire has, which is *Meekness*, wherein there is a Desire of *Love*, where then, in the Love-desire, another Will is understood than that which the Fire has.[1]

Law is at least as explicit on the mutual dependence of the two wills and their ultimate unity:

. . . the Father has His distinct manifestation in the fire, which is always generating the light; the Son has His distinct manifestation in the light, which is always generated from the fire; the Holy Ghost has His manifestation in the spirit, that always proceeds from both, and is always united with them.[2]

Blake gave pictorial expression to the Two Principles in his allegorical illustration of James Hervey's *Meditations Among the Tombs*. In one corner of the painting, to the left of God the Father, Blake wrote 'Wrath'; in the other corner, 'Mercy'; and directly to the left of God, 'God out of Christ is a Consuming Fire.' This again suggests that Blake characteristically thought of Wrath in Boehme's sense, for in *Aurora* (ch. 14, sec. 49), we find: 'But in the Outspeaking of his Word, wherein the Nature of the Spiritual World exists . . . and wherein *God calls himself an angry*, zealous or *jealous God, and a consuming Fire*, therein indeed God has *known the Evil* from Eternity . . . but therein is he *not called God*, but a consuming Fire.'[3]

The Two Principles are analogous to Blake's contrary states of Innocence and Experience. Meekness is apposite to the visionary poet in one State, Wrath in the other.[4] The poet

---

[1] *Aurora*, ch. 11, sec. 92, *Works of Jacob Behmen*, i. 99.

[2] 'An Appeal', *Selected Mystical Writings of William Law*, ed. Stephen Hobhouse (New York, 1948), p. 46.

[3] *Works*, i. 138. The allusion is to Hebrews 12 : 29: 'For our God is a consuming fire.' Blake's addition of 'out of Christ' has exactly Boehme's significance. The epitome of Hervey's *Meditations* is reproduced, with commentary, in Damon's *Blake Dictionary*, pl. xi and pp. 183–4.

[4] I should note that Gerald E. Bentley, Jr., suggests, without going further into this subject, that 'The question of "The Tyger" is whether the wrath

of Experience must endeavour, like Boehme and Law, to show that Wrath is the self-executing judgement of God in a fallen world. By doing so, he will pass 'beyond' Experience into inspired prophecy. The Tyger shows the way to this, embodying the Wrath of the First Principle unfolded in history as the great human upheaval of the French Revolution. Angels call it evil. The poet aspiring towards prophecy perceives and fixes its terrible energies as sublime.

Terror, as we have seen, was commonly considered the highest manifestation of sublimity. Burke (p. 58) went so far as to say that 'terror is in all cases whatsoever, either more openly or latently the ruling principle of the sublime'. Dennis had tried to explain why this was so.

. . . the Care, which Nature has inrooted in all, of their own Preservation, is the Cause that Men are unavoidably terrify'd with any thing that threatens approaching Evil. 'Tis now our Business to shew how the Ideas of Serpents, Lions, Tygers, &c. were made by the Art of those great Poets, to be terrible to their Readers, at the same time that we are secure from their Objects.[1]

The chief effect of the sublime is 'astonishment', which Burke defines as 'that state of the soul, in which all its motions are suspended, with some degree of horror', and 'the mind is so entirely filled with its object, that it cannot entertain any other, nor by consequence reason on that object which employs it' (p. 57). These effects are produced when we contemplate dangerous objects which we know cannot harm us. Like Dennis, Burke finds examples of this which bring Blake's poem to mind: 'We have continually about us animals of a strength that is considerable, but not pernicious. Amongst these we never look for the sublime: it comes upon us in the gloomy forest, and in the howling wilderness, in the form of the lion, the tiger, the panther, or rhinoceros' (p. 66).

These writers found the literature of the Old Testament particularly rich in the sublime of terror:

Now of all these Ideas none are so terrible as those which shew the Wrath and Vengeance of an angry God; for nothing is so wonderful

principle and the love principle emanate from the same eternal being' ('William Blake and the Alchemical Philosophers', p. 216).
[1] *The Grounds of Criticism in Poetry*, in *Critical Works*, i. 362.

in its Effects: and consequently the Images or Ideas of those Effects must carry a great deal of Terror with them, which we may see was *Longinus's* Opinion, by the Examples which he brings in his Chapter of the Sublimity of the Thoughts.[1]

Dennis goes on to produce examples of Wrath from Habbakuk and Psalms, comparing them with passages from Homer to the advantage of the former (pp. 366–8). Lowth writes, in a similar vein:

Nothing, however, can be greater or more magnificent than the representation of anger and indignation, particularly when the Divine wrath is displayed. Of this the whole of the prophetic Song of Moses affords an incomparable specimen [cites Deut. 32 : 40–2, followed by Isa. 63 : 4–6] . . . The display of the fury and threats of the enemy, by which Moses finely exaggerates the horror of their unexpected ruin, is also wonderfully sublime [cites Exod. 15: 9–10].[2]

Of the Biblical passages which Dennis, Lowth, Burke, and others display as instances of the sublime, many have in common with Blake's poem the depiction of wrath in terms of fire, beasts of prey, or both. Lowth, for example, comments on

. . . the sublimity of those passages . . . in which the image is taken from the roaring of a lion, the clamour of rustic labourers, and the rage of wild beasts:

> JEHOVAH from on high shall roar,
> And from his holy habitation shall he utter his voice;
> He shall roar aloud against his resting-place,
> A shout like that of the vintagers shall he give
> Against all the inhabitants of the earth.
>
> And I will be unto them as a lion;
> As a leopard in the way will I watch them:
> I will meet them as a bear bereaved of her whelps:
> And I will rend the caul of their heart:
> And there will I devour them as a lioness;
> A beast of the field shall tear them.[3]

---

[1] *The Grounds of Criticism in Poetry*, in *Critical Works*, i. 361.

[2] Lowth, *Lectures*, i. 379–81. See Monk, *The Sublime*, pp. 79–80.

[3] Op. cit. 363. Jer. 25 : 30; Hos. 13 : 7, 8. My own Biblical citations are from the Authorized Version, but in an instance such as this one where the author provides his own translation, I reproduce the text as he gives it, unless otherwise noted.

William Smith, in the notes to his translation of Longinus (p. 127), gave a number of examples of sublimity, among them this passage from Psalm 18: 'There went up a smoke out of his nostrils, and fire out of his mouth devoured: coals were kindled at it. . . . And he rode upon a Cherub, and did fly, and came flying upon the wings of the wind.'

The most powerful manifestations of 'the Sublime of the Bible' were in descriptions of divine wrath and power; the single book of the Bible which was considered most sublime in the eighteenth century, and which was also to be the subject of Blake's great pictorial interpretation in old age, was Job. Lowth declared of the book as a whole:

> Not only the force, the beauty, the sublimity of the sentiments are unrivalled; but such is the character of the diction in general, so vivid is the expression, so interesting the assemblage of objects, so close and connected the sentences, so animated and passionate the whole arrangement, that the Hebrew literature itself contains nothing more poetical. (i. 313)

Almost all of Lowth's Lecture XIV, 'Of the Sublime in General', is devoted to Job, in addition to three lectures on the work itself. Burke (p. 63) found Job 4 : 13–17 'a passage amazingly sublime . . . principally due to the terrible uncertainty of the thing described'. The same passage served Smith (p. 151) as an example of the sublime of horror, and Blake used part of it as the theme for his ninth illustration to Job—'Then a Spirit passed before my face: the hair of my flesh stood up . . . Shall mortal Man be more just than God?' Section V of Burke's *Enquiry*, 'Power', draws numerous examples of its subject from Job. Among these are the descriptions of Behemoth and Leviathan, symbolic beasts to which the Tyger is related as an embodiment of sublime power.

In his later writings and paintings, Blake portrays Leviathan as a demonic parody of the sublime, but this change in his symbolism, reflecting his changed view of revolution after the rise of Napoleon, occurred long after 'The Tyger' was written. To ignore this fact in linking Tyger and Leviathan is to distort the meaning of the poem. At this point we should rather think of the tiger-striped Leviathan of *The Marriage of*

Heaven and Hell, which advances from the direction of Paris 'with all the fury of a spiritual existence' (E 40). The Tyger is like the Leviathan of Job in that both are fiery images of divine energy:

Out of his mouth go burning lamps, and sparks of fire leap out.
Out of his nostrils goeth smoke, as out of a seething pot or caldron.
His breath kindleth coals, and a flame goeth out of his mouth.
In his neck remaineth strength, and sorrow is turned into joy before him. (41 : 19–22)

Such power cannot be explained; it can only be evoked, as by the questions which the Lord asks Job from the whirlwind, or by those which Blake's speaker asks in 'The Tyger'.[1] 'Did he who made the Lamb make thee?' no more demands an explicit answer than 'Who hath divided a water-course for the overflowing of the waters, or a way for the lighting of thunder?' Leviathan is the culminating image of God's speech to Job because as an embodiment of power it completes the process of raising the Job problem out of the realm of ethical discourse, inducing an attitude of awe, wonder, and astonishment which the eighteenth century called sublime. This is the function of 'The Tyger' in the *Songs of Experience*.

4

The Tyger

Tyger Tyger, burning bright,
In the forests of the night;
What immortal hand or eye,
Could frame thy fearful symmetry?

In what distant deeps or skies
Burnt the fire of thine eyes!
On what wings dare he aspire?
What the hand, dare seize the fire?

And what shoulder, & what art,
Could twist the sinews of thy heart?
And when thy heart began to beat,
What dread hand? & what dread feet?

[1] Erdman, *Blake*, p. 103, suggests a possible indirect connection between the two through a paraphrase in James Hervey's *Theron and Aspasio* (1775).

What the hammer? what the chain,
In what furnace was thy brain?
What the anvil? what dread grasp,
Dare its deadly terrors clasp?

When the stars threw down their spears
And water'd heaven with their tears:
Did he smile his work to see?
Did he who made the Lamb make thee?

Tyger, Tyger burning bright,
In the forests of the night:
What immortal hand or eye,
Dare frame thy fearful symmetry?[1]

A responsive contemporary reader would have seen the sublimity of 'The Tyger' not only in its theme but in its rhetoric
and its imagery as well. First there are the questions of which
Blake's poem entirely consists, and which I have compared
to those of Job: in both cases sublimity lies in the form as well
as in the content. For example, Edward Young wrote in a
note to his own verse-paraphrase of Job: '*Longinus* has a
chapter on interrogations, which shews that they contribute
much to the sublime. This speech of the Almighty is made up
of them.'[2] Smith, commenting on that same chapter (xviii) in
Longinus, remarked: 'To these Instances may be added the
whole 38th Chapter of *Job*; where we behold the Almighty
Creator expostulating with his Creature . . . There we see
how vastly useful the Figure of Interrogation is, in giving us
a lofty Idea of the Deity, whilst every Question awes us into
Silence, and inspires a Sense of our own Insufficiency' (p. 154).
Blake's poem has other sublime elements as well. Richard
Hurd associated sublimity with 'apostrophes and invocations'[3]

---

[1] In one copy of the *Songs*, line 12 was altered to 'What dread hand Formd
thy dread feet?' (Copy P, in Geoffrey Keynes and Edwin Wolf, *William Blake's
Illuminated Books: A Census* (New York, 1953), p. 61). Malkin printed the
line as 'What dread hand forged thy dread feet?' Damon, *William Blake*, p.
279, thinks this emendation was Blake's own. Bateson, *Selected Poems*, p. 118,
notes that 'forged' is the reading in Wordsworth's Commonplace Book.

[2] *The Works of the Author of the Night-Thoughts* (London, 1792), i. 188 n.
See also Lowth, op. cit., i. 357.

[3] Quoted by Miles, *Eras and Modes in English Poetry*, p. 66, from *On the Idea
of Universal Poetry*, in *The Works of Richard Hurd, D.D.*, ii (London, 1811), 9.

—'The Tyger' is, of course, both. (Hurd also wrote that poetry 'calls up infernal spectres to terrify, or brings down celestial natures to astonish, the imagination'.) As for diction, Blake's exhibits the qualities which Lowth praised in Hebrew poetry—'sparing in words, concise, and energetic' (ii. 250). One could easily apply to 'The Tyger' the statement that 'The sublimity of the matter is perfectly equalled by the unaffected energy of the style' (ii. 251); Lowth is speaking of Psalm 29, in which 'The voice of the LORD divideth the flames of fire. The voice of the LORD shaketh the wilderness; the LORD shaketh the wilderness of Kadesh' (7–8). Such a comparison was made more or less explicitly by Malkin, who in discussing Blake's *Songs* observed: 'The devotional pieces of the Hebrew bards are clothed in that simple language, to which Johnson with justice ascribes the character of sublimity' (p. xxxi). Among later writers on the poem, only Gilchrist made use of this hint. Also, in addition to being simple and energetic, Blake's diction employs what Professor Miles (p. 57) so aptly calls the 'vocabulary of cosmic passion and sense impression' which characterizes the sublime poem of the late eighteenth century. Vistas open in 'distant deeps or skies', penetrated by the 'immortal hand or eye' of a being who dares 'aspire' on 'wings'; 'the stars' and 'heaven' participate in the cosmic drama. Other expressions, in stanzas 3 and 4, belong to the vocabulary of the sublime of terror: 'dread hand', 'dread grasp', and 'deadly terrors'. In his use of sublime language, as Professor Miles has demonstrated, Blake is very much a poet of his era.

Having discussed the sublimity of 'The Tyger', we must turn to the symbolic meanings which its images represent. It is here, of course, that Blake differs from poets who merely imitated the Bible. Blake's images have meanings which may in part be construed from the internal logic of the poem, but which also depend at least in part upon meanings established elsewhere, in Blake's other poems or in the traditional sources from which he drew. We learn to understand Blake's forests, tears, fire, stars, and furnaces as we do Shelley's veils, boats, rivers, and caves, or Yeats's spindles and swans. Meaning is affected by context, though not entirely determined by it.

Fire, for example, has a different significance for Blake when
it gives both heat and light than when it gives heat alone, and
furnaces may be creative or destructive, depending on what
is going on in them. In interpreting these images, we must
beware of assigning sources too narrowly, or of mechanically
transferring a meaning from one context to an entirely
different one. We should, instead, try to understand what
each image contributes to the effect of the poem as a whole.

The Tyger embodies the *contrarium* of Wrath in the Godhead, 'Burning bright' with Prophetic fire and perceived as
a sublime phenomenon. He is God's judgement upon the
world of Experience. In Blake's Notebook he appears after
the moral terrain of that world has been charted in terms of
the hapless soldier, the blackening church, the harlot, the
chimney-sweep. This debased and corrupt order produces a
contrary to the Lamb of Innocence in the Tyger. But Contraries
are not Negations. The Tyger is not 'a symbol of competitive,
predacious selfhood'. Wrath is a vice only in the unfallen
world of Innocence; in our world, in the London or Paris of
1792, Mercy and the other virtues of Innocence are vices.

> I heard an Angel singing
> When the day was springing
> Mercy Pity Peace
> Is the worlds release
>
> Thus he sung all day
> Over the new mown hay
> Till the sun went down
> And haycocks looked brown
>
> I heard a Devil curse
> Over the heath & the furze
> Mercy could be no more
> If there was nobody poor
>
> And pity no more could be
> If all were as happy as we
> At his curse the sun went down
> And the heavens gave a frown

> Down pourd the heavy rain
> Over the new reapd grain
> And Miseries increase
> Is Mercy Pity Peace[1]

The Tyger, ultimate product of Experience, shows the way out of Experience to the earthly paradise of *The Marriage of Heaven and Hell*:

> Then the perilous path was planted:
> And a river, and a spring
> On every cliff and tomb;
> And on the bleached bones
> Red clay brought forth.   (E 33)

But man's attempt to create such a paradise on earth came in the bloody aspect of the French Revolution. 'One might as well think of establishing a republic of tigers in some forest of Africa',[2] declared Sir Samuel Romilly after the September Massacres, and Wordsworth in the autumn of 1792 found Revolutionary Paris

> . . . . a place of fear
> Unfit for the repose which night requires,
> Defenceless as a wood where tigers roam.[3]

In *The Book of Ahania* (1795), where the energy principle temporarily overthrows repressive reason, 'Fuzon, his tygers unloosing, / Thought Urizen slain by his wrath.'[4] The image of the tiger seems to have been almost inevitable.

Night, forests, and stars are frequently used by Blake as symbols of the old order, *l'épaisse nuit gothique* of Holy Europe. 'Thy Nobles have gather'd thy starry hosts round this rebellious city', declares warlike Burgundy to the King

---

[1] E 461–2. (A Notebook poem contemporary with *Songs of Experience*.)

[2] Quoted by Asa Briggs in *The Age of Improvement* (London, 1960), pp. 134–5.

[3] *The Prelude* (1805), ed. Ernest de Selincourt (Oxford, 1959), p. 370. For the date of composition of 'The Tyger' (autumn of 1792), see Erdman, *Blake*, pp. 167 n. and 174; Nurmi, *PMLA*, lxxi. 671 n.

[4] See my 'Method and Meaning in Blake's *Book of Ahania*', *BNYPL*, lxx (1966), 27–33.

in *The French Revolution* (1791, E 282–96), 'To rouze up the ancient forests of Europe, with clarions of cloud [loud?] breathing war' (ll. 100–1). He fears that the revolutionaries will 'mow down all this great starry harvest of six thousand years' (l. 90) and that 'the ancient forests of chivalry' will be 'hewn' (l. 93). In the same poem, Orleans, speaking for the popular cause, talks of 'the wild raging millions, that wander in forests, and howl in law blasted wastes' (l. 227). This is similar, too, to 'The Argument' of *The Marriage of Heaven and Hell*, where 'the just man rages in the wilds / Where lions roam' (E 33). In *Europe* (1794), 'The night of Nature' is eighteen centuries of history which culminate in the war of 1793, when 'The Tigers couch upon the prey & suck the ruddy tide' (E 65). In the same poem man enmeshed in material error hides 'In forests of night' (E 62). There is, perhaps, a suggestion of Dante's *selva oscura* in the image, and of Spenser's Wood of Error. It may also recall Thomas Taylor's use of woods as a symbol of material nature,[1] and, as was pointed out earlier, the Prophets sometimes use the forest to stand for the corrupt order which God will burn. Blake need not have consciously borrowed his forest symbol from any of these sources to have been aware of its meanings in them. Such awareness, together with a feeling of affinity, influences the conceptions of a poet and makes traditional symbols viable in his work, as we see again in Blake's use of the stars.

Lines 17–18 have several related meanings. The literal image is of starlight and dew; Frederick Pottle suggests 'When the stars faded out in the dawn and the dew fell.'[2] On the historical level, the stars represent the armies of monarchy; as early as the *Poetical Sketches* and as late as *Jerusalem*, Blake associates the stars with tyranny and war:

> The stars of heaven tremble: the roaring voice of war, the trumpet, calls to battle! ('Prologue to King John', E 430)

> Loud the Sun & Moon rage in the conflict: loud the Stars Shout in the night of battle & their spears grow to their hands

---

[1] See Harper, *The Neoplatonism of William Blake*, pp. 157 and 169.
[2] *Explicator*, viii (1950), no. 39.

With blood, weaving the deaths of the Mighty into a Tabernacle
For Rahab & Tirzah; till the Great Polypus of Generation
　　covered the Earth.　　　　　　(*Jerusalem*, 67 : 31–4, E 218)[1]

'The stars threw down their spears' appears in Night V of
The Four Zoas, where, as Erdman points out, Urizen's words
refer to the defeat of the counter-revolutionary armies at
Yorktown and Valmy:

I calld the stars around my feet in the night of councils dark
The stars threw down their spears & fled naked away
We fell . . .　　　　　　　　　　　　　(64 : 26–8, E 377)[2]

(Also compare the defeat of the British as described in *America*
15 : 4–5: 'The millions sent up a howl of anguish and threw off
their hammerd mail, / And cast their swords & spears to
earth, & stood a naked multitude.') The meaning of these
stars derives in part from Revelation. In 12 : 4 the stars are
Satan's legions: 'And his tail drew the third part of the stars
of heaven, and did cast them to the earth'; while in the apocalypse of chapter 6, after the Lamb of God opens the sixth
seal, 'the stars of heaven fell unto the earth, even as a fig
tree casteth her untimely figs, when she is shaken of a mighty
wind' (13). Coleridge, who like Blake saw the French
Revolution as an apocalyptic event, uses this latter image
in *Religious Musings*:

　　　　And lo! the Great, the Rich, the Mighty Men,
　　　　The Kings and the Chief Captains of the World,
　　　　With all that fixed on high like stars of Heaven
　　　　Shot baleful influence, shall be cast to earth[3]

'This passage', Coleridge noted (p. 121), 'alludes to the
French Revolution . . . I am convinced that the Babylon of the

---

[1] Cf. *Jerusalem*, 55 : 27, where 'The Stars in their courses fought' (E 202),
echoing Judges 5 : 20. Several lines after this, the Eternals name the Eighth
Eye of God, but 'he came not, he hid in Albions Forests' (33). In this later phase
of his thought, Blake believes that the destructive wrath of revolution should
be restrained; therefore the Words of the Eternals are described as 'Curbing
their Tygers with golden bits & bridles of silver & ivory' (35).

[2] See Erdman, *Blake*, p. 178.

[3] Written in 1794. *Complete Poetical Works*, i. 121.

Apocalypse does not apply to Rome exclusively; but to the union of Religion with Power and Wealth, wherever it is found', a statement which could have been made by Blake as well. Revelation 6 ends, significantly, 'For the great day of his wrath is come; and who shall be able to stand?' (17).

Blake also thought of the stars as symbols of oppression because they were associated both with the mechanism of the Newtonian universe and with the instrumentality of fate. The defeat of the stars signifies the casting off of both cosmic and internal constraint, freeing man to realize his potentially divine nature. This is also a theme in Paracelsus and Boehme. Boehme (*Threefold Life*, ch. 11, sec. 38) wrote:

> For *the outward life* is fallen quite under the power of the Stars, and if thou wilt withstand them, thou must enter into God's will, and then they are but as a shadow, and cannot bring that to effect which they have in their power: *neither do they desire it*, but the Devil only desireth it: For the whole Nature boweth itself before the will of God: For the Image of God in Man is so powerful and mighty, that when it wholly casteth itself into the will of God, it overpowereth Nature, so that the Stars are *obedient* to it, and do rejoice themselves in the Image . . . at which the Heaven rejoiceth, and so the Anger of God in the Government of this world is *quenched*; for when that is burning, Man's wickedness is guilty of it, in that Men kindle it in the Spirit of this world.   (*Works*, ii. 116)

According to Paracelsus,

> The stars are subject to the philosopher, they must follow him, and not he them. Only the man who is still animal is governed, mastered, compelled, and driven by the stars, so that he has no choice but to follow them. . . . But the reason for all this is that such a man does not know himself and does not know how to use the energies hidden in him, nor does he know that he carries the stars within himself . . . and thus carries in him the whole firmament with all its influences.[1]

After the failure of the peasants' revolt, Paracelsus declared: 'The peasants have submitted to the stars, and have been beaten by them. Whoever trusts the stars, trusts a

---

[1] *Selected Writings*, ed. Jolande Jacobi (New York, 1951), p. 228.

traitor.'[1] In 'The Tyger', the opposite happens: the stars are beaten and desert their order. Man's fate suddenly becomes of his own making, and the 'just man' of 'The Argument' can create a human society, symbolized by the covering of the bleached bones of the Old Adam with the red clay of the New.

The weeping stars of Blake's poem owe something perhaps to the anonymous lyric 'Tom of Bedlam', reprinted in Joseph Ritson's *Ancient Songs* of 1792:

> I behold the stars at mortal wars,
> In the wounded welkin weeping

The tears in Blake's poem are doubtless the 'tears such as Angels weep' in *Paradise Lost*, I. 620, but of Angels in the Blakean sense—they are tears of frustration, hypocrisy, repression. This is the burden of meaning carried by tears in other *Songs of Experience*. In 'The Human Abstract', Cruelty 'waters the ground with tears' in order to make the Tree of Mystery grow. The speaker of 'The Angel' (E 24) uses tears as a defence against feeling:

> And I wept both night and day
> And he wip'd my tears away
> And I wept both day and night
> And hid from him my hearts delight
>
> So he took his wings and fled:
> Then the morn blush'd rosy red:
> I dried my tears & armd my fears,
> With ten thousand shields and spears.

In the Lambeth prophecies, Urizen is often depicted as weeping because life cannot keep his iron laws. 'And he wept, & he called it Pity / And his tears flowed down on the winds' (*Book of Urizen*, E 81). Pity, as I have said, is a vice in the world of Experience. It is the error of La Fayette in the poem Blake wrote about him not long after 'The Tyger':

> Fayette beheld the King & Queen
> In curses & iron bound

[1] Quoted in Henry M. Pachter, *Paracelsus: Magic Into Science* (New York, 1957), p. 107.

But mute Fayette wept tear for tear
And guarded them around.   (E 491)

Erdman suggests a parallel to this in Paine's condemna-
tion of Burke's pity for Marie Antoinette—'He pities the
plumage, but forgets the dying bird.'[1] If the just man is to
find his way out of the forest around him, he must give up his
modest stillness and humility and imitate the action of the
tiger.

Having discussed the tiger–fire images in the poem and the
stars–forest–tears constellation, we must now turn to the
third important group of images, those concerned with
metal-working.

> What the hammer? what the chain,
> In what furnace was thy brain?
> What the anvil? what dread grasp,
> Dare its deadly terrors clasp?

These instruments—hammer, chain, furnace, and anvil—are
in Blake's prophetic writings assigned to Los, Eternal
Prophet, and symbol of the Imagination.[2] It is the function of
Los to create the imaginative constructs which give form to
human perception. On Plate 6 of *Jerusalem* he is pictured with
all four instruments mentioned in 'The Tyger', and in *The
Book of Los* (1795, E 93) he forges the sun with them.

> Roaring indignant the bright sparks
> Endur'd the vast Hammer; but unwearied
> Los beat on the Anvil; till glorious
> An immense Orb of fire he fram'd
>
> Oft he quench'd it beneath in the Deeps
> Then survey'd the all-bright mass. Again
> Siezing fires from the terrific Orbs
> He heated the round Globe, then beat[,]
> While roaring his Furnaces endur'd
> The chaind Orb in their infinite wombs.[3]

[1] *Blake*, p. 168, from *Rights of Man* (London, 1791), 4th ed., p. 26.
[2] As noted by Hazard Adams, *Blake and Yeats: The Contrary Vision* (Ithaca,
N.Y., 1955), p. 238.
[3] This similarity is discussed in my Brown Univ. master's thesis, 'William
Blake's Revolutionary Symbolism' (1957), p. 7, and in Miner, *Criticism*, iv.
67–8.

The furnace in which the energy-symbols of Sun and Tyger
are created is the prophetic imagination: the hammer is the
divine Word. The meanings of these images are supported
by, though they do not depend on, their use in the Bible,
Paracelsus, and Boehme. In Ezekiel 22 : 17–22, the furnace
is a simile for the wrath of God:

> And the word of the Lord came unto me, saying,
>
> Son of man, the house of Israel is to me become dross: all they
> are brass, and tin, and iron, and lead, in the midst of the furnace;
> they are even the dross of silver.
>
> Therefore thus saith the Lord God; Because ye are all become
> dross, behold, therefore I will gather you into the midst of Jeru-
> salem.
>
> As they gather silver, and brass, and iron, and lead, and tin, into
> the midst of the furnace, to blow the fire upon it, to melt it; so will
> I gather you in mine anger and in my fury, and I will leave you there,
> and melt you.
>
> Yea, I will gather you, and blow upon you in the fire of my wrath,
> and ye shall be melted in the midst thereof.
>
> As silver is melted in the midst of the furnace, so shall ye be
> melted in the midst thereof; and ye shall know that I the Lord have
> poured out my fury upon you.

But the furnace does more than melt down; it also purifies:
'Behold, I have refined thee, but not with silver; I have
chosen thee in the furnace of affliction' (Isa. 48 : 10). The furnace can be creative as well as destructive, as we see in Psalm
12—'The words of the Lord are pure words: as silver tried
in a furnace of earth, purified seven times.' The destructive
fire of wrath is also the energy of purification. Paracelsus,
who believes that destruction perfects that which is good,
regards the work of the alchemist's furnace as analogous to
this divine activity: 'For in the same way as God created the
heaven and the earth, the furnace with its fire must be constructed and regulated.' 'But the sun receives light from no
other source than God Himself, Who rules it, so that in the
sun God Himself is burning and shining. Just so it is with this
Art. The fire in the furnace may be compared to the sun. It
heats the furnace and the vessels, just as the sun heats the

vast universe. For as nothing can be produced in the world without the sun, so also in this Art nothing can be produced without this simple fire.'[1] Blake carries the alchemical analogy into symbolism—the imaginative activity of the poet–prophet in raising the perceptions of mankind is, metaphorically, the Great Work of turning base metals into gold. Blake's furnace is a perpetual source of power for transforming a dead world. The hammer, the active force of the *Logos*, beats out the changes. 'Is not my word like as a fire? saith the LORD; and like a hammer that breaketh the rock in pieces?' (Jer. 23 : 29). Boehme speaks of the Spirit of God as 'the right Hammer' which strikes in the soul and makes it long for the love of God. 'Such a Soul is *easy* to be awakened . . . especially when the Hammer of the Holy Ghost sounds through the Ears into the Heart, then the Tincture of the soul receives it *instantly*; and there it goes forth through the whole soul.'[2] As if in answer to the closing questions of 'The Tyger', in *Jerusalem*, Plate 73, all things are created in Los's furnaces, including 'the tyger' and 'the wooly lamb' (E 226); and in *The Book of Los*, after creating the sun, 'Los smild with joy' (E 93).

I do not suggest that we must literally find answers to the questions of Blake's poem in his sources or in his other writings. What these materials can do is reinforce and corroborate our sense of what the poem means; they also indicate its place in Blake's thought. Created by Los, the Tyger is an educt of the prophetic imagination. As an incarnation of divine Wrath, it calls to mind the Prophets' representations of God as a beast of prey, the Greyhound of Virgil's prophecy in canto i of the *Inferno*, and the Lion of the tribe of Juda in Revelation 5:5.[3] Its fearful symmetry derives from the dialectical tension of Boehme's First and Second Principles.

---

[1] 'Concerning the Spirits of the Planets', *Hermetic and Alchemical Writings*, i. 85, 74 resp.

[2] *The Threefold Life of Man*, ch. 18, sec. 49, in *Works*, ii. 194.

[3] Cf. the 'Christ the tiger' of Eliot's 'Gerontion', in which several other lines also recall Blake:

> . . . . Virtues
> Are forced upon us by our impudent crimes.
> These tears are shaken from the wrath-bearing tree.
> The tiger springs in the new year. Us he devours . . .

It inaugurates a Day of Wrath in which man will be tried by fire, but its ultimate function is to create a world in which a higher Innocence will be possible. Those who follow vision through the fallen world of Experience, like the parents of 'The Little Girl Found', will discover this.

> Then they followed,
> Where the vision led:
> And saw their sleeping child,
> Among tygers wild.

3

Heroic Fatality: The Lambeth Books
(1793–1795)

The mainspring of revolt . . . is the principle of superabundant activity and energy.

CAMUS: *The Rebel*

Two years after moving to Lambeth in 1791, Blake began to publish the 'Bible of Hell' which he had promised his readers in *The Marriage*. The six illuminated books which he produced from 1793 to 1795 project a central myth, the 'boundaries' of which are, in Frye's words, 'creation, fall, redemption and apocalypse'.[1] In these poems the concepts of Energy, represented by the symbolic figures Orc and Fuzon, and of Imagination, represented by Los, are once more very important, but their meanings are considerably modified. Dismayed by the violent suppression of liberty in France,[2] Blake had become increasingly aware of the ambiguous nature of Energy and had even begun to doubt the efficacy of the prophetic Imagination. Consequently, in *The Book of Urizen* (1794), Los binds Orc with the Chain of Jealousy, the Imagination mistakenly trying to limit the claims of Energy as a threat to its autonomy. In *America* (1793) a double perspective is maintained, suggesting the ambiguity of Orc by his two forms: human and serpent: Energy hovers between redemptive potentiality and the will-to-power. In *The Book of Ahania* (1795), this ambiguity gives way to a completely ironical view; Energy is now seen not as an apocalyptic, redemptive force, but as bound into the betrayals of history. Concomitantly, there is a shift in the meaning of Wrath,

---

[1] *Fearful Symmetry*, p. 124.
[2] See Erdman, *Blake*, p. 288.

which becomes separated from its divine source in the dark
world of fallen nature.

1

The Lambeth books compose a Bible of Hell in that they reveal the archetypal configurations which Blake saw as underlying human events. With the speculative mythologists who
were his predecessors and contemporaries, Blake believed
that all existing myths were variants of a single universal one.
For Blake, the events which that original myth referred to
were mental; history, sacred and secular, was a recapitulation
of these events in the external world. In the Lambeth books,
the myth is re-created as a symbolic narrative with several
levels of meaning. This mode of presentation is derived from
the medieval fourfold method of exegesis, as a comparison
with Dante will show.

In his letter to Can Grande della Scala, Dante gives a fourfold exposition of the Psalmodic text 'When Israel went
out of Egypt, the house of Jacob from a people of strange
language, Judah was his sanctuary, and Israel his dominion.'
This literal statement, says Dante, allegorically signifies our
redemption wrought by Christ; morally, the conversion of
the soul from sin to a state of grace; anagogically (mystically
or supernaturally), the departure of the soul 'from the slavery
of this corruption to the liberty of everlasting glory'.[1] Blake's
treatment of the same Biblical situation occurs at the end of
The Book of Urizen:

> So Fuzon call'd all together
> The remaining children of Urizen:
> And they left the pendulous earth:
> They called it Egypt, & left it.
> (28: 19–22, E 82)

Historically, Fuzon is Moses leading Israel (the children of
Urizen) to the Promised Land. The 'allegorical' extension of
this meaning is its parallel in Blake's own time, the French
Revolution. The psychological dimension in Blake is analogous

---

[1] Charles Sterrett Latham, *A Translation of Dante's Eleven Letters* (Cambridge, Mass., 1892), p. 193.

to the moral one in Dante: Fuzon is the Energy principle
that will redeem man from the bondage of Urizen's repressive
law. The combined effect of these events upon human destiny
is the meaning which corresponds to Dante's anagoge. Here
it is the restoration of man to prelapsarian unity, which for
Blake at this time is the meaning of the soul's salvation. Thus
we have a myth created syncretically from many sources,
creating a figural situation with historical, political, and
psychological meanings. The Lambeth books are, as Schorer
remarks, 'Blake's first complete attempt to state, by means
of an explicit myth, the simultaneity of cosmic, historical and
psychological events.'[1]

Blake's great model for the mythological-symbolic poem in
English was, of course, *The Faerie Queene*. 'Spenser', Frye
observes, 'treats Arthurian and Biblical mythology with equal
freedom as equally relative to an archetypal myth.'[2] By Blake's
time this mode of poetry had long seemed obsolete. As
Basil Willey has shown, following the triumph of the
Cartesian spirit there had remained, temporarily, 'one
source, and one only, from which the seventeenth century
protestant poet could draw images and fables which were not
only "poetic" but also "true": the Bible'.[3] It is precisely
this distinction between the 'poetic' and the 'true' which
Blake seeks to obliterate in *All Religions Are One* and in his
account of the genesis of the gods in *The Marriage*. All
religions are 'true' *because* 'poetic'; all are deceptions when
their myths are understood literally. This includes the religion Milton invented when he wrote *Paradise Lost*—'If
historical facts can be written by inspiration Miltons Paradise
Lost is as true as Genesis. or Exodus . . .' Blake's point, of
course, is that *none* of these should be read for their 'historical
facts'.

I cannot concieve the Divinity of the ⟨books in the⟩ Bible to
consist either in who they were written by or at what time or in the
historical evidence which may be all false in the eyes of one man &
true in the eyes of another but in the Sentiments & Examples which

---

[1] *William Blake*, p. 82.

[2] p. 143.

[3] *The Seventeenth Century Background* (New York, 1934), p. 227.

whether true or Parabolic are Equally useful as Examples given to us of the perverseness of some & its consequent evil & the honesty of others & its consequent good[1]

All scriptures, therefore, have a claim to figurative validity, for 'The Religeons of all Nations are derived from each Nation's different reception of the Poetic Genius which is every where call'd the Spirit of Prophecy.'[2] The spirit of prophecy did not cease with the end of the Bible but continues to animate the imaginations of all true poets. Sometimes the poet may have to be rescued from his own Corporeal Understanding, as Blake rescued Milton, for the truth of his statement is not necessarily what he thinks he intends; it is the underlying meaning revealed by a figurative reading of the poem. The function of prophecy is not to predict the future but to expose the otherwise hidden motives and consequences of human decisions.

Prophets in the modern sense of the word have never existed Jonah was no prophet in the modern sense for his prophecy of Nineveh failed Every honest man is a Prophet he utters his opinion both of private & public matters Thus If you go on So the result is So He never says such a thing Shall happen let you do what you will. a Prophet is a Seer not an Arbitrary Dictator.[3]

It is in this sense that Blake subtitles two of his Lambeth books 'A Prophecy' and calls Los 'the Eternal Prophet'.[4]

2

Los is the time-bound form of an 'Eternal', Urthona, whose name combines Greek roots meaning 'original' and 'clay' and puns on 'Earth-owner'. He is at once the unfallen Adam, the alchemical *prima materia*, and man in possession of the

---

[1] From Blake's annotations, written in 1798, to Bishop Watson's *Apology for the Bible*, E 607. Cf. Blake's later remark that 'The antiquities of every Nation under Heaven, is no less sacred than that of the Jews. They are the same thing as Jacob Bryant, and all antiquaries have proved' (E 534).

[2] *All Religions Are One* (E 2). Cf. Blake's correction of Bacon's statement that 'the religion of the heathen consisted rather in rites and ceremonies, than in any constant belief: for you may imagine what kind of faith theirs was, when the chief doctors and fathers of their church were the *poets*'; to which Blake rejoined: 'Prophets' (E 611).

[3] Annotations to Watson, E 606–7.

[4] *Book of Los*, E 90; *Song of Los*, E 65.

earth. Los, his name in the fallen world, puns on the loss of
this possession. But the prelapsarian unity can be regained:
Los is an anagram of *Sol*, and, Bentley points out, 'To the
physical alchemists Sol stood for gold, the highest form of
matter, but according to Boehme, "*Sol* signifies the word
which became Man".'[1] As a worker in metals, Los also suggests the divinity Vulcan, which Paracelsus takes to be a
symbol of the celestial alchemist:

> The artist working in metals and other minerals transforms them
> into other colours, and in so doing his operation is like that of the
> the heaven itself. For as the artist excocts by means of Vulcan, or
> the igneous element, so heaven performs the work of coction
> through the Sun. The Sun, therefore, is the Vulcan of heaven
> accomplishing coction in the earth.[2]

Smelted in the crucible of creative imagination, Los becomes
the *Logos* as, in Blake's later works, the Imagination becomes
the indwelling Christ. (The reinforcing of one mythological
derivation by another, frequently with punning, is typical of
Blake's practice in finding names for his pantheon.) Such an
identification of Los with the transcendent Imagination is not
made, however, until late in *The Four Zoas*. In the Lambeth
books he is an embodiment of the Poetic Genius of *The
Marriage* and *All Religions Are One*: the imagination both
in its prophetic sense and as 'the true faculty of knowing',
'the faculty which experiences' (E 2) and by which we construct a reality from our experience. These two functions
are really one, for the prophet's insight into cause and effect—
'If you go on So, the result is So'—is merely one instance of
the mind's constructive power. Potentially, this power can
raise men to a perception of the infinite; but as a result of
the Fall, it too suffers from, even contributes to, the limiting
of perception and desire.

3

Blake's first myth of the Fall is recounted in *The [First] Book
of Urizen* (1794) and *The Book of Los* (1795), works which are

---

[1] Erdman, *Blake*, p. 234; Damon, *William Blake*, p. 69; Bentley, *William
Blake and the Alchemical Philosophers*, p. 161.
[2] *Hermetic and Alchemical Writings*, i. 22 n.

at once Blake's Genesis and his *Timaeus*.[1] Although the elements which the myth incorporates may be found in various occult sources, it is particularly Gnostic in spirit, being a subversively ironical and pessimistic interpretation of its Old Testament prototype. In typical Gnostic manner, the Creation is viewed as a fall from a pre-existing harmony.

> Earth was not: nor globes of attraction
> The will of the Immortal expanded
> Or contracted his all flexible senses.
> Death was not, but eternal life sprung
>
> (3 : 36–9, E 70)

Blake need not have gone to esoteric sources for knowledge of this and other Gnostic doctrines, for they are summarized in J. L. Mosheim's *Ecclesiastical History*, first published in English translation in 1764.[2] He could also have found a succinct exposition of Gnostic theology reprinted from Mosheim in Priestley's *Matter and Spirit*. The passage is worth quoting in full, for it contains the basic doctrines of Blake's cosmological myth:

According to the Oriental philosophers, the eternal nature, infinitely perfect, and infinitely happy, having dwelt from everlasting in profound solitude, produced at length from itself two minds of different sexes, which resembled the supreme parent in the most perfect manner. From the prolific union of these two beings arose others, which were also followed by succeeding generations; so that, in the process of time, a *celestial family* was formed in the *pleroma*. This divine progeny being immutable in its nature, and above the power of mortality, was called by the philosophers *oeon*. How many in number these oeons were, was a point much controverted among the Oriental sages.

Beyond the mansions of light lies a rude mass of *matter*, agitated by innate, irregular motions. One of the celestial natures descending from the pleroma, either by a fortuitous impulse, or by the divine mind, reduced into order this unseemly mass, created men and inferior animals of different kinds, and corrected its malignity, by mixing with it a certain portion of divine light. This author of

---

[1] See Frye, p. 254; Harper, pp. 215–16.

[2] See Helen White, *The Mysticism of William Blake*, University of Wisconsin Studies in Language and Literature, no. 23 (1927), pp. 159–62.

the world is distinguished from the supreme Deity by the name of *demiurge*. His character is a compound of shining qualities, and insupportable arrogance. He claims dominion over the new world he has formed, as his sovereign right, and, excluding the Deity from all concern in it, demands from mankind, for himself and associates, divine honours.[1]

Blake's 'Eternals' correspond to the Gnostic 'Eons'; his demiurge is, of course, Urizen. This name has been traced to the Greek ὁρίζειν; there is also a pun on 'horizon' and 'your reason'.[2] In Eternity Urizen sows the seed of Eternal Science, but in 'obscure separation' he becomes the repressive Reason Blake sees behind all orthodoxies which promulgate 'One King, one God, one Law' (*Urizen*, E 71). In the history of the individual mind, he is the *principium individuationis* which supersedes the oceanic consciousness of the infant. According to Blake's myth, the process by which the 'Selfhood' or ego is formed in the child, resulting in an expulsion from the paradise of Innocence, is a differentiation of consciousness which recapitulates its cosmic analogue: the fall of part of the Eternal Mind and the consequent creation of the phenomenal universe.

In their division and fall, Urizen and Los are precipitated into a condition of Wrath:

> The Prophetic wrath, strug'ling for vent
> Hurls apart, stamping furious to dust
> And crumbling with bursting sobs; heaves
> The black marble on high into fragments
>
> .   .   .   .
>
> The Immortal revolving; indignant
> First in wrath threw his limbs, like the babe
> New born into our world . . .[3]

This is no longer the First Principle of Wrath in the Godhead, but the condition which Boehme and Law describe as following the fall of Lucifer. 'Lucifer could will strong might

---

[1] Priestley, *Disquisitions*, pp. 264–5 (from Mosheim, i. 72).

[2] F. E. Pierce, 'Etymology as Explanation in Blake', *PQ*, x (1931), 395–6; see Erdman, *Blake*, p. 164.

[3] *Book of Los*, 4: 19–22, 37–9, E 91. See Milton O. Percival, *William Blake's Circle of Destiny* (New York, 1938), pp. 166–7.

and power, to be greater than the light of God made him, and so he brought forth a birth of might and power, that was only mighty wrath and darkness, a fire of nature broken off from its light'.[1] Now fire and light are no longer burning bright in dialectical tension but the opposed principles of divided worlds. God is manifest in the light-world as Love, but the dark world is Satan's, the judgement of the Satanic will upon itself. 'He [Lucifer] stept back out of the *Meekness* into the anxious *Fire-will*, and fell into Darkness'.[2] Urizen is surrounded by fires, 'But no light from the fires. all was darkness / In the flames of Eternal fury' (*Urizen*, 5 : 17–18, E 72). Consequently the dark world of Nature comes into being:

... The fire is an Eternal darkness and gnawing in itself, and that is called *the Eternal Death*, concerning which the Scripture witnesseth throughout.

> The Eternals said: What is this? Death[.]
> Urizen is a clod of clay.[3]

Urizen himself regards the Fall as a heroic enterprise in which the Selfhood—'I alone, even I!'—inures itself to an alien world which it has created from 'A void immense, wild dark & deep, / Where nothing was; Natures wide womb'.[4] But the real condition of this world and of the mind which now perceives it is Wrath, 'a fire of nature broken off from its light'.

As Urizen's reason and Los's 'faculty of knowing' make up the functions of a single mind, the fall of Urizen brings about the fall of Los:

> Los wept howling around the dark Demon:
> And cursing his lot; for in anguish,
> Urizen was rent from his side ...
> (*Urizen*, 6 : 2–4, E 72)

---

[1] *Selected Mystical Writings of William Law*, ed. Stephen Hobhouse (New York, 1948), p. 47.

[2] Boehme, *Aurora*, 'Law edition', 15 : 41.

[3] *The Threefold Life of Man*, 7 : 81; *Urizen*, 6 : 9–10, E 73.

[4] Compare the 'heroic' attitude of Milton's Satan. The passage quoted particularly resembles the description of Satan about to venture into Chaos: 'The Womb of nature and perhaps her Grave' (*P.L.* II. 910 ff.). For the possible influence of Boehme on Milton, see Margaret Lewis Bailey, *Milton and Jakob Boehme, a Study of German Mysticism in Seventeenth-Century England* (New York, 1914).

Anguish (*Angst*) is Boehme's term for the third 'quality' of the
First Principle; it is a 'whirling confusion' identified with
the element sulphur. 'In anguish dividing & dividing' (14:52),
the faculty of knowing falls with Reason into the Wrath of the
phenomenal universe. The Eternal Mind, which is also every
individual mind early in its development, becomes an isolated
consciousness in the *Angst* of the Wrath principle.

> The eternal mind bounded began to roll
> Eddies of wrath ceaseless round & round,
> And the sulphureous foam surging thick
> Settled, a lake, bright, & shining clear:
> White as the snow on the mountains cold.
>
> (*Urizen*, 10:19–23, E 74)

This occurs as Los binds Urizen with the linked chain of time
which he has forged with his hammer, tongs, and bellows.
Time is 'created' by the human mind as it falls into Selfhood,[1]
and Los too is imprisoned in the time-bound consciousness
he has created.

After the initial fall into material existence comes a further
fall into sexuality. Los and the other Eternals, originally
androgynous, divide into male and female.

> All Eternity shudderd at sight
> Of the first female now separate
> Pale as a cloud of snow
> Waving before the face of Los
>
> (*Urizen*, 18:9–12, E 77)

Blake follows Boehme, the Kabbala, and the tale of Aristo-
phanes in the *Symposium* in presenting the androgynous
human body as a symbol of libidinal freedom.[2] Discrete
sexual identity is seen as the freezing up of a free flow of

---

[1] An analogy to this part of *Urizen* may be found in Blake's painting of
Michael binding Satan. Bentley remarks that 'The Michael of Blake's myth is
Los, who guards the imprisoned soul, to keep its wrath from consuming the
eternals' (*William Blake and the Alchemical Philosophers*, p. 193; see also Damon,
William Blake, p. 222).

[2] See Brown, *Life Against Death*, p. 310.

energy; instead of an eternity of erotic delight there is now
the yearning and teasing of the romantic agony.

> But Los saw the Female & pitied
> He embrac'd her, she wept, she refus'd
> In perverse and cruel delight
> She fled from his arms, yet he followd

> (19 : 10–16, E 78)

Los is now subject to all the limitations of the fallen world,
where his function is debased to 'Choosing forms of worship
from poetic tales', as *The Marriage* puts it. In *The Song of
Los* (1795), 'They saw Urizen give his Laws to the Nations /
By the hands of the children of Los' (3 : 8–9, E 65). All religions are 'children of Los', creations of the imagination, but
the limited fallen mind can frame its religious conceptions
only as Urizenic law. Those who receive the Law—Moses,
Trismegistus, Brama, Jesus, Mahomet, and Odin, among
others—are 'legislators' in the eighteenth-century sense.

> In all periods [Rousseau wrote] the Fathers of their country have
> been driven to seek the intervention of Heaven, attributing to the
> Gods a Wisdom that was really their own, in order that the People,
> subjected to the laws of the State no less than to those of nature,
> and recognizing in the creation of the City the same Power at
> work as in that of its inhabitants, might freely obey and might bear
> with docility the yoke of public happiness. The legislator, by put-
> ting into the mouths of the immortals that sublime reasoning which
> is far beyond the reach of poor mankind, will, under the banner of
> divine authority, lead those to whom mere mortal prudence would
> ever be a stumbling-block.[1]

'Good Advice for Satan's Kingdom', Blake might well have
written on Rousseau's title-page as he had on Bacon's. To
Blake, the Church-and-State religions are indeed created that
the people 'might freely obey' and bear their yoke with docility.
'Man is born free, and everywhere he is in chains.' To Blake
the chains are the 'forms of worship' men have created, inevitably evolving into repressive institutions:

> These were the Churches: Hospitals: Castles: Palaces:
> Like nets & gins & traps to catch the joys of Eternity

---

[1] Trans. Gerard Hopkins, in *Social Contract*, ed. Sir Ernest Barker (New
York, 1962), p. 208.

And all the rest a desart;
Till like a dream Eternity was obliterated & erased.

(4 : 1–4, E 66)

The notion of a Social Contract is just such a trap, 'a sort of political Adam', Paine had written, 'in whom all posterity are bound for ever.'[1] If Blake read Godwin's *Enquiry Concerning Political Justice*, published in 1793, he must have concurred with Godwin's assertion that there was no such thing as a social contract and with his attack on the authoritarian aspect of Rousseau. Social contracts, for Blake, are, like religious codes, creations of the fallen mind. The most recent and most limited 'religion' invented by this mind is the system that Blake calls Deism:

Thus the terrible race of Los & Enitharmon gave
Laws & Religions to the sons of Har binding them more
And more to Earth: closing and restraining:
Till a Philosphy of Five Senses was complete
Urizen wept & gave it into the hands of Newton & Locke.

(4 : 13–17, E 66)

Blake's quarrel with Lockian epistemology and Newtonian science has been discussed at length by Frye, Blackstone, and others;[2] as Frye says, '. . . His unfavourable comments on science always relate to certain metaphysical assumptions . . .'[3] Like Goethe, Blake held the philosopher or scientist responsible for the psychological and aesthetic implications of his theories. Erich Heller's summary of Goethe's view would also do very well for Blake's:

. . . every scientific theory is merely the surface rationalization of a metaphysical substratum of beliefs, conscious or unconscious, about the nature of the world. And it is these beliefs too, these models of reality constructed in human minds and souls, which live and prosper for vast stretches of history in perfect pragmatic integrity, and, to a remarkable extent, *create*, not find and accept, the shape of the external world.[4]

[1] *Rights of Man*, 2nd ed. (London, 1791), p. 15.
[2] *Fearful Symmetry*, pp. 3–29; Blackstone, *English Blake*, pp. 328–45; Fisher, pp. 101–21.
[3] Op. cit., p. 28. [4] *The Disinherited Mind* (New York, 1957), p. 26.

Blake's attack on Newton is akin to Goethe's in that Blake, too, regards 'the mathematico-analytical scientist' as 'imprisoned "within the hypothetical limitations of an obstinately self-willed and narrow-minded individuality".'[1] An emblem of this is Blake's colour print of Newton, at the Tate Gallery: the magnificent figure is hunched over his compasses in an attitude similar to Urizen's in the famous frontispiece to *Europe*.[2] Both are more than half-way towards the on-all-fours position of the bestial Nebuchadnezzar on the last plate of *The Marriage*. 'Self destroying beast formd Science' (*Four Zoas*, ix. 120 : 40)—science as a discrete category of knowledge—is opposed to 'Eternal Science' (*Ahania*, 5 : 34, E 88), science as related to a complete human identity. The evolution of 'a Philosophy of Five Senses' indicates that the mind of Europe is approaching the futhermost limit of error, worshipping its own ego under the name of Supreme Being. A Second Coming must be at hand; Energy is once more about to break free into history. Therefore 'Africa', the first part of *The Song of Los*, ends with the first line of *America*:

> Clouds roll heavy upon the Alps round Rousseau & Voltaire:
> And on the mountains of Lebanon round the deceased Gods
> Of Asia; & on the desarts of Africa round the Fallen Angels
> The Guardian Prince of Albion burns in his nightly tent
>
> (4 : 18–21, E 67)

---

[1] *The Disinherited Mind* (New York, 1957), p. 30.

[2] Sometimes called 'The Ancient of Days', or 'God Creating the Universe'. Damon, *William Blake*, p. 348, points out that this illustrates *P.L.* VII. 226–31. Once more, the interpretation is ironic—cf. Blake's epigram 'To God':

> If you have formd a Circle to go into
> Go into it yourself & see how you would do (E 508)

The source of the compasses is, of course, *P.L.* VII. 224–7:

> . . . in his hand
> He took the golden Compasses, prepar'd
> In Gods Eternal store, to circumscribe
> This Universe, and all created things. . . .

Professor Merritt Hughes notes the source of this in turn as Proverbs 8 : 27 and an analogue in Dante, *Paradiso* xix. 40–2 (*Paradise Lost* (New York, 1962), p. 171 n.). He adds that 'the divine hand drawing a circle in Chaos was a familiar printer's ornament . . .' We must remember that Blake would have taken the word 'circumscribe' in his own sense.

4

Orc, ork . . . 1590. [In sense 1, a. F. *orque*, ad. L. *orca*, a kind of whale.] 1. A cetacean of the genus *Orca*, family *Delphinidæ*; esp. the killer (*O. gladiator* Gray). Formerly applied to more than one vaguely identified sea-monster. 1611. 2. Occas. more vaguely (cf. L. *Orcus*, Rom. *orco*, and see OGRE): A devouring monster, an ogre 1590. Also (in sense 1) O·rca.

Shorter Oxford English Dictionary

To the blown *Baltic* then, they say,
The wild Waves found another way,
Where *Orcas* howls, his wolfish Mountains rounding;
Till all the banded West at once 'gan rise,
A wide wild Storm ev'n Nature's self confounding,
With'ring her Giant Sons with strange uncouth
Surprise.

COLLINS: *Ode to Liberty*

The hero of Energy in the Lambeth books first appears as a manifestation of sublime Wrath, like the Tyger:

Red rose the clouds from the Atlantic in vast wheels of blood
And in the red clouds rose a Wonder o'er the Atlantic sea;
Intense! naked! a Human fire fierce glowing, as the wedge
Of iron heated in the furnace; his terrible limbs were fire.

(*America*, 4 : 6–9, E 52)

Here Orc recalls the fourth figure seen by Nebuchadnezzar in the burning fiery furnace, and also Robert Southwell's vision of 'A pretty Babe all burning bright' who declares,

My faultlesse breast the furnace is, the fuell wounding thornes:
Loue is the fire, and sighs the smoake, the ashes shames
and scornes;
The fewell Iustice layeth on, and Mercie blowes the coales,
The metall in this furnace wrought, are mens defiled soules:
For which, as now on fire I am to worke them to their good,
So will I melt into a bath, to wash them in my blood.[1]

Orc as divine child represents the revolutionary possibility

---

[1] 'The burning Babe', *Saint Peters Complaint* (London, 1602) p. 74.

of humanizing society. In order to release the flow of desire, he must destroy the Law created 'To keep the gen'rous from experience till the ungenerous / Are unrestraind performers of the energies of nature' (11 : 8–9, E 54). Yet we are soon made aware that Orc has another aspect: he is also the serpent 'wreath'd round the accursed tree' (8 : 1); after he appears, 'heat but not light went thro' the murky atmosphere' (4 : 11). Throughout the Lambeth books he appears variously as divine child, human fire, demon and serpent; and sometimes this ambiguity is conveyed in apparent contradictions between illustration and text. This ambiguity is purposeful, for, as Camus observes, a dominant theme in Blake is that 'The romantic hero . . . brings about the profound and, so to speak, religious blending of good and evil'. Camus calls the result of this blending 'fatality'. The romantic hero is 'fatal' because 'fate confuses good and evil without man being able to defend himself . . . to the extent that he increases in power and genius, the power of evil increases in him'.[1] Thus the imagery of Orc oscillates from the sublime to the grotesque, reflecting his paradoxical potentiality of either redeeming human energy or betraying it to the cycle of history.

In *The Book of Urizen*, Blake attempts to account for the ambiguity of revolutionary Energy by making Orc a child of Los and Enitharmon. As an embryo, he is first a 'worm', then a 'serpent', and finally, after passing through 'Many forms of fish, bird & beast',[2] an infant. Like the child of 'Infant Sorrow', Orc enters this world in anguish, and his parents immediately begin to teach the infant consciousness the demarcations of 'reality':

Delving earth in his resistless way;	My mother groand! my father wept.
Howling, the Child with fierce flames	Into the dangerous world I leapt:
Issu'd from Enitharmon.	Helpless, naked, piping loud;
. . . . . .	Like a fiend hid in a cloud.

---

[1] *The Rebel*, p. 44.

[2] 19 : 34, E 78. Bernard Blackstone suggests that Blake learned about embryonic development through reading Erasmus Darwin (*The Consecrated Urn* (New York, 1959), pp. 26–7).

No more Los beheld Eternity.

	Struggling in my fathers hands:
In his hands he siez'd the infant	Striving against my swadling
He bathed him in springs of	bands:
sorrow	Bound and weary I thought best
He gave him to Enitharmon.	To sulk upon my mothers
	breast.
(19 : 44–6; 20 : 2–5, E 78–9)	('Infant Sorrow', E 28)

This situation is also the subject of one of Blake's illustrations to Young's *Night Thoughts*, where the father is shown
measuring the infant with the span of his hand.[1] Measure-
ment, baptism, and swaddling bands all symbolize a limitation imposed upon the oceanic consciousness of the infant.
The limitation is internalized as Orc grows 'fed with milk
of Enitharmon' and then is bound by Los with the Chain of
Jealousy.

Blake uses the term 'Jealousy' to signify both love-as-
possession and a religious attitude which conceives God to
be punitive and repressive. Urizen is the 'Father of Jealousy'
who in 'Earth's Answer' possesses the Earth as jealous lover.
The Chain is at the same time the 'tenfold chains' of the
Commandments and the internalized repression of desire that
makes men bear their yoke with docility—'the mind-forg'd
manacles' of 'London' and the 'heavy chain' of 'Earth's
Answer', 'That free Love with bondage bound'. Afflicted
with this Chain of Jealousy, Los as the Poetic Genius of the
Mosaic dispensation binds Orc—'The fiery joy, that Urizen
perverted to ten commands'[2]—to the Rock of the Decalogue.
This event is presented so as to suggest the myth of the
exposure of the hero, the chaining of Prometheus, and the
Crucifixion:

> They took Orc to the top of a mountain.
> O how Enitharmon wept!
> They chain'd his young limbs to the rock

[1] No. 44 in the watercolour series, p. 23 in the Edwards edition of *Night
Thoughts*, published in 1797. See my forthcoming 'Blake's *Night Thoughts*: an
Exploration of the Fallen World', *William Blake: Essays for S. Foster Damon*,
ed. Alvin Rosenfeld (Providence, 1969).

[2] *America*, 8 : 3, E 53.

> With the Chain of Jealousy
> Beneath Urizens deathful shadow
>   (20 : 21–5, E 79)

But as 'to the devourer it seems as if the producer was in his chains, but it is not so' (*Marriage*, E 39), the repressed energy cannot be destroyed:

> The dead heard the voice of the child
> And began to awake from sleep
> All things. heard the voice of the child
> And began to awake to life. (20 : 26–9)

This links back to the situation of the Preludium to *America*, where the chained Orc is guarded by the shadowy Daughter of Urthona and struggles to invest her with his energy.

The daughter of Urthona is material Nature, a creation of the imagination, shadowy because Los has done the work of Urizen in creating the illusion of an external nature distinct from man. She is 'nameless' and 'dumb'—'Where man is not nature is barren'[1]—until she is raped by Orc. Once possessed by Energy, the natural world recognizes her human lover.

> I know thee, I have found thee, & I will not let thee go;
> Thou art the image of God who dwells in darkness of Africa;
> And thou art fall'n to give me life in regions of dark death.
>   (2 : 7–9, E 51)

'The image of God who dwells in darkness of Africa' refers to Swedenborg's statement that 'The Gentiles, particularly the Africans, entertain an Idea of God as of a Man, and say that no one can have any other idea of God'; on which Blake commented, 'To think of holiness distinct from man is impossible to the affections. Thought alone can make monsters, but the affections cannot'.[2] The four animal forms in which Orc is manifest appear monstrous only to those who fear the affections:

> I see a serpent in Canada, who courts me to his love;
> In Mexico an Eagle, and a Lion in Peru;
> I see a Whale in the South-sea, drinking my soul away.
>   (2 : 12–14, E 51)

---

[1] *Marriage*, E 37.

[2] Annotations to Swedenborg's *Wisdom of Angels Concerning Divine Love and Divine Wisdom*, E 593.

This practice of representing the feelings as animals Blake also derived from Swedenborg, according to whom 'The things of the will they [the most ancient people] compared to and called *beasts*, and those of the understanding, birds: and they distinguished between the good and evil affections; comparing the former to lambs, sheep, kids, goats, rams, cows and oxen . . .' By fierce beasts, such as wolves, bears, foxes, and swine 'are represented divers lusts and vices'; reptiles and creeping things are 'sensual desires and gratifications', while birds are intellectual things, both true and false.[1] Blake, of course, invests these images of correspondence with his own meaning—to him Swedenborg's 'lusts and vices' are potentially the joys and graces of eternity, and Orc's animal forms are symbols of liberated desire.

Before the energy of Orc, Albion's armies helplessly throw down their weapons, like the stars in 'The Tyger':

The British soldiers thro' the thirteen states sent up a howl
Of anguish: threw their swords & muskets to the earth & ran
From their encampments and dark castles seeking where to hide
From the grim flames; and from the visions of Orc . . .

(13 : 6–9, E 55)

This triumph is 'mental' as well as 'corporeal', and one aspect of Orc's 'thick-flaming, thought-creating fires'[2] is the writings of Thomas Paine. Defending Paine against Bishop Watson, Blake asked, 'Is it a greater miracle to feed five thousand men with five loaves than to overthrow all the armies of Europe with a small pamphlet?' (E 606). Paine appears to Blake as an incarnation of Energy: 'Paine is either a Devil or an Inspired man. Men who give themselves to their Energetic Genius in the manner that Paine does are no ⟨Examiners⟩' (E 603). Blake even applies to Paine the parallelism of Biblical and modern situations that he employs through the Lambeth books—'Let the Bishop prove that he has not spoken against the Holy Ghost who in Paine strives with Christendom as in Christ he strove with the Jews'

---

[1] *Arcana Coelestia* (New York, 1873), i. 251, 254, 267 (pars. 715, 719, 746). See also White, *The Mysticism of William Blake*, p. 147.
[2] *The Song of Los*, 6 : 6, E 67.

(E 604). The American Revolution as seen by Blake is an apocalyptic event, the millennial transformation that would be continued after twelve years, 'when France reciev'd the Demons light' (16 : 15, E 56). His hope was shared by other 'friends of freedom, and writers in its defence' addressed by Dr. Richard Price in his *Discourse on the Love of Our Country* in 1789:

> The times are auspicious. Your labours have not been in vain. Behold kingdoms, admonished by you, starting from sleep, breaking their fetters, and claiming justice from their oppressors! Behold, the light you have struck out, after setting AMERICA free, reflected to FRANCE, and there kindled into a blaze that lays despotism in ashes, and warms and illuminates EUROPE![1]

Thus Orc once again breaks into history in *Europe* (1794), 'And in the vineyards of red France appear'd the light of his fury' (15 : 2, E 65).

In *Europe* we are again confronted with the ambiguity of Energy. A bitterly pessimistic view of Energy as bound into the cycle of recurrence is voiced by the nameless shadowy female in the Preludium:

> Unwilling I look up to heaven! unwilling count the stars!
> Sitting in fathomless abyss of my immortal shrine.
> I sieze their burning power
> And bring forth howling terrors, all devouring fiery kings.
>
> Devouring & devoured roaming on dark and desolate mountains
> In forests of eternal death, shrieking in hollow trees.
> Ah mother Enitharmon!
> Stamp not with solid form this vig'rous progeny of fires.
>
> (2 : 1–8, E 59–60)

Such a view was described by Hume in his *Dialogues Concerning Natural Religion* as 'nothing but the idea of a blind nature, impregnated by a great vivifying principle, and pouring

---

[1] *A Discourse on the Love of Our Country* (London, 1789), p. 50. Erdman suggests that the interval of twelve years may refer to 'the time between Yorktown (1781) and the execution of Louis XVI (1793)', rather than being an error in calculating the interval between the two revolutions ('William Blake's Exactness in Dates', *PQ*, xxviii (1949), 470).

forth from her lap, without discernment or parental care, her
maimed and abortive children!'[1] In the Preludium this nightmarish vision is countered by the promise of a divine child
who will end the cycle of recurrence:

> And who shall bind the infinite with an eternal band?
> To compass it with swaddling bands? and who shall cherish it
> With milk and honey?
> I see it smile & I roll inward & my voice is past.
>
> $\qquad\qquad\qquad\qquad\qquad$ (2 : 13–16, E 60)

The prophecy is fulfilled with the birth of Christ, but there
follows 'The night of Nature', eighteen centuries of history
during which Orc lies bound. With the American and French
Revolutions, Orc breaks free. He is called a 'horrent Demon'
(4 : 15) but on the same page is pictured as a naked youth
with a bright nimbus. Is his demonic nature merely a
delusion of the Angelic mind? Or does the grinning, coiled
Orc serpent of the title-page suggest that although Energy
promises apocalyptic freedom, it actually betrays man to the
cycle of history? Once more, Orc holds in paradoxical suspen-
sion the two possibilities that 'The times are ended' and that
'the times are return'd upon thee'.[2]

Orc's complexity is increased by the fact that his serpent
form is not a mere evil aspect but is itself ambiguous, suggesting renewal as well as finitude. Erasmus Darwin observed
that the serpent was an ancient symbol for renovated youth
and that 'a serpent was wrapped round the large hiero-
glyphic egg in the temple of Dioscuri, as an emblem of the
renewal of life from a state of death'.[3] In the last Chorus of
Hellas, Shelley uses the serpent image in just this sense:

> The world's great age begins anew,
> $\quad$ The golden years return,
> The earth doth like a snake renew
> $\quad$ Her winter weeds outworn:

---

[1] Ed. Henry D. Aiken (New York, 1960), p. 79.

[2] The words of Orc and of Albion's Angel, respectively, in *America*, 8 : 2, E
52 and 9 : 19, E 53.

[3] *The Botanic Garden*, i (1791), Additional Notes, 56. For this book, Blake
engraved Fuseli's picture of Anubis bestriding the Nile. Darwin's source of
information on the serpent, Bryant's *New System*, also illustrated by Blake,
is later referred to in the *Descriptive Catalogue*.

But, Shelley writes in his note to this lyric, 'Prophecies of wars, and rumours of wars, etc., may safely be made by poet or prophet in any age, but to anticipate however darkly a period of regeneration and happiness is a more hazardous exercise of the faculty which bards possess or feign.'[1] The thought of serpentine renewal leads to the thought of serpentine recurrence:

> Oh, cease! must hate and death return?
> Cease! must men kill and die?
> Cease! drain not to its dregs the urn
> Of bitter prophecy.

In the Bible itself, the Serpent appears not only as tempter, but also as healer, idol, and type of Christ. Moses cured the serpent wounds of the people with a 'fiery serpent' of brass raised on a pole (Num. 21:9; cf. *Song of Los*, 7:28, where Orc is 'Like a serpent of fiery flame!'). Blake, however, sees an ironical meaning in this situation, and in his painting of this episode pictures Moses with the serpent coils beginning to enfold him, while other human figures are completely entwined by smaller serpents. Later worshipped idolatrously, the brazen serpent was broken into pieces by the reforming king Hezekiah (2 Ks. 18:4); it reappears in the fourth gospel: 'And as Moses lifted up the serpent in the wilderness, even so must the Son of man be lifted up: That whosoever believeth in him should not perish, but have eternal life' (John 3:14–15). According to Frye,

> The energy of Orc which broke away from Egypt was perverted into the Sinaitic moral code, and this is symbolized by the nailing of Orc in the form of a serpent to a tree. This was a prototype of the crucifixion of Jesus, and the crucifixion, the image of divine visionary power bound to a natural world symbolized by a tree of mystery, is the central symbol of the fallen world.[2]

This is true when we view the serpent figure from the retrospect of *The Four Zoas*. However, the 'Orc cycle' does not exist as a completed pattern in the Lambeth books so far.

[1] *The Complete Poetical Works of Percy Bysshe Shelley*, ed. Thomas Hutchinson (London, 1960), p. 479.   [2] *Fearful Symmetry*, p. 137.

There persists the alternate possibility of the apocalyptic transformation of society. The first poem in which Blake does take an entirely ironical and pessimistic view of the fate of Energy is *The Book of Ahania* (1795), written after the Terror and the rise and fall of Robespierre. Yet Blake was not willing to commit himself permanently to such a view even then: he left scope in his myth for the eventual redemption of Energy, should the authoritarian aspect of the Revolution have turned out a temporary aberration, by making the fatal hero of *Ahania* not Orc but a surrogate, Fuzon.

5

Fuzon is one of the four elemental sons born in *The Book of Urizen* (E 80), where he is pictured as a flaming face in the sky on Plate 24. His name is related to fire, *feu*, and nature, φύσις.[1] As we have seen, he appears as a liberating figure at the end of *Urizen*, leading an Exodus from 'Egypt'. In *Ahania* he suggests, at one point or another, several prototype figures in addition to Moses: Satan, Absalom, Prometheus, Jesus, St. Sebastian, Odin, Adonis, and Robespierre! Like all his prototypes, Fuzon struggles with and eventually succumbs to the Urizen principle. This conflict between energy and repressive reason, taking the form of a myth of the hero and the primal father, takes place in the divided fallen mind. The outcome is ironical: the energy principle triumphs only to become similar to what it rebelled against, so that repressive reason achieves the final victory.

At the beginning of *Ahania*, Fuzon reminds us of Satan rising from the burning lake in *Paradise Lost*:

> Fuzon, on a chariot iron-wing'd
> On spiked flames rose; his hot visage
> Flam'd furious! sparkles his hair & beard
> Shot down his wide bosom and shoulders.
> On clouds of smoke rages his chariot
>
> (2 : 1–5, E 83)

[1] Ibid., p. 214.

> Forthwith upright he rears from off the Pool
> His mighty Stature; on each hand the flames
> Drivn backward slope their pointing spires, and rowld
> In billows, leave i' th' midst a horrid Vale.
> Then with expanded wings he stears his flight
> Aloft . . .   (*P.L.* i. 221–6)

Like Satan, Fuzon will rebel against a father-god in the name of a freedom which is tyranny. 'Moulding into a vast Globe his wrath', he challenges Urizen–Jehovah:

> Shall we worship this Demon of smoke,
> Said Fuzon, this abstract non-entity
> This cloudy God seated on waters
> Now seen, now obscur'd; King of sorrow?
>   (2 : 10–14, E 83)

The Globe of wrath, hurled at Urizen, becomes 'a pillar of fire to Egypt'. Here as in *Urizen* Fuzon is Moses as liberator. His beam of fire is the revolutionary energy of Orc, who in *The Song of Los* 'Arose like a pillar of fire above the Alps' (E 68). His eighteenth-century analogue is Rousseau, or the libertarian aspect of Rousseau's thought. Against the fiery beam Urizen raises a shield forged ten winters in his mills of reason,[1] but as 'Active Evil is better than Passive Good' (E 581), Fuzon's weapon pierces the shield and wounds Urizen. Up to this point it seems we are to have another celebration of the heroic ambiguity of energy, as in *America*. But instead of proceeding 'forward' towards apocalypse, the action begins to diverge into a cyclical pattern. The fiery beam, dividing 'the cold loins of Urizen' (cf. 'the frozen loyns' of 'the populous North', *P.L.* i. 351–2), separates him from Ahania, his emanation. The casting-out of Ahania, Pleasure,[2] is the ironic result of the victory of energy:

> He groand anguished & called her Sin,
> Kissing her and weeping over her;

---

[1] Compare Urizen's shield with the shield of Satan, *P.L.* I. 284 ff.

[2] Damon, *William Blake*, p. 360, suggests that Blake may have had in mind the discussion of Reason and Pleasure in Part I of Plato's *Philebus*. (This dialogue was published in Sydenham's translation in 1779.) In her lament later in the poem, Ahania also calls to mind the Divine Wisdom of Proverbs, especially 8 : 30: 'Then I was by him, as one brought up with him: and I was daily his delight, rejoicing always before him . . .'

> Then hid her in darkness in silence;
> Jealous tho' she was invisible.
>
> (2 : 34–7, E 83–4)

'He who desires but acts not, breeds Pestilence', and Ahania becomes 'The mother of Pestilence'. Urizen can now prepare the black Bow of moral law and the rock of the Decalogue as weapons against Fuzon, who has set himself up as a new tyrannical father-principle:

> While Fuzon his tygers unloosing
> Thought Urizen slain by his wrath.
> I am God. said he, eldest of things!
>
> Sudden sings the rock, swift & invisible
> On Fuzon flew, enter'd his bosom . . .
>
> (3 : 36–40, E 85)

In creating an authoritarian revolutionary order, Fuzon has succumbed to Urizen's repressive Law.

Satan, says Blake in a lyric, is worshipped under the names Jesus and Jehovah; Moses chained with the Ten Commandments the people he had liberated from servitude in Egypt; Rousseau's disciple Robespierre removed the goddess Reason from Notre Dame and set the Supreme Being in her place.[1] With respect to each of these analogues, Blake's view is that Energy has congealed into a repressive system that is ironically similar to the one it displaced. Another such analogue is the story of Absalom in 2 Samuel, from which Blake had previously drawn an emblem for *The Gates of Paradise*— 'My Son! my Son!'[2] Absalom promised justice ('Oh that I were made judge in the land, that every man which hath any suit or cause might come unto me, and I would do him justice!'), but he metaphorically became his father when he seized David's house and went into his concubines (15:4, 16:21). Blake's Adonis-like Fuzon is also modelled after the Absalon of *David and Bethsabe* by George Peele, a play which

---

[1] See Erdman, *Blake*, pp. 288–9.

[2] As pointed out by Chauncy Brewster Tinker, *Painter and Poet* (Cambridge, Mass., 1939), pp. 111–12. Blake's text for this picture in the later 'Keys of the Gates' is 'My Son! my Son! thou treatest me / But as I have instructed thee' (E 266). In the picture (E 261), the son attacks his father with a spear.

has echoes in *America* and *Visions of the Daughters of Albion* as well.[1] Blake's Absalom, like Peele's, is an Adonis figure.

> His beautiful visage, his tresses,
> That gave light to the mornings of heaven
> Were smitten with darkness, deform'd
> And outstretch'd on the edge of the forest
> (3 : 41–4, E 85)

> O, let my beauty fill these senseless plants
> With sense and pow'r to loose me from this plague,
> And work some wonder to prevent his death,
> Whose life thou mad'st a special miracle.

> .   .   .   .

> See, where the rebel in his glory hangs:–
> Where is the virtue of thy beauty, *Absalon?*
> Will any of us now fear thy looks?
> Or be in love with that thy golden hair,
> Wherein was wrap'd rebellion 'gainst thy sire . . .?[2]

'Paradise was open'd in his face', according to Dryden's treatment of the Absalom story as an historical archetype,[3] but it was a false paradise. Robespierre turned the promised earthly paradise of the Republic into a tyranny of Virtue, expelling one false religion in order to install another. Myth and politics converge in Blake's image of Fuzon crucified on the Tree of Mystery.

The growth of the Tree of Mystery, Blake's symbol for the network of Church-and-State religion—the Church as political body and the State as religious object—is also recounted in 'The Human Abstract' of *Experience*. This Tree 'grows . . . in the Human Brain', representing the internalization of socially instituted authority. Fuzon is, as Frye remarks (p. 215), a sacrifice to himself. Nailed by Urizen to the Tree, he is also a type of St. Sebastian.

---

[1] See 'Method and Meaning in Blake's *Book of Ahania*', p. 31, n. 15.

[2] *The Love of King David and Fair Bethsabe: with the Tragedy of Absalon*, in *The Origin of the English Drama*, ed. Thomas Hawkins (Oxford, 1773), ii. 179, 181. The first speaker is Absalon, the second a soldier. Also compare Blake's painting *The Pardon of Absalom* (reproduced in Wright, ii, plate 62).

[3] On Dryden's Absalom as an embodiment of Energy and an aspect of Milton's Satan, see Price, *To the Palace of Wisdom*, pp. 52–63.

> Forth flew the arrows of pestilence
> Round the pale living Corse on the tree
> (4:9–10, E 86)

The image of the arrow-pierced St. Sebastian was used as an
icon against disease in the Middle Ages,[1] the metaphor of
arrows of disease having been drawn from Psalm 38:

> O Lord, rebuke me not in thy wrath: neither chasten me in thy hot
> displeasure.
> For thine arrows stick fast in me, and thy hand presseth me sore.
> There is no soundness in my flesh because of thine anger; neither
> is there any rest in my bones because of my sin.
>
> . . . .
>
> For my loins are filled with a loathsome disease: and there is no
> soundness in my flesh.

To Blake there is a terrible irony in the identification of the
disease with the cure. The martyrdom of Fuzon is really the
result of his own 'Cold fury' (an expression Blake uses elsewhere with reference to Robespierre):[2] the cost of the triumph
of the revolutionary will in France was the suppression of
liberty and the repression of desire in the Republic of Virtue.
Blake believed that a true revolution would free man to
realize his full sexual identity and that desire, in the words of
The Marriage, 'being restrained . . . by degrees becomes passive till it is only the shadow of desire', while 'the restrainer
or reason usurps its place & governs the unwilling'. The hero,
having limited the scope of energy to power, succumbs to the
pestilence bred by the denial of desire—he becomes a 'pale
living Corse', something less than human. When Fuzon
sets himself up as 'God, eldest of things', he moves from the
state of ambiguity or fatality to the state Blake later calls
Satan. ('I alone am God', Blake's Satan declares in *Milton*,
38:56, E 139). The will-to-power of the Selfhood is now
revealed. As Camus says of the romantic hero, 'To the extent
that he increases in power and genius, the power of evil

---

[1] See Louis Réau, *Iconographie de l'art chrétien* (Paris, 1958), iii, pt. 3, 1191.
[2] Letter to Richard Phillips, 14 October 1807, K 865.

increases in him.' The last plate of *Ahania* depicts severed heads and mangled limbs, leavings of the guillotine.[1]

*   *   *

William Hazlitt, in an essay written some twenty-five years after the Lambeth books, addressed himself to a subject that had come to occupy Blake with increasing insistence during the 1790s:

I affirm, Sir, that poetry, that the imagination, generally speaking, delights in power, in strong excitement, as well as in truth, in good, in right, whereas pure reason and the moral sense approve only of the true and good. I proceed to shew that this general love or tendency to immediate excitement or theatrical effect, no matter how produced, gives a bias to the imagination often inconsistent with the greatest good, that in poetry it triumphs over principle, and bribes the passions to make a sacrifice of common humanity . . . .—'Do we read with more pleasure of the ravages of a beast of prey, than of the shepherd's pipe upon the mountain?' No; but we do read with pleasure of the ravages of the beast of prey, and we do so on the principle I have stated, namely, from the sense of power abstracted from the sense of good; and it is the same principle that makes us read with admiration and reconciles us in fact to the triumphant progress of the conquerors and mighty hunters of mankind, who come to stop the shepherd's pipe upon the mountains, and sweep away his listening flock.[2]

This passage, which so impressed Keats that he copied it into his journal-letter of February–May 1819,[3] brings into sharp focus the dilemma of the relation of energy or power to the imagination. Elsewhere Hazlitt wrote that 'The language of poetry naturally falls in with the language of power'.[4] Hazlitt, like Blake, was a libertarian in a dark time; like Blake, he affirmed the power of imagination in painting and in poetry; but for Hazlitt the operation of imagination in the realm of human events was disturbingly equivocal,

---

[1] See Erdman, *Blake*, p. 289. I am indebted to Professor Erdman for a colour reproduction of this plate, made from the unique copy of *Ahania* in the Lessing J. Rosenwald Collection of the Library of Congress.

[2] 'Letter to William Gifford', *The Complete Works of William Hazlitt*, ed. P. P. Howe (London and Toronto, 1931), ix. 37.

[3] *The Letters of John Keats*, ed. Maurice Buxton Forman (London, 1960), pp. 307–8.

[4] 'Coriolanus', *Works*, iv. 214.

'because our vanity or some other feeling makes us disposed to place ourselves in the situation of the strongest party'.[1]

When we consider such images of power as Leviathan, Tyger, and Orc, it may seem as if Blake was tending toward a similar view in the 1790s. It is true that Blake denies morality any place in the creations of the imagination. 'If Homers merit', he says in his annotations to Henry Boyd's *Historical Notes* on Dante, 'was only in these Historical combinations & Moral sentiments he would be no better than Clarissa'. Against Boyd's argument that Shakespeare is a better moral teacher than the philosophers, Blake asserts

the grandest Poetry is Immoral the Grandest characters Wicked. Very Satan. Capanius Othello a murderer. Prometheus. Jupiter. Jehovah, Jesus a wine bibber

Cunning & Morality are not Poetry but Philosophy the Poet is Independent & Wicked the Philosopher is Dependent & Good[2]

However, as we see from the examples of Jesus and Prometheus, 'Wicked' is used here with characteristic Blakean irony. To Urizen, the 'enormous forms of energy' are 'All the seven deadly sins of the soul' (*Urizen*, 4:48–9, E 71); it is the Angel who projects a terrifying apparition of Leviathan in *The Marriage*. These demonic masks are created by fear and repression. Conversely, to Blake brute power is not in itself sublime. The 'num'rous hosts' of Albion's Angel in *America* are powerful, or appear to be, but they are not sublime, while the Tyger is sublime not because he is merely powerful but because his power embodies a divine purpose too great for the eye of man. Orc exists in two forms precisely because the sense of power may be abstracted from the human ends which power should serve; Fuzon, in whom this process is completed, is the subject of irony, not of awe or sympathetic identification.

In his political writings, Hazlitt is consistent in his distrust of the 'exclusive' nature of the imaginative faculty. '. . . The whole drift of Mr. Burke's theory', he wrote,

---

[1] Ibid., p. 215.
[2] E 623. Boyd's *Inferno* was published in Dublin in 1785. Keynes (p. 900) conjecturally assigns the date 1800 to the annotations on the assumption that the book was a gift from Hayley.

went to make politics a question or department of the imagination
. . . this could never be true, because politics treat of the public
weal and the most general and wide-extended consequences, whereas
the imagination can only be appealed to by individual objects and
personal interests, and must give a false verdict in all other cases.[1]

Although Blake would have agreed with Hazlitt's condemna-
tion of Burke's politics, he could not have agreed with the
reason for it, or with Hazlitt's belief that the welfare of
millions 'could never be brought forward by the imaginative
faculty and could only be weighed in the balance of abstract
truth and reason'.[2] For Blake the imagination or Poetic
Genius, being 'the faculty which experiences', is cognitive,
and it reveals the archetypal or figural reality in the configuration of concrete historical events. Formerly it had perceived
in the French Revolution a potential fulfilment of millennial
anticipation. In the latter 1790s, Blake had to recognize the
failure of this hope, but he did not yet abandon it; nor did he
renounce the claim of poetry to the Prophetic function. He
began, instead, to contemplate the creation of a new, expanded
myth, one which would both account for the failure of energy
to redeem the world and, at the same time, redefine the nature
and function of the imagination.

[1] *The Life of Napoleon Buonaparte, Works*, xiv. 274.
[2] Loc. cit.

4

The Dream of Reason

The Dream of Reason Produces Monsters.
GOYA: *Caprichos*

THE last of the Lambeth books were etched in 1795. Most of
Blake's time and labour in the following year must have been
spent in the enormous task of illustrating Young's *Night
Thoughts*, for which Blake painted 537 water-colour designs
and engraved forty-three folio-sized plates.[1] Many of the
pictorial themes of this series are those of the Lambeth books:
the illustrations to Young also describe the nature of life in
a fallen world, the limitations set upon energy and desire,
and the apocalypse to come.[2] The major symbolic characters
of the Lambeth books—Los, Enitharmon, Urizen, and Orc—
also appear prominently in these illustrations; two more will
be encountered in Blake's next long poem, where they are
called Luvah and Vala. Numerous other images and personages
are shared by these designs and Blake's own poems, including the compasses, the serpent, the chain, and the wheel;
Nebuchadnezzar, Leviathan, and Rahab. All this shows that
after finishing the Lambeth books, Blake did not even temporarily abandon the mythology he had created. Rather, he
employed it in a new mode, investing an un-Blakean poem
with Blakean symbolism. By 1797, after the completion of
the *Night Thoughts* pictures, he was free to begin a long
illustrated poem of his own, arranged like Young's in nine
'Nights'. This new 'Bible of Hell, in Nocturnal Visions collected'[3] would present an inclusive myth of the fall and redemption of humanity, drawing upon, adding to, or changing
the material of the Lambeth books where necessary.

[1] See Alexander Gilchrist, *The Life of William Blake*, ed. Ruthven Todd
(London, 1942), pp. 116–17, 377–8.
[2] See 'Blake's *Night Thoughts*: an Exploration of the Fallen World'.
[3] Inscribed on the back of a drawing, followed by 'Vol. I. Lambeth'. See
K 897.

In writing the poem he originally called *Vala*, Blake had to confront two problems of consistency. One was that although the structure he had chosen demanded an apocalyptic termination in the ninth night, a termination which had earlier been identified with the American and French Revolutions, by 1797[1] the deliverance of the world by revolutionary energy seemed a remote prospect. The vineyards of red France had been pruned by the Directory, which consolidated its power in the *coup d'état* of Fructidor,[2] and Napoleon's army was waging a successful war of expansion in Italy. The slave was still grinding at the mill; the deserts had not blossomed. The second problem was of Blake's own making. In the Creation–Fall narratives of *Urizen* and *Los*, he had created a sort of involuntary dualism, a myth with implications that in some ways conflicted with his own beliefs. Blake's intuition of the goodness of the body in general and of sexual love in particular had not weakened—the magnificently sensuous lament of *Ahania* shows this, as does the Fairy's song prefixed to *Europe*;[3] but the dualistic structure of the Lambeth myth seems to imply that physical life is inherently evil. Blake tried to solve both these problems and at the same time to create a more comprehensive frame of action by changing his myth of the Fall. To the two components of the psyche in the Lambeth books, Los and Urizen, he added two more: Luvah and Tharmas, representing respectively the emotions and the sensations of the body. Orc was made the operative form of Luvah in the fallen world, so that now the redemptive capacity of energy, revolutionary and erotic, depended on the reintegration of the disorganized Fallen Mind. Now the role of imagination, in the sense in which we have used the word so far, could be described more precisely in the relations between Los and Tharmas.

---

[1] The date on the title-page of Blake's manuscript. On the poem's dates of composition, see *William Blake's Vala*, ed. H. M. Margoliouth (Oxford, 1956), pp. xxiii–xxv; and *Vala or The Four Zoas*, ed. G. E. Bentley, Jr. (Oxford, 1963), pp. 157–66. See also Bentley, 'The Date of Blake's *Vala* or *The Four Zoas*', *MLN*, lxxi (1956), 487–91; and 'The Failure of Blake's *Four Zoas*', *Texas Studies in English*, xxxvii (1958), 102–13.

[2] 4 September 1797. See Erdman, *Blake*, p. 285 n.

[3] *The Book of Ahania*, E 87–9; *Europe*, E 58–9.

The reality of these four 'Zoas'—I use Blake's later term[1] as most convenient—is explicitly psychological:

> in the Brain of Man we live, & in his circling Nerves.
> this bright world of all our joy is in the Human Brain.[2]

Each Zoa is in some way responsible for the Fall, but in the new myth the ultimate responsibility is assigned to Luvah:

> The Eternal Man takes his repose: Urizen sleeps in the porch
> Luvah and Vala woke & flew up from the Human Heart
> Into the Brain; from thence upon the pillow Vala slumber'd.
> And Luvah siez'd the Horses of Light, & rose into the Chariot
> of Day   (5v: 8–11, M 78)

Passion subverts the place of Reason, taking over its function of directing the will, in a mythological rendering which draws upon Plato's *Phaedrus* (the two steeds) and Ovid's story of Phaeton.[3] The account is considerably expanded in Night III, where the Eternal Man worships Luvah, 'a Shadow from his wearied intellect' (20v: 3, M11), as god of the natural world. Again, the Fall is a consequence:

> And Luvah strove to gain dominion over the Eternal Man.
> They strove together above the Body where Vala was inclos'd
> And the dark Body of Man left prostrate upon the crystal
> pavement
> Coverd with boils from head to foot, the terrible smitings
> of Luvah   (21R: 13–16, M12)

---

[1] The first 'datable mention' of Zoas, as Bentley (*Vala or The Four Zoas*, p. 156) points out, is in Blake's letter to Ozias Humphrey dated 18 January 1808 ('Four Living Creatures filled with Eyes', K 444).

[2] *William Blake's Vala*, ed. Margoliouth, p. 79. This edition, which presents the text 'before erasures, deletions, additions, and changes of order had brought it to the state in which we know it today as *The Four Zoas*' (p. xi), will be the principal one used for *Vala*. All quoted or cited passages have been compared with the Bentley edition (indicated as B) of the entire *Four Zoas* and with the Erdman text. Any pertinent differences will be noted, except for those matters of capitalization or of punctuation which do not affect meaning. M's pagination is according to leaf and recto or verso. These will be given, followed by line number and page number. The above passage is 6R: 13–14, M 79. Los is the speaker.

[3] See Harper, *The Neoplatonism of William Blake*, p. 175; and Percival, *William Blake's Circle of Destiny*, p. 30.

Here the situation corresponds to that of Blake's design 'Satan Smiting Job with Sore Boils', first executed as a tempera painting in or about 1799.[1] Luvah has become a Satanic will, and the account of Luvah's fall in Night III recalls the degeneration of Urizen in the Lambeth books:

> Luvah & Vala
> Went down the Human Heart where Paradise & its joys abounded
> In jealous fears in fury & rage, & flames roll'd round their fervid feet
> And the vast form of Nature like a Serpent play'd before them
> (21v: 10–13, M12)

Once more, with the serpent and flame images, we have a fall into Wrath,[2] but this time it is the affections rather than reason which assert their independence of the whole human identity. Consequently the passional self is cut off from fulfilment in the natural world, with which it hopelessly desires complete union:

> Luvah was cast into the Furnaces of affliction & sealed
> And Vala fed in cruel delight, the furnaces with fire
> (13R: 10–11, M4)

Passion now turns, in frustration and despair, from love to hatred: 'I am love & hatred ⟨awakes⟩ in me' (14R : 13, M4). Thus, long before the birth of Orc in Night V, the poem postulates the perversion of energy to destructive fury, anticipating Albion's statement in Night IX that 'War is Energy enslavd'.

A similar description of the Fall as a psychological event occurs in Book IX of *Paradise Lost*.

> Thir inward State of Mind, calm Region once
> And full of Peace, now tost and turbulent:
> For Understanding rul'd not, and the Will

---

[1] See Darrell Figgis, *The Paintings of William Blake* (London, 1925), pl. 61.

[2] Percival writes of Boehme, 'Observing that the spirit and the body are in correspondence, he asserted that "the image of man cometh to be the image of the serpent"' (p. 166). The reference is to *The Threefold Life of Man*, 6 : 58.

Heard not her lore, both in subjection now
To sensual Appetite, who from beneathe
Usurping over sovran Reason claimd
Superior sway . . .[1]

The conceit of the mind as a council or kingdom whose proper order may be subverted by an alliance between the senses and the emotions is frequently encountered in Renaissance and seventeenth-century literature. Boehme wrote of a 'Princely Council' made up of Sight, Hearing, Smell, Taste, and Feeling, 'which fifth Counsellor arises also from all the Powers of the Body in the Spirit, into the Head' (*Aurora*, 5 : 55). Boehme warns that 'if one Member stirs *too much*, and at any Time *hurts* a princely Counsellor . . . it would be in love with that it *ought not* to be in love with '(5 : 64). He gives the examples of Lucifer and Eve; Luvah and Vala are close analogues of these. The general conception is that heart and brain communicate by means of vital spirits which ascend, become spirits of sense, and bring a report on the forms encountered in the fantasy back to the heart, where the appropriate affections are moved. When one of the faculties does not function properly, a disruption of the hierarchy of the psyche results:

> The genius and the mortal instruments
> Are then in council; and the state of man,
> Like to a little kingdom, suffers then
> The nature of an insurrection.
>
> (*Julius Caesar* ii. i. 66–9)

Such a condition occurs in a state of irrational passion, when the emotions and the senses rebel against reason, inflame the imagination, and seize control of the will. By means of 'motions' of animal spirits, the will is propelled by the passions into an irrational course of action. Mental disturbance (what the Elizabethans call 'perturbation') and physical illness, even death may result.[2] This explanation is frequently used to describe what happens in the 'madness' of love for an

---

[1] Lines 1125–31. See Denis Saurat, *Blake and Milton* (London, 1935 (1920)), p. 112.

[2] See Ruth Leila Anderson, *Elizabethan Psychology and Shakespeare's Plays*, Univ. of Iowa Humanistic Stud., III (1927), 69–153; and Hardin Craig, *The Enchanted Glass* (New York, 1936), pp. 113–38.

unworthy object,[1] as, for example, in Shakespeare's *Troilus and Cressida*. Troilus, like Blake's Eternal Man, becomes the victim of his senses and emotions, so that he must deny not only the evidence of reason but also, ultimately, the evidence of his senses themselves. In the case of Albion, the unworthy object is Vala—the illusion or 'veil' of Nature; Luvah, passion, rises into the brain and drives the chariot of slumbering reason, the will. Man, suffering 'the torments of Love & Jealousy' (Blake's later subtitle), falls into the sleep of earthly existence and dreams what is going on within him.

The psychology of *Vala* seems less arbitrary when it is thus regarded as a version of medieval and Renaissance accounts of how mind and body act in relation to each other. Ultimately, the sources of this psychology are in Plato's *Republic* and Aristotle's *De Anima*; there are analogues to the Zoas in the four elements of Greek science and in Paracelsus; the 'scatter'd portions' of Albion's immortal body suggest, as G. M. Harper points out (p. 231), the dispersion of Bacchus in the phenomenal world, a Neoplatonist doctrine that Blake might have learned through Thomas Taylor. Other figures similar to Blake's Eternal Man are the Kabbalistic Adam Kadmon, who contained in his body all living creatures, and the Celestial Man of the Corpus Hermeticum ('The Man moves through air and fire . . . sees his own reflection in the waters, and falls in love with it. He jumps to embrace his image and in doing so becomes ordinary man').[2] What concerns us here is not the priority of any particular source as such, for Blake's method, as we have seen, was to work diverse materials into a unified myth. In *Vala*, the vehicle of the myth is Renaissance faculty psychology. Once this is recognized, the genre of the poem also becomes clear: it is a *psychomachia*.

The early *psychomachia*, as C. S. Lewis has described it in *The Allegory of Love*, takes the form of an allegorical battle of abstract Virtues and Vices. It is assumed in these works that man's inner nature is a divided one.

---

[1] Anderson, pp. 71, 92–131.
[2] John Senior, *The Way Down and Out* (Ithaca, N.Y., 1959), p. 24.

War rages, horrid war
Even in our bones; our double nature sounds
With armèd discord.[1]

Professor Lewis calls this one of the few affecting passages in Prudentius and suggests that it demonstrates, on the part of Prudentius's contemporaries, a 'daily and hourly experience of the *non simplex natura*' (p. 73). In the medieval morality plays, such an awareness is dramatized in the form of battles and sieges which represent the moral struggle of Christian life. With their *sedes* and *platea*, their three-levelled stage, and their non-Aristotelian conventions of time and space, these plays suggest the exciting possibility of objectifying a symbolism of the life of the mind. At their best, as in *The Castle of Perseverance* or *Mankind*, they occasionally do so or seem about to do so. But without allowing for a *natura* much more *non simplex*—and this would have meant abandoning the plays' ostensibly homiletic purpose—there was little the morality playwrights could do to add to the interest of the plays, except to depart into irrelevant realistic or comic modes. It remained for Spenser to use the *psychomachia* as a subtle literary device. The stated theme of the *Faerie Queene* is 'to fashion a gentleman'; this is the great theme of Castiglione, of the Platonizing Renaissance—but in Spenser's poem, who is the gentleman? It is of course the mind (and body) in which the events of the poem take place, and the quests and battles are episodes in the making of that mind. The typical rhythm of the episodes is disjunction, quest and struggle, unity; the unity may be broken again, but the poem clearly demands the entelechy of all twelve Aristotelian virtues in the last canto.[2]

In writing *Vala*, Blake freely adapted the method of Spenser. The attempts of the Zoas to reunite with their separated

[1] *The Allegory of Love* (Oxford, 1938), p. 72 (Prudentius, *Psychom.* 740–2).

[2] Spenser declared that 'in the person of Prince Arthure I sette forth magnificence in particular, which vertue, for that (according to Aristotle and the rest) it is the perfection of all the rest, and conteineth in it them all, therefore in the whole course I mention the deedes of Arthure applyable to that vertue which I write of in that booke' (*Complete Poetical Works* (Cambridge, Mass., 1936), pp. 136–7). 'The stories of Arthur', Blake wrote in his *Descriptive Catalogue* of 1809, 'are the acts of Albion, applied to a Prince of the fifth century . . .' (E 534). For Blake's relation to Spenser, see Frye, op. cit., pp. 142–3, 318–19.

female counterparts recall Spenser's knights in quest of their lost or abducted ladies. Blake's subject, like Spenser's, is the making of a whole man. Both use the conventions of the *psychomachia* to define the mind's division against itself. Where Blake goes beyond Spenser is in making the poem more of a projection of the mind's processes and less of a moralized allegory. Blake's heroes fight, not Saracens and monsters, but one another (as, to be sure, Spenser's do occasionally). 'A dissociation of thought and feeling' would be a legitimate if over-familiar way of putting it; for on one level, as we shall see, Blake's meaning applies to the mind of Europe at a particular point in its history; and as in the Lambeth books, there are parallel cosmic, political, and psychological meanings.

In *Vala* all the Zoas are fallen. The fall of Urizen occurs in Night III, which in this respect corresponds to *Ahania*. Once more, Ahania (Pleasure) is cast out by Urizen. Luvah's fall has occurred previously, and is related retrospectively by Ahania in this Night. It is the antecedent fall of Luvah that causes Urizen to reject his own female counterpart.

His visage changd to darkness & his strong right hand came forth
To cast Ahania to the Earth he siezd her by the hair
And threw her from the steps of ice that froze around his throne
Saying Art thou also become like Vala. thus I cast thee out
Shall the feminine indolent bliss, the indulgent self of weariness
The passive idle sleep the enormous night & darkness of Death
Set herself up to give her laws to the active masculine virtue
Thou little diminutive portion that darst be a counterpart
Thy passivity thy laws of obedience & insincerity
Are my abhorrence.   (22R : 2–11, M 12–13)

The whole man has previously succumbed to the passions' invading his brain while reason slept.[1] The dream of reason produces monsters: identifying pleasure with the irrational, Urizen casts Ahania out. Reason will now deny erotic pleasure in order to guard against passion. Urizen's proper function of illuminating the will has been abandoned. 'Thou sitst in harmony for God hath set thee over all',[2] declares

[1] 'When Urizen slept in the porch & the Eternal Man was smitten' (20R: 15, M 11).

[2] 19R : 10, M 10. B 38 indicates that this line was later deleted.

Ahania, but Urizen's 'immortal steeds of light' have been taken by Luvah. Reason's consequent identification of Eros with the irrational is what brings about Urizen's fall. Attempting to withdraw into self-containment, he descends to the world of Tharmas, of sensation.

Tharmas has already fallen. As Urizen enters his world, Tharmas laments the loss of Enion, his own rejected female counterpart. The beginning of his speech is curiously like the lines from Prudentius ('War rages, horrid war / Even in our bones . . .') cited earlier: 'fury in my limbs. destruction in my bones & marrow' (22v : 23, M 14). Later, Blake added an account of the separation of Tharmas and Enion to the beginning of Night I. S. Foster Damon interprets this fall of Tharmas as meaning that

the Body is losing its exultation in life, and is out of communication with the Earth Mother (Enion). Already the sense of Sin, of self-analysis, has crept in; and Tharmas (the Body) is divided by the sophistication of Ethics and becomes a Spectre, or Reasoning Force. . . . Tharmas sinks into the Sea of Time and Space, and his Spectre alone remains to accuse and torture Enion.[1]

A further, epistemological interpretation is advanced by Fisher:

. . . Blake's 'fall' is a fall in perception, or a fall in the relationship of the observer and the observed. This is, initially, the fall of Tharmas, who becomes the consolidation of fallen man's relationship to the immediate data of experience, that is, his instincts and sensations. . . .

Tharmas, the original faculty of altering the data of experience, becomes the fixed data of fallen experience—the body of man and the instincts and habits which regulate its functions. Enion, his emanation, becomes the forces of nature as the field of organic life and growth.[2]

In what sense may it be true that man has lost touch with the body of the earth, that a 'fall in perception' has taken place? In one way, Blake's meaning is similar to Wordsworth's in the 'Intimations' ode. The adult's recollection of his early perceptions and the contrast between them and his present ones convince him that 'there hath past away a glory

---

[1] Damon, *William Blake*, p. 156.   [2] *Valley of Vision*, p. 232.

from the earth'. To account for the disappearance of the
'celestial light' that had clothed all objects of perception,
Wordsworth employs the Platonic myth of the pre-existence
and descent of the soul. Blake's myth of division and fall has,
in part, a similar purpose. It also has, I believe, a second
meaning, one having to do with the history of philosophy, or
perhaps more precisely, with what Owen Barfield has termed
the 'history of human consciousness'.[1] The tendency of
epistemology from Descartes on had been to remove the
'secondary qualities'—the colour, taste, smell, and feel of
a thing—from the object of perception and to locate them in
the perceiver himself. The mind was no longer thought to be
in contact with a 'real' world through the senses; it was now
considered a passive observer of 'phantasms', images received in its *camera obscura*. E. A. Burtt has described the
implications of such a view in *The Metaphysical Foundations
of Modern Physical Science* (London, 1950):

> Space was identified with the realm of geometry, time with the
> continuity of number. The world that people had thought them-
> selves living in—a world rich with colour and sound, redolent with
> fragrance, filled with gladness, love and beauty, speaking every-
> where of purposive harmony and creative ideals—was now crowded
> into minute corners in the brains of scattered organic beings. The
> really important world outside was a world hard, cold, colourless,
> silent, and dead; a world of quantity, a world of mathematically
> computable motions in mechanical regularity. The world of quali-
> ties as immediately perceived by man became just a curious and
> quite minor effect of that infinite machine beyond. In Newton the
> Cartesian metaphysics, ambiguously interpreted and stripped of its
> distinctive claim for serious philosophical consideration, finally
> overthrew Aristotelianism and became the predominant world-
> view of modern times.   (pp. 236–7)

Blake had commented on the nature of such a universe as
early as the Annotations to Lavater:

> deduct from a rose its redness, from a lilly its whiteness from a
> diamond its hardness from a spunge its softness from an oak its
> heighth from a daisy its lowness & rectify every thing in Nature as

---

[1] *Saving the Appearances* (London, 1957), p. 13.

the Philosophers do. & then we shall return to Chaos & God will
be compelld to be Excentric if he Creates O happy Philosopher
(E 584–5)

In defending the view that qualities, or at least some qualities, inhere in their objects, Blake even uses the terms of
Scholastic philosophy:

. . . if Rafael is hard & dry it is not his genius but an accident
acquired for how can Substance & Accident be predicated of the
same Essence! I cannot concieve   (E 585)

Here Blake is already on his way toward his later notion of
'Mental Forms' which become reified in objects. The abstract
universe which man's mind creates by 'deducting' the
qualities from things is the hell that Blake will call 'Ulro'—
'Abstract Philosophy warring . . . against Imagination'. The
postulation of the kind of world that Burtt describes is metaphorically, for Blake, a 'fall'. It corresponds to the 'fall' in
perception of every human being as he grows out of childhood, and both these falls create the world as it appears to the
European mind at the end of the eighteenth century.

2

Into the world generated by the fall of Tharmas and Enion
are born Los and Enitharmon. They do not fall as the others
do, for as Time and Space they are the 'children' of the world
that the antecedent falls have created.

He could controll the times & seasons, & the days & years
She could controll the spaces, regions, desart, flood & forest
They wanderd long, till they sat down upon the margind sea.
(5R:13–15, M 78)

Los in *Vala* is once more 'the faculty which experiences' and
potentially 'the true faculty of knowing';[1] as in the Lambeth
books, he makes Urizenic errors in his fallen state. In Night

---

[1] *All Religions Are One*, E 2.

IV, confronting Tharmas, he declares himself a slave of repressive Reason:

> Los answerd in his furious pride sparks issuing from his hair
> Hitherto shalt thou come. no further. here thy proud waves
>   cease
> We have drunk up the Eternal Man by our unbounded power
> Beware lest we also drink up thee rough demon of the waters
> Our God is Urizen the King. King of the Heavenly hosts
> We have no other God but he thou father of worms & clay
> And he is falln into the Deep rough Demon of the waters
> And Los remains God over all. weak father of worms & clay
> I know I was Urthona keeper of the gates of heaven
> But now I am all powerful Los & Urthona is but my shadow[1]

Here imagination—if Los can even be called that in these early parts of the poem—attempts to dictate a containing reality to watery Tharmas, 'the *streamy* Nature of Association', as Coleridge put it, 'which Thinking = Reason, curbs & rudders . . .'[2] But the bounds which Los tries to impose are too restrictive; he is overwhelmed by the waters of Tharmas and separated from Enitharmon, indicating, as in *Urizen*, a further degeneration of the mind's constructive power.

Los is now a 'Dark Spectre', the skeletal outline of metaphysics.[3] Tharmas and the spectral Los exhange recollections of the Fall and lament the loss of the harmony of Beulah:

> O why did foul ambition sieze thee Urizen Prince of Light
> And thee O Luvah prince of Love till Tharmas was divided
> And I what can I now behold but an Eternal Death
> Before my Eyes & an Eternal weary work to strive
> Against the monstrous forms that breed among my silent waves
> Is this to be A God far rather would I be a Man
> To know sweet Science & to do with simple companions
> Sitting beneath a tent & viewing sheepfolds & soft pastures
> $\hspace{4cm}$ (26R : 24–31, M 19)

Tharmas enlists the Spectre in the binding of Urizen, 'Lest he should rise again from death in all his dismal power'. His mistaken hope is that by limiting the claims of Reason he can

---

[1] 24v : 11–20, M 16–17. 'Eternal' in line 13 was originally intended as 'Ancient' (B 47).

[2] *The Notebooks of Samuel Taylor Coleridge 1794–1804*, ed. Kathleen Coburn, i (New York, 1957), no. 1770. [3] See Damon, *William Blake*, p. 379.

save some portion of the lost bliss of the undivided self. Instead, the result threatens to deliver the mind to a stream of undifferentiated sensation, without meaning or value:

> Now all comes into the power of Tharmas. Urizen is falln
> And Luvah hidden in the Elemental forms of Life & death
> Urthona is My Son O Los thou art Urthona & Tharmas
> Is God. The Eternal Man is seald never to be deliverd
> I roll my floods over his body my billows & waves pass over him
> The sea encompasses him & monsters of the deep are his companions
> Dreamer of furious oceans cold sleeper of weeds & shells
> Thy Eternal form shall never renew my uncertain prevails
> against thee   (26R : 12–19, M 19)

'Urthona is My Son'—the imagination, Tharmas in effect declares, is a function of sensation. Likewise the first 'Natural Religion' tractate asserts that 'The desires & perceptions of man untaught by any thing but organs of sense, must be limited to objects of sense'; but the second begins with Blake's own view that 'Mans perceptions are not bounded by organs of perception. he percieves more than sense (tho' ever so acute) can discover' (E 2). As the mind in which Night IV of *Vala* takes place is limited to objects of sense, Los, instead of assuming 'the Poetic or Prophetic Character', is a slave of Tharmas; and Night IV ends with a long description of Los's binding of Urizen. An important difference between this episode and the earlier version of it in *The Book of Urizen* is that, as Margoliouth says, 'In BU the binding of Urizen seems a necessary act of limitation to save from something worse: in *Vala* it is a malevolent act in which Tharmas and the Spectre rejoice and Los is an unwilling but helpless agent' (M 119). As Los binds Urizen, he becomes more and more like him, one repressive principle being much like another. 'He became what he was doing he was himself transformd.'[1] The imagination, enlisted in the work of

---

[1] 28R : 17, M 22. This is a Neoplatonist conceit also employed by Shelley; Milton Wilson, *Shelley's Later Poetry* (New York, 1959), pp. 73–4, notes examples in *Prometheus Unbound* and *Prince Athanase*, as well as in Blake's later works and in Paine's *Rights of Man*. The ultimate source is *Republic* III; Percival, p. 319, compares Plotinus: 'Souls, while they contemplate diverse objects, are and become that which they contemplate.'

repression, will continue that work by binding energy in Night V.

3

The first four Nights of *Vala* make up Blake's revised and expanded myth of the creation as fall. By making Luvah, who will be explicitly identified with Orc in Night V, the over-reacher who throws the microcosm into chaos, Blake significantly changed the meaning of Orc before he even appeared in the poem. I have suggested that the reason for this was Blake's need to account mythically for the failure of energy to redeem the world after the French Revolution. With this change in the poem's symbolism, its theme changes as well: from the eruption of revolutionary energy into the world to the restoration of the original hierarchy of the fallen mind. Still, Blake at first envisioned Orc's energies as contributing to such a goal, as Urizen's speech of Night III indicates:

> O bright Ahania, a Boy is born of the dark Ocean
> Whom Urizen doth serve, with Light replenishing his darkness
> I am set here a King of trouble commanded here to serve
> And do my ministry to those who eat of my wide table
> All this is mine yet I must serve & that Prophetic boy
> Must grow up to command his Prince & all my Kingly power[1]

Three Nights of *Vala* (V, VIIa, and VIIb) recapitulate the history of Orc given in the Lambeth books, making certain important changes and additions which we will presently discuss. At first the action seems to progress toward, or at least leave room for, revolution-as-apocalypse; but as such a possibility became more and more remote with Napoleon's accession to and consolidation of power, Blake found himself engaged in a series of extensions and revisions which explained what had happened according to the politics of eternity, but which at the same time cost the poem whatever unity it might have had. Consequently, no interpretation of *Vala* can hope to be wholly consistent; what we can do is attempt to account for the poem's inconsistencies.

[1] 19v : 2–7, M 10. Margoliouth's note compares the fears of Herod in Matthew 2.

The generation of Luvah has been announced by Tharmas in Night IV: 'And Luvah hidden in the Elemental forms of Life & death' (26R : 13, M 19). The event itself occurs in Night V where, as in *Urizen*, Orc is born to Los and Enitharmon. At this point, Enitharmon as Space corresponds to the Eternal Female who groans in travail in the Preludium to *Europe*. Weary with conceiving 'all devouring fiery kings', the Eternal Female was given hope by a vision of the divine child to come. But the Orc born in *Vala* is to be identified not with Christ but with the First Principle, as Blake's imagery tells us:

The groans of Enitharmon shake the skies the labring Earth
Till from her heart rending his way a terrible Child sprang forth
In thunder smoke & sullen flames & howlings & fury & blood[1]

The 'Enormous Demons' of instinctual life which awaken at the birth of Orc hail him as an incarnation of Luvah:

The Enormous Demons woke & howld around the new born king
Crying Luvah King of Love thou art the King of rage & death
(29v : 21–2, M 24)

These lines have two ironic allusions. One is to the Wesleyan hymn 'Hark! the herald angels sing / Glory to the new born king': 'New born' replaced an earlier 'youthful' in order to echo Charles Wesley's lines (see M 122) in a parody of the Nativity. After the birth of the 'secret child' in *Europe*, 'War ceas'd, & all the troops like shadows fled to their abodes' (E 60), but in *Vala* the Demons' song calls for 'Clarions of war' (30R:18, M 24). Their greeting to Orc,

---

[1] 29v : 16–18, M 24. Cf. the later addition to Night I:
> Distracted Luvah
> Bursting forth from the Loins of Enitharmon, Thou fierce Terror
> Go howl in vain, Smite Smite his fetters Smite O wintry hammers
> Smite Spectre of Urthona, mock the fiend who drew us down
> From heavens of joy into this deep.   (8v : 8–12, M 81)

Note that in Night IV, Orc is born from the heart. Bentley suggests that 'Blake's "red Orc" seems to come from Boehme's disobedient son, who is occasionally called *Cor*.' Bentley, *William Blake and the Alchemical Philosophers*, p. 195, cites Boehme's statement that the third quality 'is well called *Cor* or the Heart' (*Aurora* 8 : 47).

'King of Love thou art the King of rage & death', parodies
the beginning of Richard Crashaw's 'Hymn to the Name and
Honour of the Admirable Saint Teresa': 'Love, thou art
absolute sole lord / Of life and death.'[1] Crashaw's poem is
a text for the familiar emblem of the transfixing of St.
Teresa's heart by the Dart of Love; to Blake this would be
a symbol of the self-destroying nature of a Luvah that delights in its own suffering. In the 'Preludium' to *America*,
Orc's union with Nature was one of erotic fulfilment, but in
Night VIIa of *Vala* it will be mutually destructive. Another
echo in the Demons' nativity song, 'now the times return
upon thee' (30R : 17, M 24), employs the words of Albion's
Angel in *America*. In the earlier poem, the Angel's assertion
that Orc's revolutionary energy was part of the bound circle
of history was opposed and (dramatically, at least) outweighed
by Orc's great proclamation of revolution as apocalypse
('The times are ended; shadows pass, the morning 'gins to
break . . .'). In *Vala* there is no such alternative. The failure
of the Republic to preserve political liberty at home and its
aggressive, expansionist military policy abroad[2] had forced
Blake to resolve another of Orc's ambiguities.

As in *Urizen*, Orc grows 'fed with the milk / Of Enitharmon', the mother's milk of things-as-they-are. Fourteen
years pass, bringing 'the fiery boy' to his age in the Preludium of *America*. Now comes the time for the binding of Orc
by Los, who has suffered 'anguish fierce', in Boehme's sense
of a 'quality' of the Wrath-world. One of the important
respects in which *Vala* changes the myth of the binding of
Orc is that Orc is now no longer an unoffending victim.

> . . . Los beheld the ruddy boy
> Embracing his bright mother & beheld malignant fires
> In his young eyes discerning plain that Orc plotted his death
>   (30v : 7–9, M 25)

Los has already built Golgonooza, the city of art, 'in dark
prophetic fear' of the fires of revolution. He is in danger of
becoming like the senile Har of *Tiriel*, an embodiment of

---

[1] *The Poetical Works of Richard Crashaw* (Edinburgh, 1793), p. 720b.
[2] See, for example, Erdman, *Blake*, pp. 284–8.

escapist art who sings 'in the great cage'. Orc's energy threatens to destroy the brittle universe that Los created when he bound Urizen. To prevent the destruction of 'reality', the imagination doing the work of repressive reason binds energy in the chains of Time:

He siezd the boy in his immortal hands
While Enitharmon followd him weeping in dismal woe
Up to the iron mountains top & there the jealous chain
Fell from his bosom on the mountain. The spectre dark
Held the fierce boy Los naild him down binding around his limbs
The dismal chain   (30v : 24–9, M 25)

Energy can be repressed but not destroyed. In his annotations to Lavater, Blake had underlined the aphorism 'He alone has *energy that cannot be deprived of it*' (E 580), and in *The Marriage* he had written:

The Giants who formed this world into its sensual existence and now seem to live in it in chains, are in truth. the causes of its life & the sources of all activity, but the chains are, the cunning of weak and tame minds. which have power to resist energy . . .
. . . to the devourer it seems as if the producer was in his chains, but it is not so, he only takes portions of existence and fancies that the whole.   (E 39)

Orc, though bound, is bathed in a stream of instinctual life:

His limbs bound down mock at his chains for over them a flame
Of circling fire unceasing plays to feed them with life & bring
The virtues of the Eternal worlds ten thousand thousand spirits
Of life rejoice around the Demon going forth & returning
At his enormous call they flee into the heavens of heavens
And back return with wine & food. Or dive into the deeps
To bring the thrilling joys of sense to quell his ceaseless rage[1]

The description, modelled after Daniel's vision of the Ancient of Days ('A fiery stream issued and came forth from before him: thousand thousands ministered unto him, and

---

[1] 31R : 10–16, M 25–6. 'Rejoice' in line 13 was later changed to 'lament' (B 61). For an interesting conjecture as to the source of this passage, see Damon, *William Blake*, p. 376.

ten thousand times ten thousand stood before him' (7 : 10),
suggests that Orc yet retains, at least in potential, his divine
regenerative capacity. So do the animal images woven into
the passage, some of which recall the manifestations of Orc
in the 'Preludium' to *America*:

> His nostrils breathe with fiery flame. his locks are like the forests
> Of wild beasts there the lion glares the tyger & wolf howl there
> And there the Eagle hides her young in cliffs & precipices
>
> (23–5, M 26)

Images of fertility suggest that Orc may still turn the earth
into man's garden:

> there waves the harvest & the vintage rejoices. the springs
> Flow into rivers of delight. . . .
>
> .   .   .   .
>
> His loins inwove with silken fires, are like a furnace fierce
> As the strong Bull in summer time when bees sing round the
>   heath
> Where the herds low after the shadow & after the water spring
> The numrous flocks cover the mountain & shine along the valley
>
> (31R : 27–8; 31V : 1–4, M 26)

The situation appears to be that of the 'Preludium': Orc will
shortly break free, invest the shadowy Female with his
energies, and restore Adam to Paradise. But at this point
Blake makes a highly significant change in the nature of 'the
bloody chain of nights & days' with which Orc is bound. Los
and Enitharmon, repentant, try to unchain Orc but cannot.

> Nor all Urthonas strength nor all the power of Luvahs Bulls
> Tho they each morning drag the unwilling Sun out of the deep
> Could uproot the infernal chain. for it had taken root
> Into the iron rock & grew a chain beneath the Earth
> Even to the Center wrapping round the Center & the limbs
> Of Orc entering with fibres. became one with him a living Chain
> Sustaind by the Demons life.   (31V : 30–2; 32R : 1–4, M 27)

Some seventeen years later, Shelley would use a similar image
in explaining the failure of the French Revolution and its
significance for his own time:

> It has ceased to be believed that whole generations of mankind
> ought to consign themselves to a hopeless inheritance of ignorance

and misery, because a nation of men who had been dupes and slaves for centuries were incapable of conducting themselves with the wisdom and tranquillity of freemen so soon as some of their fetters were partially loosened. . . . If the Revolution had been in every respect prosperous, then misrule and superstition would lose half their claims to our abhorrence, as fetters which the captive can unlock with the slightest motion of his fingers, and which do not eat with poisonous rust into the soul.[1]

Shelley's metaphor has political and moral reference; Blake's is political and psychological. For Blake the fates of Revolution and of psychic energy are mutually involved: the first is a manifestation of the second, and one cannot change without affecting the other as well. The chain which becomes internalized by Orc indicates a change in the fate of energy both in the microcosm of the psyche and in the macrocosm of society. This part of Blake's Orc myth anticipates the Freudian description of the development of the superego, in which the same situation is described in discursive language. In his 'Philosophical Inquiry Into Freud', *Eros and Civilization*,[2] Herbert Marcuse summarizes Freud's account as follows:

In the course of the development of the ego another mental 'entity' arises: the *superego*. It originates from the long dependency of the infant on his parents; the parental influence remains the core of the superego. Subsequently, a number of societal and cultural influences are taken in by the superego until it coagulates into the powerful representative of established morality and 'what people call the "higher" things in human life.' Now the 'external restrictions' which first the parents and then other societal agencies have imposed upon the individual are 'introjected' into the ego and become its 'conscience'; henceforth, the sense of guilt—the need for punishment generated by the transgressions or by the wish to transgress these restrictions (especially in the Oedipus situation)—permeates the mental life. 'As a rule the ego carries out repressions in the service and at the behest of its superego.' However, the repressions soon become unconscious, automatic as it were, and a 'great part' of the sense of guilt remains unconscious.

[1] Preface to *The Revolt of Islam*, *The Complete Poetical Works of Percy Bysshe Shelley*, ed. Thomas Hutchinson (London, 1960), p. 33.
[2] Boston, 1955, pp. 31–2.

The Orc myth has just these components. Dependence on parents is represented by the nursing of Orc: 'Coverd with gloom. the fiery boy grew fed by the milk / Of Enitharmon' (3OR:27–8, M 25). Oedipal guilt—Orc is seen 'Embracing his bright mother' and plotting his father's death. To further emphasize these motifs, Blake later added one line to the end of his description of the binding of Orc, making it read:

> Giving the Spectre sternest charge over the howling fiend
> Concenterd into Love of Parent Storgous Appetite Craving
> $\qquad\qquad\qquad\qquad\qquad$ (61 : 9–10, E 334)

Damon notes that *Storgous* is 'an adjective derived by Blake from "storge", meaning Parental Love, used by Blake in preference to the more violent word, "incestuous"'.[1] The ingrowing of the chain represents the internalization of repression; the chain cannot be struck off, for the psyche now contains its own principle of repression, the 'mind-forg'd manacles' of 'London'. When Orc does break loose later in the poem, it will be to impose a new oppressive reality upon society.

> In every revolution [observes Marcuse] there seems to have been a historical moment when the struggle against domination might have been victorious—but the moment passed. An element of *self-defeat* seems to be involved in this dynamic (regardless of the validity of such reasons as the prematurity and inequality of forces). In this sense, every revolution has also been a betrayed revolution.
> $\qquad\qquad\qquad\qquad\qquad\qquad\qquad\qquad$ (pp. 90–1)

The French Revolution, to Blake, had promised total freedom; an apocalyptic transformation of the conditions of human life. Its betrayal and the self-betrayal of energy, the subjects of Nights VIIa and VIIb, are first explained by Blake in the psychological myth of Night V.

Night V ends with the lament of Urizen, fallen into 'the deep dens of Urthona', where Orc lies chained. The Fall is again recounted, this time with an emphasis upon Urizen's

---

[1] *William Blake*, p. 375.

responsibility in not having guided man with the light of Reason.

> I went not forth I hid myself in black clouds of my wrath
> I calld the stars around my feet in the night of councils dark
> The stars threw down their spears & fled naked away
> We fell. (32v : 25–8, M 28)

'Did he smile his work to see?' This time there could be no answer, not even a question, for Urizen's descent into Wrath merely allows the passions, Luvah, to subvert the will.

> Then thou didst keep with Strong Urthona the living gates of
>   heaven
> But now thou art bowd down with him even to the gates of hell
>
> Because thou gavest Urizen the wine of the Almighty
> For steeds of Light that they might run in thy golden chariot of
>   pride (33R : 3–6, M 28–9)

Hearing the howls of Orc, Urizen surmises that in the fallen world where all things turn to their opposites, the agent of the Fall may become the agent of redemption: 'When Thought is closd in Caves. Then love shall shew its root in deepest Hell' (33R : 12). He decides to explore the caverns and find 'that deep pulsation' which, Frye suggests, is 'really the throbbing heart and lungs of the fallen Albion'.[1]

Night VI records Urizen's journey through the caves of the Fallen Mind, analogous to the flight of Satan through Chaos in Book II of *Paradise Lost*. In his wandering he encounters Tharmas, who, in despair over the chaos of the fallen world, would prefer the extinction of the mind to its present divided existence:

> Withhold thy light from me for ever & I will withhold
> From thee thy food so shall we cease to be & all our sorrows
> End & the Eternal Man no more renew beneath our power[2]

The 'food' of Reason is perception; without Tharmas's stream of sensation, Reason will be 'starvd upon the void' (line 22), while perception unillumined by intellect is merely

---

[1] *Fearful Symmetry*, p. 221.
[2] 35R : 15–17, M 31. 'Cease' was an earlier reading for 'end' (B 68).

a chaos without relationship or meaning. In the prelapsarian world, according to Blake's myth, the two mutually
informed each other; but they are now in conflict, abstract
reason setting up claims to knowledge over the wisdom of
the body and the senses drawn with the passions into irrational pursuits. But the destiny Blake has given the faculties
is integration rather than mutual destruction; Albion will say
in Night IX:

> In enmity & war first weakend then in stern repentance
> They must renew their brightness & their disorganizd functions
> Again reorganize till they resume the image of the human
> Cooperating in the bliss of Man obeying his Will
> Servants to the infinite & Eternal of the Human form
>   (63v : 13–17, M 59)

Urizen goes on, 'with a Globe of fire / Lighting his dismal
journey thro the pathless world of death' (35v : 1–2, M 32).
This again calls attention to the transition from Boehme's
Second (Light) to First (Heat) Principles as a result of the
Fall, for the unfallen Urizen was the Prince of Light. (In the
succeeding Night, Orc will recall 'how I stole thy Light & it
became Fire consuming'.[1]) As he goes still deeper into the
Wrath-world, Urizen meets with degenerate forms of energy:

> Then he beheld the forms of tygers & of Lions dishumanizd men
> Many in serpents & in worms stretchd out enormous length
>   (35v : 28–9, M 33)

As Urizen enters Orc's 'Cavernd Universe of flaming fire' in
Night VII, more images of Wrath appear:

> fierce his lions
> Howl in the burning dens his tygers roam in the redounding
>   smoke
> In forests of affliction.   (39R : 8–10, M 38)

---

[1] N.B. Percival: 'Blake's conception of fire would seem to unite the ancient
tradition which makes fire the substance of mind, with that of Jacob Boehme,
who saw in it the dark, wrathful first principle. The fusion is accomplished by
making light, which Boehme called an emanation of the wrathful fire, the unfallen
mind. When the mind falls, it slips back into its dark fire-source—the world of
experience in which ignorance and passion are compelling forces. . . . In *The
Four Zoas* we are told that when Luvah stole Urizen's light it became a "consuming fire"' (p. 209).

Urizen's stolen steeds of light are here, 'bound to fiery mangers', and the plough and harrow, with which he should sow the seed of Eternal Science, have been perverted to waging corporeal war.

> The plow of ages & the golden harrow wade thro fields
> Of goary blood the immortal seed is nourished for the slaughter
>
> (39R : 14–15)

Instead of creating an earthly Paradise, France has followed the will-to-power, and so has fallen into the condition of the First Principle. 'No other living thing,' says Urizen to the bound Orc, 'Dare thy most terrible wrath abide' (39v : 19–20, M 39). Yet, he is amazed to find, the dream of paradise persists:

> Yet thou dost laugh at all these tortures & this horrible place
> Yet throw thy limbs these fires abroad that back return upon thee
> While thou reposest throwing rage on rage feeding thyself
> With visions of sweet bliss far other than this burning clime
> Sure thou art bathd in rivers of delight on verdant fields
> Walking in joy in bright Expanses sleeping on bright clouds
> With visions of delight so lovely that they urge thy rage
> Tenfold with fierce desire to rend thy chain & howl in fury
>
> (39v : 32–9)

In the words of *The Marriage*, 'the Messiah fell. & formed a heaven of what he stole from the Abyss' (E 34). As energy still preserves this hope of ultimate unity of being, it remains preferable to repressive reason. 'I rage in the deep,' says Orc, 'for Lo my feet & hands are naild to the burning rock / Yet my fierce fires are better than thy snows.'[1]

It must be remembered that Urizen is not 'Reason' in all its senses, but repressive authority which may act through reason *or* through irrational dogma—'religion', 'Mystery'. The Renaissance notion of 'intuitive' reason is proper to his prelapsarian state, but the fallen Urizen is capable only of

---

[1] 40R : 1–2, M 39. Cf. Marcuse: 'Whereas the ego was formerly guided and driven by the *whole* of its mental energy, it is now to be guided only by that part of it which conforms to the reality principle. This part and this part alone is to set the objectives, norms, and values of the ego; as *reason* it becomes the sole repository of judgment, truth, rationality . . .' (pp. 141–2).

discursive reason; and even the more imaginative aspects of this—logic and metaphysics, for example—are functions of the Spectre of Urthona. Urizen, as the Greek root of his name indicates, is the fixer of limits: limits to energy (' . . . Reason is the bound or outward circumference of Energy'[1]), to desire ('The bounded is loathed by its possessor'[2]), to human aspiration. In the eighteenth century, these limits are set in the name of Reason as they had previously been set as religious dogma; therefore Urizen can represent both, seemingly opposed, principles. He writes 'dreadful letters' —the Ten Commandments—in his books of iron, and the Tree of Mystery once more springs up under his heel, as in *Ahania*. The Tree soon becomes a system of 'intricate labyrinths'—a 'Church'[3] with its own theology, law, and political structure. The snows and storms of Urizen's repressive activity 'beat to cool the flames of Orc' (39v:3, M 38).

Orc is, or has been up to now, the metaphysical rebel who denies all limits. He is the Prolific, Urizen the Devourer. These two ought to be spiritual enemies, and Orc at first rejects the wisdom of Urizen: 'Thy Pity I contemn scatter thy snows elsewhere'. But the repressive principle, as symbolized by the ingrowing of the chain, has become part of Orc, and France's domestic and foreign policies no longer seem very different from England's. Orc is ready to learn from Urizen.

> Urizen answerd Read my books explore my Constellations
> Enquire of my Sons & they shall teach thee how to War
> Enquire of my Daughters who accursd in the dark depths
> Knead bread of Sorrow by my stern command for I am God
>   (40R : 20–3, M 40)

We are entering the France of the Consulate and the Constitution of the Year VIII, which followed Napoleon's *coup d'état* of 18 Brumaire in November 1799.[4] The administration of government was centralized to an even greater extent than it had been under the Bourbons; censorship of the press and of the theatre was instituted; labour activities were put

---

[1] *The Marriage*, E 34.   [2] *There Is No Natural Religion* [b], E 2.
[3] See Damon, *William Blake*, p. 378.
[4] See Erdman, *Blake*, p. 291.

under police surveillance.[1] In the spring of 1800, French armies took the offensive in Germany and Italy. These are, no doubt, some of the 'arts' which Urizen teaches Orc. 'Bread of sorrow' has particular significance. What Blake elsewhere calls 'our Real Taxed ⟨ Substantial Money bought ⟩ Bread'[2] was, as Erdman has shown,[3] an immediate index to the effect of war on the lives of the labouring poor. The price of the quartern loaf had soared to 1*s.* 9*d.* by the end of 1800, while the people were demanding a price of 6*d.* the quartern.[4] The government took measures to discourage consumption, forbidding the sale of new bread and of fine wheaten bread; someone was even commissioned to invent a paste that would serve as a cheap flour substitute.[5] Bread of sorrow indeed! Blake was not alone in blaming the war for high bread prices; in 1800, Pitt castigated his Whig opponents for stirring popular discontent by doing the same thing.[6] Urizen has a programme for dealing with such dissatisfactions:

> Compell the poor to live upon a Crust of bread by soft mild arts
> Smile when they frown frown when they smile & when a man
>   looks pale
> With labour & abstinence say he looks healthy & happy
> And when his children sicken let them die there are enough
> Born even too many & our Earth will be overrun
> Without these arts   (40v:2–7, M40)[7]

The doctrine is in part Malthusian. Malthus's *Essay on the Principle of Population* had been published by Johnson in 1798; Urizen incorporates in his argument what Malthus terms the 'positive check to population'—the fact that

. . . it has been very generally remarked by those who have attended to bills of mortality that of the number of children who die

---

[1] See Leo Gershoy, *The French Revolution and Napoleon* (New York, 1933), p. 354.

[2] Annotations to Thornton's *The Lord's Prayer, Newly Translated* (1827), E 658.   [3] *Blake*, pp. 315–19.   [4] Ibid., p. 317.

[5] Ibid., p. 340; John Ashton, *The Dawn of the Nineteenth Century in England* (London, 1886), pp. 19, 29.

[6] *The War Speeches of William Pitt the Younger*, selected by R. Coupland (Oxford, 1940), p. 287. See also Erdman on Pitt, *Blake*, p. 341.

[7] See Schorer, p. 325.

annually, much too great a proportion belongs to those who may be supposed unable to give their offspring proper food and attention, exposed as they are occasionally to severe distress and confined, perhaps, to unwholesome habitations and hard labour.[1]

Urizen does not propose, with Malthus, the abolition of parish and poor laws, as he has a use for charity and no wish to free the labour market.

> . . . . If you would make the poor live with temper
> With pomp give every crust of bread you give with gracious cunning
> Magnify small gifts reduce the man to want a gift & then give with pomp
> Say he smiles if you hear him sigh If pale say he is ruddy
> Preach temperance say he is overgorgd & drowns his wit
> In strong drink tho you know that bread & water are all
> He can afford Flatter his wife pity his children till we can
> Reduce all to our will as spaniels are taught with art
>   (40v : 7–14, M 40–1)

Malthus, too, had said that 'A man who might not be deterred from going to the ale-house from the consideration that on his death, or sickness, he should leave his wife and family upon the parish might yet hesitate in thus dissipating his earnings if he were assured that, in either of these cases, his family must starve or be left to the support of casual bounty'.[2] Although, as Erdman observes, 'Malthus did not add the idea of "moral restraint" until his 1803 edition',[3] what Malthus calls the 'preventive check'—'a foresight of the difficulties attending the rearing of a family' (p. 22)—is already close to the later idea. 'The labourer who earns eighteen pence a day and lives with some degree of comfort as a single man, will hesitate a little before he divides that pittance among four or five, which seems to be but just sufficient for one' (p. 23).

---

[1] *Population: the First Essay*, by Thomas Robert Malthus (Ann Arbor, Mich., 1959), p. 25.

[2] Ibid., p. 31.

[3] *Blake*, p. 342 n. See also Schorer, p. 325. Blake later added, perhaps reflecting Malthus's 'moral restraint': '. . . let Moral Duty tune your tongue/But be your hearts harder than the nether millstone' (E 348).

> there are enough
> Born even too many & our Earth will be overrun
> Without these arts   (40v : 5–7, M 40)

Urizen's advice cynically combines Malthus's 'preventive' and 'positive' checks with an advocacy of the very poor relief that Malthus attacked. The poor laws, Malthus maintained, were 'strongly calculated to eradicate this spirit [of independence in England]' (p. 29). This, of course, is exactly what Urizen wants—a pauperized working class that must depend upon the government for subsistence.

Urizen begins his instruction of Orc in the second person, but by line 13 he is confident enough to use the first person plural: 'till we can / Reduce all to our will'. Orc is learning his lesson in Power: he is changing from a rebel, in Camus's sense, to a revolutionary. 'In every rebellion', says Camus, 'is to be found the metaphysical demand for unity, the impossibility of capturing it and the construction of a substitute universe' (*The Rebel*, p. 224). In *America* Orc promised total freedom, a transformation of the conditions of life. He now abandons this for the creation of a substitute reality, a new order, betraying the original impulse toward 'metaphysical unity', the apocalyptic unity of *The Marriage*. At some point, as Camus wryly observes, the Rebel calls in the police. He becomes a revolutionary and uses the repressive institutions of society to prevent others from rebelling in the name of unity. 'We have come full circle here and rebellion, cut off from its real roots, unfaithful to man in having surrendered to history, now contemplates the subjection of the entire universe' (pp. 145–6). In Blake's symbolism, this is the point where Orc becomes a serpent in *Vala* and something like an 'Orc cycle' can be said to exist.

In the Lambeth books, as we have seen, Orc had alternate human and serpent forms, an expression of his ambiguity. In *Vala* the forms are not alternate but successive. The transition from human to serpent occurs immediately after Orc receives Urizen's instruction.

> Orc answerd Curse thy Cold hypocrisy. already round thy Tree
> In scales that shine with gold & rubies thou beginnest to weaken
> My divided Spirit Like a worm I rise in peace unbound

From wrath Now when I rage my fetters bind me more
O torment O torment A Worm compelld. Am I a worm
Is it in strong deceit that man is born. In strong deceit
Thou dost restrain my fury that the worm may fold the tree

(40v : 20–6, M 41)

The Tree around which Orc folds is Urizen's church, specifically the Roman Catholic Church, to Blake the stronghold
of Mystery. (On Plate 13 of *Europe*, Urizen is pictured as
the pope enthroned, and in 'A Song of Liberty' Blake calls
upon Rome to 'Cast thy keys . . . into the deep . . .') The
symbolism here refers to the re-establishment of State
Religion in France; perhaps specifically to Napoleon's
signing a concordat with the pope on 16 July 1800. As in
Ahania, the energy principle has become something similar
to what it rebelled against. Urizen is God again.

The transition from Orc's human to his serpent body is
expressed in terms associated with Boehme's First and
Second Principles:

> So saying he began to Organize a Serpent body
> Despising Urizens light & turning it into flaming fire
> Recieving as a poisond Cup Recieves the heavenly wine
> And turning wisdom into fury & thought into abstraction
> A self consuming dark devourer rising into the heavens[1]

The meaning of this transition from light to darkness is by
now familiar enough, as is the special significance of 'self
consuming dark devourer' in Boehme's vocabulary.[2] According to Boehme, Wrath consumes itself—and the repentant
Urizen of Night IX will say 'Let Luvah rage in the dark deep
even to Consummation' (60v : 28, M 54). Orc is now a manifestation of the will-to-power, manifested in history as
Napoleon, in the psyche as the Satanic selfhood.

Night VIIb again tells the story of Orc's breaking free, but
this time from the retrospect of what had happened to the
Revolution. This Night was formerly thought to be an
earlier version of VIIa, but evidence has been offered by

---

[1] 36–40. 'Wisdom' was later changed to 'affection' (B 81), creating a much
more forceful parallelism.
[2] See above, pp. 43–5.

Margoliouth and by Bentley to show that it must have been written later, and that when the Night is read in its original form, it is seen to follow rather than replace Night VIIa.[1] VIIa ends with the birth of Vala, 'Nature in a material form',[2] to the Spectre of Urthona and the shadow of Enitharmon. The spectral imagination, 'the slave of that Creation I created' (42v : 31, M 45), creates in the world of space an illusion of Nature. Before later additions, this Night ends:

> The Spectre smild & gave her Charge over the howling Orc

This is the situation with which VIIb begins:

> Now in the Caverns of the Grave and Places of human seed
> The nameless shadowy Vortex stood before the face of Orc[3]

The 'Vortex' is Vala, 'The shadowy Daughter of Urthona' who 'stood before red Orc' in *America*. As in *America*, she is 'nameless' because she needs man to give her an identity, 'shadowy' because as an end in itself she is an illusion. Why does Blake call her a 'Vortex'? Perhaps the reference is to the implications of Descartes's theory of vortices (as M 118 suggests). The vortices were Descartes's way of accounting for gravitation as a series of whirling motions in ether. The theory has an important relation to the concept of the universe as mechanism.

It was the first comprehensive attempt to picture the whole external world in a way fundamentally different from the Platonic–Aristotelian–Christian view which, centrally a teleological and spiritual conception of the processes of nature, had controlled men's thinking for a millennium and a half. God had created the world of physical existence, for the purpose that in man, the highest natural end, the whole process might find its way back to God. Now God is relegated to the position of first cause of motion, the happenings of the universe then continuing *in aeternum* as incidents in the regular revolutions of a great mathematical machine. Galileo's daring conception is carried out in fuller detail. The world is

---

[1] What was originally the first part of the Night was later made to follow the second part. See M xiii and 139; B 162–3. For Erdman's differing view, see E 737.

[2] Damon, *William Blake*, p. 380. [3] M 46; cf. B 93.

pictured concretely as . . . mechanical rather than teleological. The stage is set for the likening of it, in Boyle, Locke, and Leibniz, to a big clock once wound up by the Creator, and since kept in orderly motion by nothing more than his 'general concourse'.[1]

The Vortex of material Nature does not greet Orc as lover and redeemer as in *America*; rather,

> that he might lose his rage
> And with it lose himself in meekness she embracd his fire
> (46R : 4–5, M 46)

'Meekness' is an attribute of Boehme's Second Principle, but here the term is used ironically (as in 'unbound / From wrath' in VIIa, when Orc says, 'Now when I rage my fetters bind me more' (40v : 22–3, M 41). To emphasize the ironical contrast with *America*, two lines from the 'Preludium' are repeated:

> Silent as despairing love & strong as Jealousy
> The hairy shoulders rend the links free are the wrists of fire[2]

In *America*, these lines were immediately followed by

> Round the terrific loins he siez'd the panting struggling womb;
> It joy'd: she put aside her clouds & smiled her first-born smile . . .
> (2 : 3–4, E 50–1)

In *Vala*, instead of the erotic union of Energy and Nature, we have the destructive attack of Wrath on the world's body:

> Red rage redounds he rouzd his lions from his forests black
> They howl around the flaming youth rending the nameless
> shadow (46R : 13–14, M. 46)

The enormous wars between France and the Coalitions begin:

> Loud sounds the war song round red Orc in his fury
> And round the nameless shadowy Female in her howling terror
> When all the Elemental Gods joind in the wondrous Song[3]

---

[1] Burtt, p. 105.
[2] 46R : 11–12, M 46. Cf. *America*, 2 : 1–2, E 50.
[3] 46R : 16–18, M 46. B 14–15 has partly reconstructed a former reading.

The song of these 'Gods', recalling the nativity song of the 'Elemental Demons' in Night V, is followed by a description of the carnage and the proclamation of a 'Victory' that turns out to be the crucifixion of Luvah:

> They vote the death of Luvah & they naild him to the tree
> They piercd him with a spear & laid him in a Sepulcher
> To die a death of Six thousand years bound round with desolation[1]

As the war rages on, Orc entirely loses the possibility of making the earth human.

> Orc rent her & his human form consumd in his own fires
> Mingled with her dolorous members strewn thro the Abyss
> (47R : 19–20, M 48)

The *disjecta membra* of the phenomenal world are scattered in 'the Abyss'—Boehme's term for what separates our dark reality from its divine source. The fires of Wrath 'consume' Orc's human form entirely, leaving only the serpent body, which in turn will be consumed in Night IX. As a crowning irony, the reptile form of Orc is now associated with the Tyger's enemy, the stars:

> No more remaind of Orc but the Serpent round the tree of Mystery
> The form of Orc was gone he reard his Serpent bulk among
> The stars of Urizen in Power rending the form of life
> Into a formless indefinite & strewing her on the Abyss[2]

Energy has constructed its substitute universe.

In the latter part of VIIb, the other three Zoas confront one another and prepare for further wars, in the service of which all energies have been perverted; even

> The fruit trees humanizing
> Shewd their immortal energies in warlike desperation
> (49v : 10–11, M 52)

All animals have become symbols of Wrath, not only 'The Lion raging in flames / The Tyger in redounding smoke'

---

[1] 46v : 13–15, M 47. Erdman, *Blake*, p. 291, suggests that Luvah is France as victim, Orc the militant France.

[2] 47R : 21–4, M 48. B *96* conjectures 'fire' as deleted for 'Power'.

(19–20), but also those which Swedenborg took to represent gentle affections:[1] 'Sullen the wooly sheep / Walks thro the battle Dark & fierce' (17–18). The very possibility of Innocence seems to have been destroyed. Enitharmon, as an embodiment of the world in anguish, calls upon the power of prophecy to exercise its function:

> Lift up Lift up O Los awake my watchman for he sleepeth
> Lift up Lift up Shine forth O Light watchman thy light is out
> O Los unless thou keep my tower the Watchman will be slain[2]

But the prophetic imagination has as yet not assumed its redemptive task, and there is no reply. Night VIIb ends with 'The Prester Serpent' urging the ranks into battle.

*   *   *

In the first eight Nights of *Vala* (I–VIIb), there is little hope of redemptive action, either by Energy or by the Imagination. Los has much the same function as in the Lambeth books, although the description of it has been amplified with the analysis of Urthona into Los, Spectre of Los, and Spectre of Urthona. Los does set bounds to the chaos created by the Fall, but he is also 'the slave of that Creation I created', binding Orc and warring with the other faculties. He is not yet associated with the term 'imagination', which has occurred only twice in the poem so far (once in connection with Urizen's 'dread fancy' (17v : 3–6, M 7). Orc, meanwhile, has changed considerably in significance, losing his human form and with it his regenerative capacity. The prophecy of Night III is unfulfilled: the 'Prophetic boy' whom Urizen fears has not grown up to command his prince. Instead, Orc's vital energy has degenerated into destructive wrath with the in-rooting of the chain, the rending of the world in war, the organization of the serpent body, and its rising among the stars of Urizen in Power. These developments have in some ways been anticipated by the anterior myth which makes Orc a manifestation of Luvah, the Zoa of

---

[1] See above, p. 77.

[2] 49v : 4–6, M 52. Cf. Psalm 127 : 1: 'Except the LORD build the house, they labour in vain that build it: except the LORD keep the city, the watchman waketh but in vain.'

passion whose overreaching precipitated the collapse of the microcosm. There are in Night VIIb, however, traces of a new hope. In this Night there appear for the first time Christian elements which are not part of added or later passages.

> Mourning the daughters of Beulah saw nor could they have
>   sustaind
> The horrid sight of death & torment But the Eternal Promise
> They wrote on all their tombs & pillars & on every Urn
> These words If ye will believe your Brother shall rise again
> In golden letters ornamented with sweet labours of love
> Waiting with Patience for the fulfilment of the Promise Divine[1]

Here is the first manifestation of the Christian hope which will become so prominent in the following Nights and in passages added to earlier ones. *Vala* is on its way to becoming *The Four Zoas*, and we are entering the terrain of Blake's later thought.

---

[1] 48R : 3–8, M 49. Line 4 echoes John 11 : 23. On this passage, see W. H. Stevenson, 'Two Problems in *The Four Zoas*', *Blake Newsletter*, no. 4 (1968), p. 7.

5

Breaking the Bound Circle: 'The Mental Traveller' and the Seven Eyes of God

> Man stands at the level of conscious life: immediately
> in front of him is the power to visualize the eternal city
> and garden he is trying to regain; immediately behind him
> is an unconscious, involuntary and cyclic energy, much of
> which still goes on inside his own body. Man is therefore
> a Luvah or form of life subject to two impulses, one the
> prophetic impulse leading him forward to vision, the
> other the natural impulse which drags him back to un-
> consciousness and finally to death.
>
> NORTHROP FRYE: *Fearful Symmetry*

THE circular folds of the Orc serpent suggest that history is
a bound circle which channels and contains energy, limiting
it to a repetition of the same dull round of promise and betrayal. Another such construct is found in 'The Mental
Traveller', a poem roughly contemporary with Night IX of
Vala,[1] where the cyclical theme is embodied in an appropriately

---

[1] The Pickering Manuscript poems, including 'The Mental Traveller', were
dated by Professor Sampson as 'composed not later than 1803, though pos-
sibly a year or two earlier' (*The Poetical Works of William Blake* (London,
1961 (1913)), p. xl). The evidence adduced for this approximate date is the
relationship of certain poems in the Pickering Manuscript to rough drafts in the
Notebook and to a letter by Blake dated 16 August 1803. However, 'The
Mental Traveller' is not one of these, and as the Pickering Manuscript is a
series of fair copies, there is no reason to assume that this poem was not
written later than some of the others. Recently Miss Kathleen Raine has
offered strong evidence to suggest that Blake wrote 'The Mental Traveller' no
earlier than 1804 (see below), and Gerald E. Bentley, Jr., has argued that the
entire manuscript was transcribed in 1805 or later ('The Date of Blake's
Pickering Manuscript or The Way of a Poet With Paper', *SB*, xix (1966), 232–
43).

circular structure. Seen in this way, history is a nightmare of recurrence. There is, however, another perspective: seen from outside the bound circle, history becomes an ever-expanding spiral from which man can leap into a transcendent reality. The two possibilities are depicted in juxtaposition as early as the *Night Thoughts* illustrations of 1795–7. The frontispiece to Night III (No. 78) shows a huge, resplendent serpent, above whose head stands a female figure, Young's Narcissa, on a crescent moon. Her arms reach upward with a sweep reinforced by the lines of the rest of her body; in contrast to the serpent, she is white, and radiance streams from her figure. On the verso (No. 79), Blake painted another female figure, this one chained inside the circle formed by a great crested serpent, holding her hands to her head with a horrified expression. Thus we have two human alternatives. The second of these is the one described in 'The Mental Traveller'; the first is the subject of a series of additions to *Vala* in which Blake introduced the symbolic construct he called the Seven Eyes of God.

1

'The Mental Traveller' is an epitome of those parts of the Lambeth books and *Vala* which have as their subject the 'Orc cycle'[1]—revolutionary Energy and its fate in history. In this poem the situations of the Orc cycle are treated retrospectively as parts of an inexorable series of events, the over-all view being that man is trapped within the bound circle which is both the subject and the structure of the poem. There is, however, a difference between the view *in* the poem and the view *of* the poem, a difference indicated by a pervasive irony. We are made aware of this almost from the first, with the lines 'And heard & saw such dreadful things / As cold Earth wanderers never knew' (E 475). These dreadful things turn out to be precisely the situations of our world presented in paradigmatic form; all through the poem the narrator pretends that his account is of an alien world, while

---

[1] *Fearful Symmetry*, pp. 228–9. See also John H. Sutherland, 'Blake's "Mental Traveller"', *ELH*, xxii (1955), 136–47.

we know it is of our own. The equivalent of a contrasting perspective is produced by this dogged literalness of statement in a poem we know from the first is symbolical. A sense of distance is created by the peculiar flatness of the diction and (as Irene H. Chayes points out[1]) by the pattern of the double circle which the narrator seems to be unaware of, describing events as if they were in simple linear succession up to the last line. The pseudo-naïve narrator is employed not only to describe our condition but to satirize our view of it. It is no more the business of this poem to supply the missing perspective than it is that of Book IV of *Gulliver* to provide a corrective view of the Houyhnhnms.

The plot of 'The Mental Traveller' pivots upon two births, one of which occurs at the beginning of the poem, the other about half-way through it. The first nativity is that of a male saviour:

> For there the Babe is born in joy
> That was begotten in dire woe
> Just as we Reap in joy the fruit
> Which we in bitter tears did sow

There is an allusion here to Psalm 126, a Psalm of Exile: 'They that sow in tears shall reap in joy. He that goeth forth and weepeth, bearing precious seed, shall doubtless come again with rejoicing, bringing his sheaves with him'.[2] The eruption of Energy into the barren material world promises sorrow for an old order, the destruction of which must precede the creation of a new one. But the redemptive hope held out by this Orc figure is immediately modified by his subjection to the limitations of physical existence.

> And if the Babe is born a Boy
> He's given to a Woman Old
> Who nails him down upon a rock
> Catches his shrieks in cups of gold   (E 475)

---

[1] 'Plato's *Statesman* Myth in Shelley and Blake', *CL*, xiii (1961), 358–69.
[2] Cf. *Four Zoas*, II. 32 : 16–17, E 315: 'Sorrowing went the Planters forth to plant, the Sowers to sow'. This line originally read 'Then went the Planters forth to plant, the Sowers forth to sow' (M 6). The change makes it refer explicitly to the Psalm.

Energy is circumscribed in the world of matter, the soul
limited in its perceptions to what filters through the screen
of the senses, the revolutionary impulse absorbed by things-
as-they-are. The meaning of the Babe's crucifixion is made
more explicit in lines 13–16:

> She binds iron thorns around his head
> She pierces both his hands & feet
> She cuts his heart out at his side
> To make it feel both cold & heat

'Every pleasure and pain', Blake must have read in Taylor's
Phaedo, 'as if armed with a nail, fastens and rivets the soul
to the body, causes it to become corporeal, and fills it with
an opinion, that whatever the body asserts is true'.[1] The
Babe can at this point be identified with Luvah, who wears a
crown of thorns in Night IX (68R : 21, M 68) and is crucified
in VIIb (46v : 13, M 47). The natural world now begins to
drain away the energy of the divine child.

> Her fingers number every Nerve
> Just as a Miser counts his gold
> She lives upon his shrieks & cries,
> And she grows young as he grows old

The danger is that the child will be assimilated into the world
he came to redeem, energy canalized and contained as in
Night V of *Vala*, where Orc's chain becomes part of his body.
But the situation quickly shifts to that of Night VIIa and of
the 'Preludium' to *America*, where Orc, guarded by the
'shadowy Daughter of Urthona' or the 'Nameless Shadowy
Vortex', gets free and rapes his keeper.

> Till he becomes a bleeding youth
> And she becomes a Virgin bright
> Then he rends up his Manacles
> And binds her down for his delight

Orc is now free to transform nature. He 'plants himself in all
her nerves'—energy pours into the vacuum at the centre of

---

[1] *Cratylus, Phaedo, Parmenides, and Timaeus*, trans. Thomas Taylor (London, 1793), p. 186.

material phenomena and begins to revolutionize every aspect of life. Orc is now a 'Husbandman' whose 'Garden' is society (as in *America* Orc makes the world fruitful by impregnating the daughter of Urthona). However, we see little of the redeeming Orc of the Lambeth prophecies in 'The Mental Traveller', for a new state is quickly reached.[1] The hero undergoes a moral change analogous to Orc's in Night VIIb. He becomes an 'aged Shadow' who tries to accumulate material wealth by dint of industry and self-denial.

> And these are the gems of the Human Soul
> The rubies & pearls of a lovesick eye
> The countless gold of the akeing heart
> The martyrs groan & the lovers sigh   (E 476)

These are not real spiritual gifts, as may at first appear, but the illusory rewards of repression. A comparison of this passage with Blake's Notebook poem 'Riches' (E 461) points up the contrast. There Blake speaks of 'The countless gold of a merry heart' and 'The rubies & pearls of a loving eye'. 'Riches' describes fulfilment—'merry', 'loving'; the 'Mental Traveller' lines describe frustration— 'lovesick', 'akeing.' Orc has become Urizen.[2] His charity should not mislead us, for we know what Blake thought of such charity.

> Pity would be no more,
> If we did not make somebody Poor:
> And Mercy no more could be,
> If all were as happy as we   (E 27)

The existence of charity demonstrates the unjust state of society. It is precisely this state that the hero now represents.

---

[1] Professor Sampson points out the applicability to 'The Mental Traveller' of Blake's doctrine of States, citing in illustration a passage from *A Vision of the Last Judgment* (1810): '⟨. . . These States Exist now Man Passes on but States remain for Ever he passes thro them like a traveller who may as well suppose that the places he has passed thro exist no more as a Man may suppose that the States he has passd thro Exist no more Every Thing is Eternal⟩' (*Poetical Works* (Oxford, 1905), p. 273; I have folowed Erdman's punctuation, E 546).

[2] See Frye, p. 229; Sutherland, *ELH*, xxii. 141. Though Orc does not become Urizen in *Vala*, he does degenerate into Urizen's spiritual ally; in Night VIII Urizen is seen 'Communing with the Serpent of Orc in dark dissimulation' 50v:32, M 84).

> He feeds the Beggar & the Poor
> And the wayfaring Traveller
> For ever open is his door
>
> His grief is their eternal joy
> They make the roofs & walls to ring

This is also the state of Urizen in Night III of *Vala*:

> I am set here a King of trouble commanded here to serve
> And do my ministry to those who eat of my wide table
>
> (19v : 4–5, M 10)

However, the hero's power begins to decline almost as soon as it reaches its height. A new birth occurs, one which will destroy the order that the aged Shadow had painfully established, just as in his role as Orc he destroyed the previous order.

The Babe who is born near the midpoint of the poem is the opposite of and counterpart to the first. She is a reincarnation of the Woman Old, a new and ever-the-same version of the old reality, as at the end of Night VIII of *The Four Zoas*.

> The Ashes of Mystery began to animate they calld it Deism
> And Natural Religion as of old so now anew began
> Babylon again in Infancy Calld Natural Religion
>
> (111 : 22–4, E 371)

The Female Babe's parodical resemblance to the male one should not mislead us. 'She is all of solid fire', but the word 'solid' indicates that hers is not the free, exuberant flow of Energy; it is, rather, the same power we see concentrated in the solid haloes of Satan (Job illus. 6) and Nelson.[1] Her 'gems & gold', taken over from the Urizen figure, reappear as the 'pestilential food' of Orc in Night VIII of *Vala*.[2] The word

---

[1] See below, pp. 195–96.

[2] 51R : 21–4, M 85:

> . . .Still the pestilential food in gems & gold
> Exuded round his awful limbs Stretching to serpent length
> His human bulk While the dark shadowy female brooding over
> Measurd his food morning & evening in cups & baskets of iron

'Female' itself is replete with negative associations in Blake, the Female Will being only one of these, and Female Babes are no exception:

> Forbid all Joy, & from her childhood shall the little female
> Spread nets in every secret path.   (*Europe*, 6 : 8–9, E 61)

William Michael Rossetti was right, on one level, in calling her 'The halo of authority and tradition, or prestige, gathering round the Idea'; another, related, aspect is Professor Damon's view of her as 'an established code of conduct . . . a Church, outward religion'; yet another is Frye's: 'the natural environment which man partially but never wholly subdues'.[1] She is also Napoleonic France, congealing revolutionary energy into an authoritarian system. Yet no single identification will do justice to the breadth of meaning of the Female Babe, who with her other manifestations as maiden and Woman Old comprises the numerous evil females of Blake's pantheon: Enitharmon as space and as Female Will; Rahab the harlot; Tirzah, binder of spirit to flesh; the daughters of Urizen, who knead the bread of materialism; and Vala. She and her lover drive out the aged Host, possessing themselves of the dead institutional shell of what revolutionary energy had once animated.

---

[1] *The Poetical Works of William Blake* (London, 1874), p. 185 n.; *William Blake*, p. 131; *Anatomy of Criticism* (Princeton, 1957), p. 322; resp. Frye earlier wrote that 'As Orc declines, his imaginative achievements are completed into a single form or "Female Babe," which is then to be used by other imaginations, just as an appletree sheds its fruit for others to eat' (*Fearful Symmetry*, p. 229). However, even at that time Professor Frye expressed dissatisfaction with this interpretation in a footnote to the passage (p. 444). Sutherland calls the Female Babe 'this splendid product of man's creative powers' (*ELH*, xxii. 143), and Martin K. Nurmi sees her as 'a kind of fierce love born of such joy as Experience provides' ('Joy, Love, and Innocence in Blake's "The Mental Traveller"', *Studies in Romanticism*, iii (1964), 114). Professor Hazard Adams attempts to invest the Female Babe with a meaning opposite to that of the Woman Old: 'As against the aged and unprolific woman she is the prolific muse, the true Jerusalem' (*William Blake: A Reading of the Shorter Poems* (Seattle, 1963), p. 94). It seems to me that none of these readings can be sustained either by what happens in the poem—the female causes a further deterioration of reality by driving the male into the desert—or by the rest of Blake's myth: *every* Vala is potentially the true Jerusalem, but in a world unregenerated by Imagination, emanations become harlots, Vala must become Rahab.

The aged Shadow now must wander through the desert of
his own being 'Untill he can a Maiden win', or impose his
identity upon nature and the material world once more. But
their relationship this time is based not upon energy but
upon abstract reason, often represented by Blake in terms of
cold:

> And to allay his freezing Age
> The Poor Man takes her in his arms
> The Cottage fades before his sight
> The Garden & its lovely Charms

The Garden with its suggestion of Eden, lost when the Female Babe drove out her aged Host, disappears altogether
when man embraces a philosophy of the five senses. Having
subjected the universe to analysis, man can no longer even
envision the possibility of Edenic harmony. The world becomes an image of the spiritual condition of its perceiver—
'The eye altering alters all'—and appears no longer infinite,
but a globe of solid matter; the heavenly bodies 'shrink away'
to the finite forms in which we perceive them. ('As a man is,
So he Sees. As the Eye is formed, such are its Powers.'[1]) All
that remains of existence is a 'dark desart'. This is Ulro, the
plane of unalloyed material being, the lowest level that the
mind can reach. Nothing is left to eat or drink because
the spirit cannot find sustenance in a universe of dead matter.
But Ulro is also the limit of contraction beyond which error
cannot go. From this point on, all progress in the cycle is
towards the original situation.

The hero discovers that he can live upon the 'food' of
sensuous experience offered by nature:

> The honey of her Infant lips
> The bread & wine of her sweet smile
> The wild game of her roving Eye
> Does him to Infancy beguile   (E 477)

We have now gone almost full circle. The revolutionary
impulse represented by the Babe, having become an orthodoxy in its own right, grew progressively more enfeebled

---

[1] Letter to Dr. Trusler, 23 August 1799 (K 793).

to the point where it had to derive new energies from the world it had formerly enriched. (Cf. *Jerusalem*, 65:59–60, E 215: 'For a Spectre has no Emanation but what he imbibes from decieving / A Victim! Then he becomes her Priest & she his Tabernacle.') With this renewal of energy, the hero has progressed along the upstroke of the second half of the cycle. The passions, represented as animals, return to the world. The hero pursues his coy mistress, and 'Labyrinths of wayward Love' spring up around them. We approach one of the two points in the cycle where a true union occurs, having ascended from the hell of Ulro to Beulah, the state of happy marriage among all things. (The first union took place when the female figure became the hero's garden in lines 23–4.)

> Then many a Lover wanders here
> The Sun & Stars are nearer rolld
>
> The trees bring forth sweet Extacy
> To all who in the desart roam
> Till many a City there is Built
> And many a pleasant Shepherds home

This state, too, is temporary. Beulah is only a 'mild & pleasant rest'[1] from the labours of Eternity. The hero must now reach the phase where once more he embodies Energy in its pure, uncompromised form, and there must follow that apocalyptic event which is the discovery of Orc, followed by his crucifixion, once more, upon the rock of Law.

'The Mental Traveller', with its pessimistic vision of flux and reflux between revolution and reaction, energy and matter, is a terrifiying poem. In it Blake seems to echo the despair of the shadowy female of *Europe*, who sees her sons as 'howling terrors, all devouring fiery kings' and prays 'Stamp not with solid form this vig'rous progeny of fires' (E 59–60). Her grief was assuaged by the birth of a divine child, but now the child is himself seen as part of the cycle. There is, at the same time, a certain ambiguity in the poem's

---

[1] See *Four Zoas*, I. 5 : 29–33, E 299. This is an added passage, not in M. Bentley suggests that 'Blake found the name not in Isaiah 62:4 . . . but in Part I of *Pilgrim's Progress*' (B. 174).

perspective. 'And all is done as I have told' implies an endless repetition of the events described; at the same time, the ability to perceive the pattern of recurrence implies some kind of freedom. If one were entirely imprisoned within the bound circle, one would not be able to see it whole—one would also be imprisoned in the illusion of the uniqueness of events. There is also the distance already mentioned between our apprehension of the poem as symbolic in mode and cyclical in structure and the narrator's presentation of it as if it were literal and linear. This distance makes us aware that there is a reality left out of the poem—as if in *Job* illustration 15 the upper level, showing Job and his children looking down through the clouds, were missing, leaving only the fish-bowl globe below with its grotesque monsters. If we ourselves were inside this fish-bowl world, it would appear to us to be the universe, like the bound circle of 'The Mental Traveller'; but both are viewed from an outside perspective, included in the Job illustration but only implied in the poem.[1]

2

In his intriguing study of the myth of the Eternal Return, *Cosmos and History*,[2] Professor Mircea Eliade traces cyclical theories and constructs of history back to the cosmogonic myths of primitive societies. Such societies, says Professor Eliade, 'refuse' to accept history by viewing events in time as a series of archetypal gestures or as a cycle of decay and regeneration.[3] Historical man—man, that is, with a consciousness of the uniqueness of events—may attempt to take refuge in one or the other of these views in order to preserve himself from the 'misfortune' of history. The cyclical conception

---

[1] Cf. Adams's remark that 'The speaker of the poem is reporting upon the fallen world from the point of view of eternity' (*William Blake*, p. 87).

[2] Translated from the French by Willard R. Trask, New York, 1959 (originally published, Paris, 1949, as *Le Mythe de l'éternel rétour: archetypes et répétition*).

[3] Professor Eliade uses the term 'archetype' in its traditional sense as meaning 'exemplary model' or 'paradigm' (p. ix), and this is the sense in which the word will be used here and in Chapters 7 and 8; no reference is intended to the Jungian 'archetypes of the collective unconscious'.

of history enters historical European culture with the popularization of the Chaldean doctrine of the 'Great Year':

> According to this doctrine, the universe is eternal but it is periodically destroyed and reconstituted every Great Year (the corresponding number of millennia varies from school to school); when the seven planets assemble in Cancer ('Great Winter') there will be a deluge; when they meet in Capricorn (i.e., at the summer solstice of the Great Year) the entire universe will be consumed by fire. It is probable that this doctrine of periodic universal conflagrations was also held by Heraclitus (e.g., Fragment 26B = 66D). In any case, it dominates the thought of Zeno and the entire Stoic cosmology. The myth of universal combustion (*ekpyrosis*) was decidedly in fashion throughout the Romano-Oriental world from the first century B.C. to the third century of our era; it successively found a place in a considerable number of gnostic systems derived from Greco-Irano-Judaic syncretism. (pp. 87–8)

One of the systems in which the myth found a place was Plato's. As Miss Chayes and Miss Kathleen Raine[1] have pointed out, Blake derived the model of history in 'The Mental Traveller' from the *Politicus*. (Taylor's translation of the *Politicus* appeared in 1804; there now seems no reason to believe that 'The Mental Traveller' was written before that year, especially if one agrees with Bentley's dating of the entire Pickering manuscript as no earlier than 1805.) In the *Politicus*, history is described as a spindle which is first wound up in one direction and then unwinds itself in the other. Each of these motions corresponds to a Great Year of the ancients. As long as the spindle unwinds, the things of the world proceed from birth to decay as we know them, but when it is wound again, the process is reversed:

> The white hairs, too, of those more advanced in years then became black, and the cheeks of those that had beards became smooth; and thus each was restored to the past flower of his age. The bodies, likewise, of such as were in the bloom of youth, becoming smoother and smaller every day and night, again returned to the nature of a child recently born. . . .[2]

---

[1] 'Blake's Debt to Antiquity', *Sewanee Review*, lxxi (1963), 406–7.

[2] *The Works of Plato*, iv (London, 1804), 123. As Miss Raine observes, this English translation by Taylor was the first. Among other similarities

Such a cyclical construct of history holds, potentially, both joy and sorrow for those who embrace it. Shelley, for example, envisioning the Greek Revolution as a new turn in the cycle, could declare,

> The world's great age begins anew,
>   The golden years return,
> The earth doth like a snake renew
>   Her winter weeds outworn:[1]

Yet the thought of recurrence involves destruction as well as regeneration—'Oh, cease! must hate and death return?'—leading Shelley to shrink from the consequences of his own prophetic vision:

> . . . if, with infirm hand, Eternity,
> Mother of many acts and hours, should free
> The serpent that would clasp her with his length.[2]

Confronting the uncoiling of the Orc serpent would mean accepting a world so constituted that, as Frye puts it, 'no cause can triumph within it and still preserve its imaginative integrity'.[3] Shelley, longing for metaphysical unity, prefers to abolish history; Nietzsche and Yeats, in contrast, greet the nightmare of recurrence with joyous acceptance. Zarathustra, having recognized his destiny as *'the teacher of the eternal recurrence'*, is told:

'Behold, we know what you teach: that all things recur eternally, and we ourselves too; and that we have already existed an eternal number of times, and all things with us. You teach that there is a great year of becoming, a monster of a great year, which must, like an hourglass, turn over again and again so that it may run down and run out again; and all these years are alike in what is greatest as in what is smallest; and we ourselves are alike in every great year, in what is greatest as in what is smallest.'[4]

between Plato's myth and Blake's poem, 'The inhabitants, too, had fruits in abundance from oaks, and many other trees, which did not grow through the assistance of agriculture, but were spontaneously given by the earth' (p. 124); 'And every Tree does shed its fruit' when the Babe is reborn.

[1] *Hellas, The Complete Poetical Works of Percy Bysshe Shelley*. ed. Thomas Hutchinson (London, 1960 (1905)), pp. 477–8.

[2] *Prometheus Unbound, Complete Poetical Works*, p. 267.

[3] *Fearful Symmetry*, p. 217.

[4] *Thus Spoke Zarathustra*, trans. Walter Kaufmann, *The Portable Nietzsche* (New York, 1954), p. 332.

'And what rough beast, its hour come round at last, / Slouches towards Bethlehem to be born?' The unwinding spindle, the reversed hour-glass, the gyres, the Orc cycle—in all these symbols of the cycle of recurrence there is a certain exaltation, as if man welcomed the prospect of being imprisoned in the bound circle of history.

> Another Troy must rise and set,
> Another lineage feed the crow,
> Another Argo's painted prow
> Drive to a flashier bauble yet.[1]

Even the destruction of civilization appears to be welcomed by these writers as the necessary prelude to the Great Year. Professor Eliade refers to 'the optimistic character of these ideas', an optimism which 'can be reduced to a consciousness of the normality of the cyclical catastrophe, to the certainty that it has a meaning and, above all, that it is never final'. The motive of such works as 'The Mental Traveller' and *A Vision* must be the consolation of locating oneself on the circle or gyre of history. Such projects are not 'theories of history as they are sometimes called, but attempts to escape from historical consciousness.

In the 'lunar perspective', the death of the individual and the *periodic* death of humanity are necessary, even as the three days of darkness preceding the 'rebirth' of the moon are necessary. The death of the individual and the death of humanity are alike necessary for their regeneration. Any form whatever, by the mere fact that it exists as such and endures, necessarily loses vigor and becomes worn; to recover vigor, it must be reabsorbed into the formless if only for an instant; it must be restored to the primordial unity from which it issued; in other words, it must return to 'chaos' (on the cosmic plane), to 'orgy' (on the social plane), to 'darkness' (for seed), to 'water' (baptism on the human plane, Atlantis on the plane of history, and so on).[2]

Unlike Shelley, who retreated from the implications of the cyclical concept, Blake accepted them; but unlike Nietzsche and

---

[1] 'Two Songs from a Play', *The Collected Poems of W. B. Yeats* (New York, 1956), pp. 239–40.
[2] *Cosmos and History*, p. 88.

Yeats, who rejoiced in these implications, Blake regarded them as partial truths produced by the limited perspective of man's fallen state. Though Blake draws upon Plato and upon Neoplatonic sources, the forms of his thought are those of the Bible, of Boehme, of Milton. There must be a meaning and purpose to the unfolding of history, a forward as well as a circular component. The myth of cosmic cycles must be adapted so as to leave each man potentially free to escape the Circle of Destiny, and man's collective experience must ultimately be defined by a Last Judgement which is not merely another periodic conflagration. Blake accomplished this by accommodating the myth of cosmic cycles to that other myth by which man escapes the nightmare of recurrence: the myth of archetypes.

3

The conception of the Seven Eyes of God was one of the additions to *Vala* which changed it into *The Four Zoas*. The nature and meaning of these changes will be our subject in the next chapter; here we are concerned with the Seven Eyes alone, as a construct of history showing the way out of the dilemma of recurrence. The term derives from Zechariah's vision of a stone with 'seven eyes' (3:9) and from John's vision of 'a Lamb as it had been slain, having seven horns and seven eyes, which are the seven Spirits of God sent forth into all the earth' (Rev. 5:6).[1] There is likewise an association with the wheels of Ezekiel's living creatures—Blake's Zoas—which were 'full of eyes' (1:18), and which provided Blake with the subject for one of his most memorable *Night Thoughts* illustrations. In *The Four Zoas*, the Seven Eyes are elected, at the end of a long addition to Night I, by the Family Divine in order to mitigate the consequences of the Fall:

. . . . Then they Elected Seven. called the Seven
Eyes of God & the Seven lamps of the Almighty

[1] See Damon, *William Blake*, p. 368. The passage in Revelation is illustrated in 'The Four and Twenty Elders Casting Down Their Crowns Before the Divine Throne' (1805; Darrell Figgis, *The Paintings of William Blake* (London, 1925), pl. 4).

The Seven are one within the other the Seventh is named Jesus
The Lamb of God blessed for ever & he followd the Man
Who wanderd in mount Ephraim seeking a Sepulcher
His inward eyes closing from the Divine vision & all
His children wandering outside, from his bosom fleeing away[1]

The names of the Eyes are given later, in Night VIII:

. . . And those in Eden sent Lucifer for their Guard
Lucifer refusd to die for Satan & in pride he forsook his charge
Then they sent Molech Molech was impatient They sent
Molech impatient They Sent Elohim who created Adam
To die for Satan Adam refusd but was compelld to die
By Satans arts. Then the Eternals Sent Shaddai
Shaddai was angry Pachad descended Pachad was terrified
And then they Sent Jehovah who leprous stretchd his hand to
    Eternity
Then Jesus Came & Died willing beneath Tirzah & Rahab[2]

The Seven Eyes are again named in *Milton* (13:17–28, E 106) and in *Jerusalem* (55:31–2, E 202). The latter passage is followed by the mention of a nameless Eighth Eye ('he came not, he hid in Albions Forests') which corresponds to the shadowy figure accompanying the Seven Angels of the Presence in *Milton*.[3] For the moment, we will consider only the Seven, returning to the shadowy Eighth later.

The Seven Eyes are, as Damon says, 'seven States . . . divinely instituted so that man should mechanically be brought back to communion with God'.[4] They are at once religious conceptions which may be held at any time and tutelary deities signifying the qualities of human consciousness during successive phases of historical development. First comes pride in the Selfhood, Lucifer; then the sacrifice of others (Molech), the Judge (Elohim), the Accuser (Shaddai), and the God of Terror (Pachad);[5] followed by

---

[1] I. 19:9–15, E 308. (I cite the Erdman text for *The Four Zoas* and will note any significant discrepancies in B.)

[2] VIII. 115:42–50, E 366. 'Their' in line 42 refers to 'Satan & his companions' after the Fall. The speaker here is Los.

[3] 15:3–7, E 108; see Damon, *William Blake*, p. 412.

[4] Ibid., p. 224; see also Frye, *Fearful Symmetry*, p. 128.

[5] These identifications derive from Damon, *William Blake*, pp. 388–9.

Jehovah, God of Law; and, seventh, Jesus, who alone willingly sacrifices not his miscalled enemies but himself. Distributed among these seven Eyes are twenty-seven lesser phases, the 'Churches' or 'Heavens' of the Mundane Shell:

> It is a cavernous Earth
> Of labyrinthine intricacy, twenty-seven folds of opakeness
> And finishes where the lark mounts . . .
>
> (*Milton*, 17:25–7, E 110)

> Just at the place to where the Lark mounts, is a Crystal Gate
> It is the enterance of the First Heaven named Luther: for
> The Lark is Los's Messenger thro the Twenty-seven Churches
> That the Seven Eyes of God who walk even to Satans Seat
> Thro all the Twenty-seven Heavens may not slumber nor sleep
>
> (35 : 61–5, E 135)

The names of the Churches themselves are given in identical passages in *Milton* and *Jerusalem*.[1] Frye has ingeniously schematized these Churches so that they constitute epicycles within the last four Eyes, the Christian era being made up of four Churches:

With the coming of Jesus or the seventh Eye the finale of history begins. The first consolidation of tyranny established to meet this new threat was the 'Church Paul', absorbing Jesus into the old Pharisaic legalism. Next comes his further absorption into the

---

[1] *Milton*, 37:35–43, E 137:

> And these the names of the Twenty-seven Heavens & their Churches
> Adam, Seth, Enos, Cainan, Mahalaleel, Jared, Enoch,
> Methuselah, Lamech: these are Giants mighty Hermaphroditic
> Noah, Shem, Arphaxad, Cainan the second, Salah, Heber,
> Peleg, Reu, Serug, Nahor, Terah, these are the Female-Males
> A Male within a Female hid as in an Ark & Curtains,
> Abraham, Moses, Solomon, Paul, Constantine, Charlemaine
> Luther, these seven are the Male-Females, the Dragon Forms
> Religion hid in War, a Dragon red & hidden Harlot

See also *Jerusalem*, 75 : 10–20, E 228–9. The two additional lines in *J* are devoted to explaining the significance of the last group: 'The Female hid within a Male: thus Rahab is reveald / Mystery Babylon the Great: the Abomination of Desolation.' Then the last line is given as above. For the sources and significance of the names and terms, see Damon, *William Blake*, p. 427.

Classical tyranny, represented by the Church Constantine, then the establishment of the female-will culture of the Middle Ages, the chivalric code and Madonna-worship associated with Charlemagne and Arthur. Finally comes the twenty-seventh Church in Luther and the Renaissance, the tyrannical precipitate of which is Deism. These twenty-seven 'Heavens,' as they are called, roll round us in a circle forever, and Deism is spiritually as far from Eden as Babylon or Egypt or Rome ever were.[1]

The twenty-seven Churches, taken together, compose a Great Year, but the Seven Eyes themselves do not form a cycle, but show the way out of the bound circle of history. The Seven Eyes are analogous to Paracelsus's seven 'astrologers' or intelligences and to Boehme's seven forms of psychic transformation.[2] Behind all such constructs lies the tradition of seven ages of man and of human history, paralleling the seven days of the Creation. Both Augustine and Luther, for example, conceive the history of the world as divided into seven ages; Luther's are named after Adam, Noah, Abraham, David, Christ, and the pope, with the seventh age to be the millennial peace of God.[3] Each age or Eye brings us closer to an apocalyptic Last Judgement. Thus, though the Churches appear to go around in a never-ending circle, the Eyes of God open towards Eternity.

Let us now return for a moment to Plato. Does the *Politicus* represent all men as trapped in the unwinding skein of history?

For, if old men tended to the nature of boys, it follows, that such as were dead, but laid in the earth, must be again restored from thence, revive again, and follow that revolution of the universe, in which generation is convolved in a contrary order; and that the earth-born race, which according to this reason is necessarily produced, should thus be denominated and defined, viz. such of them as Divinity has transferred into another destiny.[4]

---

[1] *Fearful Symmetry*, p. 134. The first three Eyes are relegated to successive falls. I do not find such an arrangement made explicitly in Blake's works; it may or may not be implied by the arrangement of Churches cited above.

[2] See Damon, *William Blake*, p. 389; Schorer, p. 127; and below, Ch. 6, pp. 169–70.

[3] See Marjorie Hope Nicolson, *The Breaking of the Circle* (New York, 1960), pp. 108–10.

[4] *The Works of Plato*, iv. 123–4.

'Such of them as Divinity has transferred into another destiny.' Professor J. B. Skemp calls this 'a clear reference to the Orphic hope of deliverance from the "sorrowful, weary wheel" of becoming and of attainment of everlasting bliss as an immortal'; he also compares it to the translation of Enoch in Hebrews 11:5: 'By faith Enoch was translated that he should not see death; and was not found, because God had translated him . . .'[1] Similar also is the doctrine of escape from the cycle of reincarnation in the *Bhagavad-Gita*, a book which had been translated into English by Charles Wilkins in 1785, and which so impressed Blake that he made it the subject of one of the sixteen pictures he exhibited in 1809: 'Mr. Wilkin [sic], translating the Geeta; an ideal design, suggested by the first publication of that part of the Hindoo Scriptures, translated by Mr. Wilkin.'[2] The *Gita*, too, projects Time as a Great Year, a circle of creation and destruction. Yet it also envisions escape from the cycle of reincarnation through *Mooktee*, or eternal release. Krishna instructs Arjuna:

> They who are acquainted with day and night, know that the day of *Brăhmā* is as a thousand revolutions of the *Yŏŏgs*, and that his night extendeth for a thousand more. On the coming of that day all things proceed from invisibility to visibility; so, on the approach of night, they are all dissolved away in that which is called *invisible*. The universe, even, having existed, is again dissolved; and now again, on the approach of day, by divine necessity, it is reproduced. That which, upon the dissolution of all things else, is not destroyed, is superior and of another nature from that visibility: it is invisible and eternal. He who is thus called invisible and incorruptible, is even he who is called the Supreme Abode; which men having once obtained, they never more return to earth: that is my mansion.[3]

The *Gita* both allows the individual soul a possible escape from the cycle of recurrence and holds out the eschatological hope of a final end to recurrence at such time when all souls

<hr>

[1] See *Plato's Statesman*, trans. J. B. Skemp (New Haven, 1952), p. 149 n.

[2] *Descriptive Catalogue*, E 539. The title of the picture is 'The Bramins.—A Drawing.' Its whereabouts is not known.

[3] *The Bhagvat-Geeta, or Dialogues of Kreeshna and Arjoon*, trans. Charles Wilkins (London, 1785), pp. 75–6. Wilkins, pp. 142–3, notes: '*A thousand revolutions of the Yŏŏgs.*—Is equal to 4320,000,000 years. An ingenious

have gone to the Supreme Abode. Blake, too, in *The Four Zoas, Milton,* and *Jerusalem,* presents a 'way out' of the cycle of history.

The cycle is embodied in the twenty-seven Churches, 'And where Luther ends Adam begins again in Eternal Circle. . . .' Liberation is of two kinds: individually, it is through re-generation from within; collectively, it is the awakening of Man as the Eighth Eye. The individual alternative of escape from recurrence is brought in immediately after the listing of the Churches in *Jerusalem.*

> But Jesus breaking thro' the Central Zones of Death & Hell
> Opens Eternity in Time & Space; triumphant in Mercy
> (75:21–2, E 229)

The collective alternative is represented in the allusions to the shadowy eighth figure we have already mentioned. His time has not yet come: 'They namd the Eighth. he came not, he hid in Albions Forests.'[1] In *Milton,* this 'Eighth Image Divine tho' darken'd' is Milton's own sleeping body.

> With him the Spirits of the Seven Angels of the Presence
> Entering; they gave him still perceptions of his Sleeping Body;
> Which now arose and walk'd with them in Eden, as an Eighth
> Image Divine tho' darken'd; and tho walking as one walks
> In sleep; and the Seven comforted and supported him.[2]

The opening of the Eighth Eye will inaugurate a Day of Man in which Jerusalem is built in England's green and pleasant land. History will be abrogated, and the process of regenera-tion will then be realized in the macrocosm. For the cyclical structure of history exists only that man may break out of it:

mathematician, who is now in India, supposes that these *Yöögs* are nothing more than astronomical periods formed from the coincidence of certain cycles, of which those of the precession of the equinoxes and the moon are two. The word *Yöög,* which signifies a *juncture* or *joining,* gives good grounds for such an hypothesis.'

[1] *Jerusalem,* 55:33, E 202. ('The emergence of man's tiger-demon from the forests is among other things the shattering emergence of history into eternity where the seven eyes become the Eighth Eye, where all are one.' Hazard Adams, *Blake and Yeats: The Contrary Vision* (Ithaca, N.Y., 1955), p. 121.)

[2] 15:3–6, E 108. See Damon, *William Blake,* pp. 412, 389.

Thus are the Heavens formd by Los within the Mundane Shell
And where Luther ends Adam begins again in Eternal Circle
To awake the Prisoners of Death; to bring Albion again
With Luvah into light eternal, in his eternal day.

(*Jerusalem*, 75:23–6, E 229)

The dialectical interplay of cyclical and linear constructs of history produces its synthesis in the Seven Eyes, allowing for both an over-all pattern of meaning to history and freedom for the individual at any point in that pattern. 'Christianity', writes Eliade,

translates the periodic regeneration of the world into a regeneration of the human individual. But for him who shares in this eternal *nunc* of the reign of God, history ceases as totally as it does for the man of the archaic cultures, who abolishes it periodically. Consequently, for the Christian too, history can be regenerated, by and through each individual believer, even before the Saviour's second coming, when it will utterly cease for all Creation.[1]

This twofold notion of regeneration, which we have seen introduced into Blake's symbolism with the Seven Eyes, is the major theme of the *Four Zoas* revisions and of *Milton*.

---

[1] *Cosmos and History*, pp. 129–30.

6

Regeneration

To be converted, to be regenerated, [wrote William James] to receive grace, to experience religion, to gain an assurance, are so many phrases which denote the process, gradual or sudden, by which a self hitherto divided, and consciously wrong inferior and unhappy, becomes unified and consciously right superior and happy, in consequence of its firmer hold upon religious realities. This at least is what conversion signifies in general terms, whether or not we believe that a direct divine operation is needed to bring such a moral change about.[1]

It is clear from Blake's own testimony that he had such an experience at Felpham, and that it was both sudden and gradual, occurring in several visionary moments during a period of perhaps three years. On 22 November 1802, he wrote to his friend and patron Thomas Butts: 'I am again Emerged into the light of day; I still & shall to Eternity Embrace Christianity and Adore him who is the Express image of God; but I have travel'd thro' Perils & Darkness not unlike a Champion' (K 815–16). In a second letter on the same day, Blake sent Butts a poem 'Composed above a twelvemonth ago', in which he tells how 'Los flam'd in my path', and he achieved fourfold vision (K 816–18). At the climactic moment of *Milton*,

> Terror struck in the Vale I stood at that immortal sound
> My bones trembled. I fell outstretchd upon the path
> A moment, & my Soul returnd into its mortal state
> To Resurrection & Judgment in the Vegetable Body
> $(42:24-7,\ \mathrm{E}\ 142)$

---

[1] *The Varieties of Religious Experience* (New York, 1911), p. 189. 'Regeneration', wrote an eighteenth-century divine, 'and Conversion, strictly taken, are not distinct Things; but these different Denominations, express the same Thing under different Views' (John Blair, 'On Regeneration', *Essays* (New York, 1771), p. 59).

This experience or series of experiences profoundly affected
the content of Blake's work. It has been remarked that previously 'He was using the Christian myth, as he used others,
as a subsidiary of his own myth';[1] but that 'in the later additions
to *The Four Zoas*, in *Milton*, and *Jerusalem*, he writes of the
cardinal Christian doctrines, the Incarnation, the Atonement,
and the Resurrection . . . as facts in the spiritual history of
man . . .'.[2] Among the important names and concepts which
appear only in the last two Nights of *The Four Zoas* manuscript or in additions to other Nights are the Seven Eyes of
God, the Council of God, the Winepress of Los, the Satanic
Selfhood, the doctrine of Individuals and States, and the
descent of Jesus in Luvah's robes of blood. *The Four Zoas* in
its final form takes for its theme the regeneration of man,
while *Milton* is about the regeneration of one man, William
Blake. In both epics the agent of regeneration is the Imagination, identified with Los, whose function is now to restore
Fallen Man to his original unity. This view of the Imagination is part of and inseparable from the theme of regeneration
in Blake's later works.

1

The notion of regeneration by the agency of a divine force
within is found previous to and concomitant with Christianity
in the mystery religions of Greece, Egypt, and the ancient
Near East: in, among others, the rites of Osiris and of Hermes
Trismegistus. In the Hermetic *Poimandres*, Hermes' son
Tat asks, 'Explain to me the manner of the regeneration',
and is answered, 'Nullify the perceptions of the body and
the birth of Deity will take place in thee.' The Osiris rituals
ended with the worshipper declaring, 'I am energized by thy
sacred name.'[3] Blake may have had some knowledge of both
these religions,[4] and if he did, it would have reinforced the

---

[1] Bentley, *Vala or The Four Zoas*, p. 174.

[2] D. J. Sloss and J. P. R. Wallis, *The Prophetic Writings of William Blake*
(Oxford, 1926), ii. 92.

[3] J. T. Marshall, 'Regeneration', *Encyclopædia of Religion and Ethics*, ed.
James Hastings (New York and Edinburgh, 1925), x. 645–6.

[4] On Hermetic parallels, see Damon, *William Blake*, pp. 294, 301, 310,
346; Raine, 'Blake's Debt to Antiquity', p. 431. Percival (pp. 17, 296)

doctrine of regeneration which he found in the New Testament and in the Christian mystics.

> Not by works of righteousness which we have done, but according to his mercy he saved us, by the washing of regeneration, and renewing of the Holy Ghost. . .   (Titus 3:5)

The word translated as 'regeneration' is παλιγγενεσία, a a term which is used by the Stoics to mean the renovation of the world following the end of a historical cycle by conflagration.[1] It occurs in Matthew 19:28, but no new cycle is to follow:

> And Jesus said unto them, Verily I say unto you, That ye which have followed me, in the regeneration when the Son of man shall sit in the throne of his glory, ye also shall sit upon twelve thrones, judging the twelve tribes of Israel.

The importance of the notion of regeneration in the New Testament, however, cannot be limited to these two appearances of the word. The conception is implicit in such important and frequently encountered doctrines as the necessity of a second birth (Christ's words to Nicodemus), the putting off of the old and the putting on of the new man (in the Pauline Epistles), and the community of believers in Christ. To emphasize the importance of the regeneration theme to his new conception of his poem, Blake cited several passages of the fourth gospel in the margin of his new beginning to Night I: John 17:21–3 and 1:14. These passages, placed in sequence, provide a parallel to Blake's own statement of his new theme as

> His [Los's] fall into Division & his Resurrection to Unity
> His fall into the Generation of Decay & Death, & his
> Regeneration by the Resurrection from the dead[2]

suggests that Blake could have known about the rituals of Osiris through Andrew Ramsay's *Travels of Cyrus*; he also calls attention to Milton's use, in *Areopagitica*, of Osiris as a symbol of Truth torn apart, dispersed, and resurrected. Damon (p. 312) notes that 'Osirification' was the term for the Egyptian doctrine 'through which all men eventually are raised to the state of gods'.

[1] Marshall, p. 639.
[2] See below, p. 149, n. 2.

That they all may be one; as thou Father, art in me, and I in thee, that they also may be one in us: that the world may believe that thou hast sent me.

And the glory which thou gavest me I have given them; that they may be one, even as we are one:

I in them, and thou in me, that they may be made perfect in one; and that the world may know that thou hast sent me, and hast loved them, as thou hast loved me.

And the Word was made flesh, and dwelt among us, (and we beheld his glory, the glory as of the only begotten of the Father), full of grace and truth.

From the New Testament, the doctrine of a new birth by which the regenerate soul in some sense participates in the divine nature passed into the tradition of Christian mysticism. 'The true and definitely directed mystical life', declares Evelyn Underhill,[1] 'does and must open with that most actual and stupendous, though indescribable phenomenon, the coming forth into consciousness of man's deeper, spiritual self, which ascetical and mystical writers of all ages have agreed to call Regeneration or Re-birth.' Miss Underhill distinguishes among three types of mystics: those of the exterior beatific vision, those of the intimate personal relation, and those especially concerned with rebirth:

Those who are conscious rather of the Divine as a Transcendent Life immanent in the world and the self, and of a strange spiritual seed within them by whose development man, moving to higher levels of character and consciousness, attains his end, will see the mystic life as involving inward change rather than outgoing search. Regeneration is their watchword, and they will choose symbols of growth or transmutation: saying with St. Catherine of Genoa, 'my Being is God, not by simple participation, but by a true transformation of my Being.'

The characteristic form of symbolic expression of such mystics, says Miss Underhill, is the 'Great Work' of the Spiritual Alchemists. The goal of these men, who attempted to combine the Christian and Hermetic traditions, was 'the production of the spiritual and only valid tincture or Philosopher's Stone, the mystic seed of transcendental life which

[1] *Mysticism* (New York, 1961 (1911)), pp. 122, 128–9, 143.

should invade, tinge, and wholly transmute the imperfect self into spiritual gold'.

At this point, in order to avoid becoming caught up in a quarrel over terminology, we should perhaps glance back at James's valuable definition, with its emphasis upon the *experience* of regeneration. There are, of course, many differences between the alchemists (and Blake) and the contemplative mystics, but they do share the attitude that the regenerate self is an attainable state, and that is what concerns us here. Another category of men, who, however much they may have differed in some other respects, shared this belief comprises those who wanted to incorporate it into common life in the secular world—Boehme, some of the evangelicals and dissenters, Whitefield, and William Law. For example, Thomas Bromley, an evangelical preacher of the late seventeenth century, defined regeneration as follows:

> As it is taken for the *Beginning* of the Work, it implies that first Change of the Soul, when in general the Frame of the Will is swayed to God and Heavenward. In it's *Progress*, 'tis the Growth and Motion of the Soul, from the Image of the Earthly toward the Image of the Heavenly. In its *End*, it is the Bringing forth of the perfect and complete Image of God in our Humanity, 1 *Cor.* 15, 49. When we attain this, we are complete in Christ, wholly new born, 2 *Cor.* 5, 17. . . .[1]

George Whitefield—one of God's 'two Servants' in *Milton*[2] —also took his text from 2 Corinthians 5 : 17, 'If any man be in Christ, he is a new Creature', asserting that neither beliefs

---

[1] *The Way to the Sabbath of Rest* (Germantown, Pa., 1759 (London, 1692)), p. 5. Bromley also speaks, in language similar to Blake's, of internal or spiritual senses which are awakened 'through the Renewal of the spiritual Body, with its five Faculties or Powers, (answering to the five Senses of the external Body)', through which 'we see spiritual Objects, as the internal Light-World, Visions of Angels, and Visions of Representation' (pp. 18–19). These similarities are probably due to the common influence of Boehme.

[2] 22 : 61–2; 23 : 1–2, E 117:

> He sent his two Servants Whitefield & Westley; were they Prophets
> Or were they Idiots or Madmen? shew us Miracles!
> Can you have greater Miracles than these? Men who devote
> Their lifes whole comfort to intire scorn & injury & death

'Westley' is John Wesley. On Blake's attitude toward 'Methodism', see my essay 'Cowper As Blake's Spectre' in *Eighteenth-Century Studies*, i (1968), 236–52.

nor sacraments could assure salvation: '. . . nothing but the Wedding Garment of a *new Nature*, can gain Admission for you at the Marriage Feast of the Supper of the Lamb . . .'[1] This same insistence on the experience of rebirth, in terms very close to Blake's, is found in *The Grounds and Reasons of Christian Regeneration* by William Law, *Works* (London, 1762):

> Now as this *Hell, Serpent, Worm*, and *Death*, are all *within us*, rising up in the Forms and Essences of our fallen Soul; so our *Redeemer*, or *Regenerator*, whatever it be, must be also equally *within us*, and spring up from as great a Depth in our Nature. . . . *Regeneration*, or the *New Birth*, is, and can be *no other* thing, but the *recovering of the Birth of the Son of God* in the fallen Soul.
>
> (vi. 40)

It is such a conception of regeneration, expressed in symbolic form, which becomes the major theme of *The Four Zoas*, in Nights VIII and IX and in additions to the preceding Nights. In one important respect, however, Blake's account of regeneration differs from that of all previous writers except Boehme. For Blake, as for Boehme, the redemptive power is the Imagination.

2

In Blake's earlier writings, the power of imagination had been loosely subsumed under the broad term 'Poetic Genius', an intuitive knowing power equated with the Spirit of Prophecy. The word 'imagination' appears only once in the works published by Blake previous to *Milton*.[2] In these works and in *Vala*, Los is one of four 'gods' or faculties who construct the inner world of man; though he is the Eternal

---

[1] *The Nature and Necessity of our New Birth in Christ Jesus, in order to Salvation*, 3rd ed. (London, 1738), p. 25.

[2] In *The Marriage*, E 38. It also occurs once in the *Island in the Moon* manuscript and twice in *Vala* before additions (once, as previously mentioned, it is associated with Urizen's phantasy). A glance under the heading 'Imagination' in the forthcoming Blake Concordance, which Professor Erdman has kindly shown me, shows a dramatic development with the letter to Dr. Trusler (23 August 1799, where it occurs eight times). Afterwards, it occurs nine times in *Milton*, sixteen times in *Jerusalem*, twelve times in 'A Vision of the Last Judgment', and frequently in Blake's other writings.

Prophet, he is conditioned by the effects of the Fall, and performs the work of Urizen in binding Orc. When at the end of VIIb Enitharmon calls, 'Lift up Lift up O Los awake my watchman for he sleepeth' (49v : 4, M 52), there is no reply. In the *Vala* manuscript, excluding additions and the very late Night VIII, Los first begins to exercise a redemptive function in Night IX, when 'Los who is Urthona rose in all his regenerate power' (69R : 34, M 71), bringing on the Great Harvest and Vintage of the Last Judgement. This last regenerative activity can only occur after the Ancient Man— later significantly altered to 'The Regenerate Man' (126 : 3, E 380)—asserts the pre-eminence of the whole human identity over its warring faculties and restores the Zoa of energy and passion to its proper place in the order of the microcosm:

> Luvah & Vala henceforth you are Servants obey & live
> You shall forget your former state return O Love in peace
> Into your place the place of seed not in the brain or heart
> If Gods combine against Man setting their dominion above
> The Human form Divine. Thrown down from their high station
> In the Eternal heavens of Human Imagination: buried beneath
> In dark Oblivion with incessant pangs ages on ages
> In enmity & war first weakend then in stern repentance
> They must renew their brightness & their disorganizd functions
> Again reorganize till they resume the image of the human
> Cooperating in the bliss of Man obeying his Will
> Servants to the infinite & Eternal of the Human form
>
> (63v : 6–17, M 59)

In accordance with this new theme of regeneration through the Imagination, Urthona is given special importance in the very last lines of the epic:

> Urthona is arisen in his strength no longer now
> Divided from Enitharmon no longer the Spectre Los
> Where is the Spectre of Prophecy where the delusive Phantom
> Departed & Urthona rises from the ruinous Walls
> In all his ancient strength to form the golden armour of science
> For intellectual War The war of swords departed now
> The dark Religions are departed & sweet Science reigns
>
> (70v : 4–10, M 72)

The Spectre and delusive Phantom are of course the forms in which Los has been encountered in the earlier Nights of *Vala*. He now regains his prelapsarian identity as Urthona, the Imagination which, Blake says in *Milton*, 'is the Human Existence itself' (32:32, E 131).

After the completion of Night IX, Blake elaborated his new conception of the redemptive activity of Imagination in additions to Nights I, VIIb, and IX and in Night VIII. In his new beginning to Night I, he made this his epic theme:

> Los was the fourth immortal starry one, & in the Earth
> Of a bright Universe, Empery attended day & night
> Days & nights of revolving joy, Urthona was his name
> In Eden; in the Auricular Nerves of Human Life
> Which is the Earth of Eden, he his Emanations propagated
> Like Sons & Daughters, Daughter of Beulah sing
> His fall into Division & his Resurrection to Unity[1]

Later, two more lines were added to this passage:

> His fall into the Generation of Decay & Death & his
> Regeneration by the Resurrection from the dead[2]

These nine lines are particularly close to the thematic statement in Boehme's treatise 'Regeneration', Book III of *The Way to Christ*:

First, What we are, and whence we are come; how we are gone forth from the Unity into Dissension, Wickedness, and Unrighteousness; how we have awakened and stirred up these Things in us.

Secondly, How we were in the Unity, when we were the children of God in *Adam* before he fell. Thirdly, How we are now in Dissension and Disunion, in Strife and Contrariety. Fourthly, Whither

---

[1] 2R:9–11, 2v:1–4, M 75. Pierce, in connection with 'the Earth of Eden', suggests that Urthona 'might mean the primitive clay from which human life—or consciousness—began' ('Etymology as Explanation', *PQ*, x (1931), 397).

[2] B 4. For references to *The Four Zoas* as distinguished from *Vala*, I will cite the generally available Erdman edition, noting any significant differences in Bentley's text (but not minor ones of spelling or orthography). The two lines referred to here are printed as one by Erdman, in a textual note (E 740, 3rd printing). As for the lines immediately preceding, 'Like Sons & Daughters' was later deleted, and a line was pencilled in calling the Emanations 'Fairies of Albion, afterwards Gods of the Heathen.'

we go when we pass out of this corruptible Being; whither we go with the immortal, and whither with the mortal Part.

In these four Points our whole Religion consisteth, *viz.* to learn to come forth from Disunion and Vanity, and to enter again into that one Tree, Christ in us, out of which we are all sprung in *Adam*.[1]

There are, of course, other parallels—for example, the myths of Bacchus[2] and of Osiris; but the relation of Boehme to Blake here is more than that of a literary influence. Blake found in Boehme an account of regeneration which fitted his own experience, and he absorbed into his own symbolic system Boehme's conception of a regeneration process going through seven 'Forms', with the active principle being the Imagination.

3

Mystics have had little use for the imagination. *The Cloud of Unknowing* adjures the reader 'for God's love be wary in this work and travail not in thy wits nor in thy imagination on nowise . . .' The 'inobedience of the Imagination' often troubles the newly converted with 'the wonderful and the diverse thoughts, fantasies, and images, the which be ministered and printed in their mind by . . . curiosity of Imagination. And all this inobedience is the pain of the original sin.'[3] James's *Varieties of Religious Experience* contains many comparable examples of deprecation of the imagination by contemplative mystics.[4] Even Boehme's English followers took such a view. Bromley wrote that 'the Soul prays and strives continually against the Power of Imagination and Activity of Thoughts, which hinder the silent Actings of the Intellect upon Eternity and supernatural Truths'. He sounds a great deal like Hobbes when he speaks of 'the false Prophet (which is irregular Imagination)',

---

[1] Pt. 8, secs. 180–2, *Works*, iv. 67.

[2] On the Bacchus myth, see Harper, pp. 236–7. I would agree with Professor Harper that 'the philosophic content of this psychological history of the Universal Man is indebted to the Bacchus story', but not that 'the Bacchus myth had become central to Blake's system'.

[3] Ed. Evelyn Underhill (London, 1956), pp. 72, 243 resp.

[4] e.g. pp. 407 (St. John of the Cross), 416 (Dionysius the Areopagite).

and a great deal like the Cambridge Platonists when he says:

. . . Phantasms, being generally drawn from corporeal Objects, cannot reach the Essence of a Spirit. And truly here the Soul plainly discovers its Fall from the divine Mind, Image and Light (in which it saw intuitively, and could give Names according to the Natures of Things) into the imaginary Spirit, which belongs to this World, and is too gross a Glass to express truly and essentially, spiritual and eternal Objects.[1]

That three men of such different philosophical and theological persuasions as Bromley, Hobbes, and John Smith could hold such similar views of the Imagination shows to what extent this was the generally received conception of it in the seventeenth century. In the next century, Law, whose thought follows Boehme's in so many other respects, derides the '*Fictions* of a *visionary* Imagination.'[2] Boehme, in contrast, believed that the Imagination might participate in the divine consciousness, as when 'the Faith of the Jews entered into the Sacrifices and Offerings, and God's Imagination entered into the Covenant'. ('Regeneration', 3:73). True, Boehme does not conceive Imagination to be *necessarily* divine, for it may be the agent of the Fall as well. The Devil 'brought his Imagination into the Image of Man, and made it so lusting, that the dark World, and also the outward World, arose in Man, and departed from the equal Agreement and Harmony, and so one over-weighed the other' (2:46). But what is important here is that to Boehme the Imagination is a creator of realities in just Blake's sense.

---

[1] *Sabbeth of Rest*, pp. 27, 32, 28–9 resp. Cf. the Cambridge Platonist John Smith: 'Our own *Imaginative Powers*, which are perpetually attending the highest acts of our Souls, will be breathing a gross dew upon the pure Glass of our Understandings, and so sully and besmear it, that we cannot see the Image of the Divinity sincerely in it' (quoted by Basil Willey in *The Seventeenth-Century Background* (London, 1946), p. 141).

[2] 'Christian Regeneration', p. 34. Stephen Hobhouse, one of the leading authorities on Boehme and Law, writes: 'The creative force of imagination, the process by which the primeval will or desire passes over from "nothing" to "something" is important to Boehme, and he loved to personify it as the Virgin *Sophia*, the divine Wisdom. Law does not seem to have been able to appreciate this side of Boehme's thought and he ignores it.' *Selected Mystical Writings of William Law* (London, 1948), p. 253.

For to know only, is no Faith, but an Hunger and Thirst after that which I desire, so that I imagine it to myself, and lay hold on it with the Imagination, and make it my own: This it is to believe.

All things are comprehended in their Eternal Forms in the Divine body of the Saviour the True Vine of Eternity The Human Imagination. . . . If the Spectator could Enter into these Images in his Imagination approaching them on the Fiery Chariot of his Contemplative Thought . . . then would he meet the Lord in the Air & then he would be happy[1]

Boehme believed that man was not doomed to stand forever in the Wrath of his divided nature but was able to return to the harmony from which he had fallen. Containing within himself both heaven and hell, man was free to choose between them. Boehme's reader is frequently exhorted to make this choice:

You must go out from the Fire into the Light; for God is no Image for us to stand before, and give good words to, *but he is a Spirit, and penetrates through the Heart and Reins*, that is, *Soul and Spirit*: He is the Fire of Love, and his Center of Nature is the Fire of Anger; and if you were in Hell among all the Devils, yet then you are in God, for the Anger is also *his, it is his Abyss*; and therefore when you go out from that, you go into the Love of God, into the Liberty that is without source [or pain].[2]

This transition from the Wrath of the First Principle to the Mercy of the Second is the subject of Blake's Notebook poem, 'Morning':

> To find the Western path
> Right thro the Gates of Wrath
> I urge my way
> Sweet Mercy leads me on
> With soft repentant moan
> I see the break of day

---

[1] 'Regeneration', 4:89, *Works*, iv. 58; 'A Vision of the Last Judgment', E 545, 550. Hobhouse considers that 'Divine *Imagination* (J. B.'s actual word) plays almost as important a part in his drama of the universe as it does in William Blake's . . .' (*Jacob Boehme* (London, 1949), p. 43 n.)

[2] *Threefold Life of Man*, pt. 11, sec. 62, *Works*, ii. 121.

The war of swords & spears
Melted by dewy tears
Exhales on high
The Sun is freed from fears
And with soft grateful tears
Ascends the sky[1]

The importance of this short lyric was first observed by Schorer, who noted that 'the repentant moan is the triumph of the imagination over selfishness . . . physical conflict, war, then gives way to the rising Sun, which is poetry and art freed from corruption, and, in a larger sense, that "mental fight" which entertains Eternals'.[2] 'Morning' is an epitome of the regeneration process which Blake described, using a more specialized vocabulary, in *The Four Zoas* and *Milton*.

For Boehme as for Blake, regeneration is an act of the Imagination which reiterates the birth of Christ in the individual soul:

For we are the Representation of the Deity, in which the Spirit of God openeth his *Wonders*: and be you rightly informed, God the Father hath begotten us again *in Christ*, that we should with our Imaginations enter again into the Word, *viz.* into the *Center* of the light flaming Heart, that the *Holy Ghost* might proceed from us again with power and works of Wonder. . . .[3]

In *Vala*, Night IX, this event occurs with the descent of the Lamb of God wearing Luvah's robes of blood.

Behold Jerusalem in whose bosom the Lamb of God
Is seen tho slain before her Gates he self renewd remains
Eternal & I thro him awake to life from deaths dark vale

. . . .

Because the Lamb of God Creates himself a bride & wife
That we his Children evermore may live in Jerusalem
Which now descendeth out of heaven a City Yet a Woman
Mother of myriads redeemd & born in her Spiritual palaces
By a New Spiritual birth Regenerated from Death[4]

---

[1] E 469. E includes this poem among lyrics written from 1800 to 1809; Keynes among those of 1800–3 (K 421). Note the similarity of line 7 to 'The war of swords departed now' in the penultimate line of *The Four Zoas*.

[2] *William Blake*, p. 308.

[3] *Threefold Life*, pt. 3, sec. 49, loc. cit.

[4] 61v: 1–3, 16–20, M 55–6 (*not* an added passage). Cf. Law, 'Two Answers to Dr. Trapp': 'If we are to have the nature of Christ regenerated in us, as the

The Lamb of God also appears in additions to Nights I, IV, and VIIa. It is in VIIa that Jesus replaces Orc as the operative form of Luvah, when Los says:

> look! behold! take comfort!
> Turn inwardly thine Eyes & there behold the Lamb of God
> Clothed in Luvahs robes of blood descending to redeem[1]

Orc, revolutionary energy, having sunk into the state called Satan, Christian brotherhood replaces revolutionary fraternity in Blake's thought as the agent of Love among men.

The sense in which Blake now uses 'Satan' is very different from that of the 'Messiah or Satan or Tempter' of *The Marriage*. Satan and the Lamb of God have become for Blake the polar identities which the soul can choose—Selfhood or Self-annihilation, Wrath or Love. 'I in my Selfhood am that Satan', declares Blake's Milton; 'I am that Evil One! He is my Spectre!' (14:30–1, E 107). He will 'go down to self-annihilation and eternal death' in order to be freed from his Selfhood and regenerated. 'Love', wrote Boehme in Book II of *The Way to Christ*, 'Dialogues on the Supersensual Life', 'hateth [Self, or] that which we call *I*, because it is a deadly Thing, and they two cannot well stand together.'[2] As was first suggested by Professor Jacques Roos, Blake's 'Selfhood' is Boehme's 'Selbheit';[3] both use the term to signify the unregenerate ego whose 'Opacity' (Blake's word) screens off from the isolated individual the knowledge that he belongs to a human community, is a member of the divine body of Albion. Blake characteristically identifies this Satanic principle with both the fallen Urizen—abstract reason—and the fallen

---

life of Adam is born in us . . . then there is an absolute necessity that that which was done and born in the Virgin Mary be also by the same power of the Holy Ghost done and born in us, by a seed of life derived into us from Christ our regenerator' (*Selected Mystical Writings*, p. 28).

[1] 87:43–5, E 355. On the lateness of this page, see B 88, 162. The addition to I was later deleted; see E 745. The other is 55:10–15 to 56:1–10, E 331. Paul Miner points out that 'robes of blood' derives from Christ's 'vesture dipped in blood' in Revelation 19:13 ('William Blake's "Divine Analogy"', *Criticism*, iii (1961), 51, n. 7).

[2] *Works*, iv. 80.

[3] He points out that the first appearance of the word in English, according to the *OED*, was in the Ellistone translation of Boehme, later used in the 'Law edition' (*Aspects littéraires du mysticisme philosophique* (Strasbourg, n.d.), p. 92).

Luvah or Orc—the will-to-power. Both are 'Spectres', separated from the whole identity that Blake calls 'Human Existence'. Blake accounts for this underlying similarity by making the distinction between States and Individuals which appears in *The Four Zoas*, *Milton*, and *Jerusalem*.

In the Lambeth books and in *Vala*, Blake did not call the conditions of human life beyond Experience 'States', but in the later parts of *The Four Zoas* he does so, adjuring the reader: 'There is a State namd Satan learn distinct to know . . . The Difference between States & Individuals of those States' (115:23–4, E 366). This distinction is necessary in order to account for the fate of Energy and still leave open the possibility of regeneration. Jesus puts on Luvah's robes of blood 'Lest the state call'd Luvah should cease'[1]—so that the vision of brotherhood will not be lost with the failure of the Revolution. That failure is also explained as a transition from one State to another: 'But when Luvah in Orc became a Serpent he des[c]ended into / That State calld Satan' (115:26–7, E 366). A gloss on this is provided by a passage in *Jerusalem*:

> Satan is the State of Death, & not a Human existence:
> But Luvah is named Satan, because he has enterd that State.
> A World where Man is by Nature the enemy of Man
> Because the Evil is Created into a State. that Men
> May be deliverd time after time evermore. . . .[2]

This is Blake's way of stating his conviction that the reign of Love on earth will be brought about by regeneration through the Imagination. The meaning of such a possibility cannot be understood by the Urizenic Selfhood.

> When Urizen saw the Lamb of God clothed in Luvahs robes
> Perplexd & terrifid he Stood tho well he knew that Orc
> Was Luvah But he now beheld a new Luvah. Or One
> Who assumd Luvahs form & stood before him opposite
>
> (101:1–4, E 358)

---

[1] Cf. Law: '. . . nothing but the incarnate life of His eternal Son, passing through all the miserable states of lost man, could regenerate his first divine life in him' (Letter IV, *Selected Mystical Writings*, p. 200).

[2] 49:67–71, E 197. (Erin speaks.)

Love has reassumed its human form, but not as Orc, who is 'a Serpent form augmenting times on times / In the fierce battle' (5–6). Urizen is 'Perplexd & terrifid' because he cannot understand the nature of the change; he makes the Satanic error of confusing States with Individuals and imputing sin to the latter. In the words of the epilogue to *The Gates of Paradise*, Satan does not know 'the Garment from the Man'. The garment which Satan mistakes for the wearer is the 'natural' or 'old' man which Paul urges be 'put off' (Eph. 4:22, 24; Col. 2:11, 3:9). Just so, the Lamb of God puts on Luvah's robes of blood, 'Bearing his sorrows & rec[iev]ing all his cruel wounds '(105:56, E 364). Thus we have, with the distinction between Individuals and States and the polar opposition of Lamb of God and Satanic Self-hood, an attempt to accommodate the symbolic structure of *Vala* to the new matter of *The Four Zoas*.

If we regard the poem with its later additions in the form in which Blake finally left it, we can see that he tried to its 'disorganiz'd functions Again reorganize' by introducing the regeneration motif into the earlier Nights. We have already remarked that in the new beginning of Night I the principal importance of Los is announced: the theme of the epic is now to be 'His fall into the Generation of decay & death, & his Regeneration by the Resurrection from the dead.' Later on in the additions to Night I, Los prophesies the birth of the Lamb of God in mortal form, 'for One must be All / And comprehend within himself all things both small & great' (E 745). Still, he exercises no redemptive function, for this part of the poem is devoted to 'His fall into division'. The division of Los is recounted in a still later addition of ninety lines, made after Blake had already written 'End of the First Night' in the manuscript. In the wars of the Zoas, Los steps back from the furnaces of his creative activity and separates into spectre, emanation, and serpent body. At the same time, the continued existence of an unfallen reality is represented in the Council of God (21:1–7, E 306), whose members behold humanity as One Man and who continue to live 'in Eden the land of life'. At the end of the added section, the Council meets again to elect the Seven Eyes of God, the meaning of

which was our subject at the end of the preceding chapter.
Another 'Council of God' passage was added toward the end
of Night IV: here the Lamb of God, once more descending in
Luvah's garments, sets the Limit of Contraction and the
Limit of Opacity, named Adam and Satan, in the bosom of
Albion.[1] These limits are the bounds beyond which the Fall
cannot go. They are the 'Egoity' and 'contracted spirit'
Boehme speaks of; together they define the state of fallen
man, Blake's 'Spectre' enmeshed in a 'Philosophy of Five
Senses'. At the same time these 'limits' prevent a further
fall into Chaos or nonentity.

In a long section added after the original end of Night VIIa,[2]
the regeneration of Los begins. First Los and his Spectre
combine—the imagination as fabricator with its own power
of abstraction. Alone, the abstracting power falls into the
delusion of Ulro, mistaking mental constructions such as
time and space for absolutes; this is why the Spectre describes himself as 'wandering / The deeps of Los the Slave of
that Creation I created'. In order to regain the unity of
Urthona, Los must first combine with his Spectre:

Thou never canst embrace sweet Enitharmon terrible Demon.
  Till
Thou art united with thy Spectre Consummating by pains &
  labours
That mortal body & by Self annihilation back returning
To Life Eternal be assurd I am thy real Self
Tho thus divided from thee & the Slave of Every passion
Of thy fierce Soul Unbar the Gates of Memory look upon me
Not as another but as thy real Self . . .[3]

Los now stands at the branching-off of two worlds.

If we unite in one[,] another better world will be
Opend within your heart & loins & wondrous brain

[1] 55:10–15; 56:1–22, E 330–1. See B 166.
[2] See E 756 and B 165.
[3] 85:32–8, E 353. 'The Spectre of Urthona', Frye comments, 'does two
things for Los: it provides him with a conscious will which makes his vision
consistent and purposeful, and it gives him a sense of the passing of time which
his imagination creates into a vision of the meaning of history' (*Fearful
Symmetry*, p. 298).

Threefold as it was in Eternity & this the fourth Universe
Will be Renewd by the three & consummated in Mental
     fires
But if thou dost refuse Another body will be prepared
For me and thou annihilate evaporate & be no more
For thou art but a form & organ of life & of thyself
Art nothing being Created Continually by Mercy & Love
     Divine[1]

The situation is analogous to that described by Boehme in his
Six Theosophical Points:

But now the original stand of the Imagination is in the first
form of Nature . . . which conducts its form through the world of
regenerated vitality as far as fire; there the desire goes through all
Forms, also makes all Forms, and propels itself into the Fire.
There is the dividing point of the Spirit, there it is born: it is now
free. Through its Imagination it may now go back to its Mother,
the world of regenerative vitality, or going forward sink down
through the anguish of Fire into death and bud forth in the light,
however it will. . . .[2]

Los chooses the way of 'self annihilation' and so regains part
of the lost unity of Eternity while yet in the fallen world. As
the liberated imagination, he is now free to engage in the
activity which most closely approximates to the 'mental war' of
Eternity: the creation of the City of Art:

. . . mingling together with his Spectre the Spectre of Urthona
Wondering beheld the Center opend by Divine Mercy inspired
He in his turn Gave Tasks to Los Enormous to destroy
That body he created but in vain for Los performd
Wonders of labour
They Builded Golgonooza Los labouring builded pillars high
And Domes terrific in the nether heavens for beneath

---

[1] 85:43–7; 86:1–3, E 354. The textual details concerning this passage are
too complex for convenient summary. See B 87–8.

[2] Quoted and translated by Bruce C. Souders in *The Reappearance of Jacob
Boehme in the Work of William Law, William Blake, and William Butler Yeats*,
unpubl. master's thesis (Columbia, 1953), p. 94. (*Six Theosophical Points* was
not included in the 'Law edition', but the substance of this passage appears
frequently in Boehme's other works. I have cited this particular passage because of its conciseness.)

Was opend new heavens & a new Earth beneath & within
Threefold within the brain within the heart within the loins
A Threefold Atmosphere Sublime continuous from Urthonas
    world
But yet having a Limit Twofold named Satan & Adam.[1]

Though 'continuous with' the unfallen world, the world they
create is 'Threefold' rather than the fourfold spiritual Eden:
Los has not yet combined with his 'Emanation', his female
counterpart. 'Turn inwardly thine Eyes', Los urges her, '&
there behold the Lamb of God / Clothed in Luvahs robes of
blood descending to redeem' (87 : 44–5, E 355). But Enitharmon does not as yet understand the principle of regeneration.
She fears Christ will come as a punisher and judge who 'Will
give us to Eternal Death fit punishment for such / Hideous
offenders Uttermost extinction in eternal pain' (87 : 55–6,
E 355). She does agree to assist Los in the labours of art, 'to
fabricate embodied semblances'. This she will do so long as
Los modulates his fires so that 'mild they burn in just proportion' and abstain from wrath:

. . . . if thou my Los
Wilt in sweet moderated fury. fabricate forms sublime
Such as the piteous spectres may assimilate themselves into
They shall be ransoms for our Souls that we may live[2]

Los will now at least temporarily subordinate his prophetic
to his artistic function. 'His hands divine inspired', Los
subdues his flames 'with the strength of Art' (90 : 25–7, E 356).
There is, again, an alchemical parallel: 'The Three Principles being enclosed in the vessel, or Athanor, which is man
himself, and subjected to a gentle fire—the *Incendium Amoris*
—the process of the Great Work, the mystic transmutation
of natural into spiritual man, can begin.'[3] The activity of the
artist is now to preserve the Divine Vision by creating the

---

[1] 87 : 2–12, E 354. 'Wondering beheld the Center opend' is a later addition,
according to B 88, as are lines 4–6. Line 5 originally had 'Los labouring inspired.' 'Urthonas' in line 11 is an addition.
[2] 90 : 21–4, E 356. Line 22 originally had 'sweet forms'; 'sweet' was deleted;
'sublime' is a late pencil addition. Line 24 was written over an erased line (B 91).
[3] Underhill, *Mysticism*, p. 145.

order of art rather than to demonstrate the causes and consequences of war to an unheeding society. Los and Enitharmon are at this point William and Catherine Blake, producing
the illuminated books.

> And first he drew a line upon the walls of shining heaven
> And Enitharmon tincturd it with beams of blushing love
> It remaind permanent a lovely form inspird divinely human[1]

In the 'embodied semblances' produced by Los the artist,
order is brought to the warring Zoas. Wrath and Pity,
Los's 'sons' Rintrah and Palamabron, are drawn out of the
ranks of war. Orc, though not free, becomes

> As Los a father to his brethren & he joyd in the dark lake
> Tho bound with chains of Jealousy & in scales of iron & brass

$$(90\!:\!48\text{–}9,\ \text{E } 356)$$

In a subsequent addition, Urizen himself comes into the
power of Los and, perceived by the artist as an infant, is
loved by him.

What an unsatisfactory development this is may easily
be seen. The arbitrary nature of the solution is such that
Erdman proposed that it must have been the result of an
unexpected historical event—the Peace of Amiens, about
which Blake had written to John Flaxman on 19 October
1801:

> I rejoice to hear that your Great Work is accomplishd. Peace
> opens the way to greater still. The Kingdoms of this World are now
> become the Kingdoms of God & his Christ,[2] & we shall reign with
> him for ever & ever. The Reign of Literature & the Arts Com-
> mences. . . .[3]

The section added to VIIa, also looking forward to a new age
of the arts, replaces the prophetic function of the artist with a

---

[1] 90:35–7, E 356. See Damon, *William Blake*, p. 409; Erdman, *Blake*,
p. 354.   [2] Rev. 11:15.
[3] K 810. See Erdman, *Blake*, p. 330. Accepting Bentley's transcription date
of 1802 need not make us reject possible reference of the added passages to the
Peace. VIIa might have been written before the preliminaries of Peace were
signed, transcribed afterwards, and augmented after the transcription but
before the renewal of the war.

purely aesthetic one; redemptive activity now consists in creating the order of art from the materials of a fallen world. This development is discordant not only with what precedes VIIa but with what follows it. In VIIb, Los is not the regenerate artist but once more the 'delusive phantom' (as Night IX calls him) of the earlier parts of the poem. 'Night or day Los follows War',[1] and he delivers a bloodthirsty war speech, 'his loins in fires of war where spears / And swords rage . . .' (96 : 22–3, E 393). The added pages also disrupt the continuity of VIIa–VIIb, and it may be that Blake reversed the two halves of VIIb in an unsuccessful attempt to disguise this. The present Night VIII, however, links closely with the new end of VIIa, indicating that when VIII was written, Blake was no longer trying to retain VIIb at all. These attempts at grafting simply do not work; the regeneration theme does not grow out of *Vala* but is superimposed on it, as Blake himself must eventually have realized.

4

Night VIII as we now have it was written, as its style and idiom show, after the other Nights.[2] Therefore we will consider it after Night IX, which was probably written, excluding additions, before the renewal of the war in May 1803. In this apocalyptic last Night, error is exposed and burned away, and humanity is prepared for the great harvest and vintage of the Last Judgement. There are some important differences between this new apocalypse and those of Blake's earlier poems, differences which point up the dilemma which he had reached during the writing of *Vala*.

The apocalypses of *The Marriage* (with 'A Song of Liberty') and *America* take place *in* history. They are eruptions of long-repressed energies, now freed to transform the conditions of life. The deserts will blossom, the deeps shrink to their fountains, the dead be resurrected. The eschatological imagery here, mostly derived from that of the Prophets, refers metaphorically to events occurring or anticipated in the

---

[1] 97 : 21, E 394; previously 'day by day' (E 763).
[2] See M 174 and B 164.

actual world. Orc's great deliverance speech in *America*, for example, is an expression of revolutionary hope in eschatological terms:

> The morning comes, the night decays, the watchmen leave their
>   stations;
> The grave is burst, the spices shed, the linen wrapped up;
> The bones of death, the cov'ring clay, the sinews shrunk & dry'd.
> Reviving shake, inspiring move, breathing! awakening!
> Spring like redeemed captives when their bonds & bars are burst;
> Let the slave grinding at the mill, run out into the field:
> Let him look up into the heavens & laugh in the bright air;
> Let the inchained soul shut up in darkness and in sighing,
> Whose face has never seen a smile in thirty weary years;
> Rise and look out, his chains are loose, his dungeon doors are
>   open.
> And let his wife and children return from the opressors scourge;
> They look behind at every step & believe it is a dream.
> Singing. The Sun has left his blackness, & has found a fresher
>   morning
> And the fair Moon rejoices in the clear & cloudless night;
> For Empire is no more, and now the Lion & Wolf shall cease.
>
>   (6:1–15, E 52)

Here even the New Testament resurrection imagery is used as a metaphor of the revolutionary society which Blake anticipates; America will become Isaiah's holy mountain where the leopard lies down with the kid, and Orc, 'the son of morning in his eastern cloud', is the child who shall lead them. Similarly, in 'The Argument' to *The Marriage*, the prophecies of Isaiah are applied to the French Revolution. The Wrath of the Tyger is a prelude to the establishment of the Kingdom—or, rather, the Republic. Blake's conception here can be described in the words R. H. Charles uses of the Prophets': '. . . this kingdom was to consist of a regenerated nation, a community in which the divine will should be fulfilled, an organised society interpenetrated, welded together, and shaped to ever higher issues by the actual presence of God.'[1] The inclusion of a resurrection of the flesh in this eschatalogical conception, as at the end of *The Song of Los*

---

[1] *Eschatology* (New York, 1963), pp. 83–4.

(E 68), also derives from Isaiah: once more, according to Charles,

> . . . When the doctrine of the blessed immortality of the faithful is connected with that of the coming Messianic kingdom, *the separate eschatologies of the individual and of the nation issue finally in their synthesis: the righteous individual, no less than the righteous nation, will participate in the Messianic kingdom, for the righteous dead of Israel will rise to share therein.* (p. 130)

Terms like these also seemed fitting to radicals in the early days of the Revolution. An anonymous French writer declared after the fall of the Bastille: 'The day of revelation is upon us. . . . The very bones have risen at the sound of the voice of French freedom; they bear witness against the centuries of oppression and death, and prophesy the regeneration of human nature and of the life of nations.'[1] Thomas Paine wrote, in *Rights of Man*, that 'The solemn and majestic spectacle of a Nation opening its commission, under the auspices of its Creator, to establish a Government; [is] a scene so new, and so transcendantly unequalled by any-thing in the European world, that the name of a Revolution is diminutive of its character, and it rises into a Regeneration of man.'[2] As we have seen from the two Nights VII of *Vala*, Blake no longer entertained such hopes. What, then, can be the meaning of the apocalypse of Night IX? of the repetition of Orc's deliverance speech, now given to Tharmas? of the harvest and vintage of the Last Judgement and the imagery of resurrection ('And every one of the dead appears as he had livd before', 122:41, E 377)? They cannot be understood in the sense of the earlier apocalypses we have mentioned. Blake, having abandoned his revolutionary hopes, no longer employs the eschatological conception of the Hebrew prophets, who had looked for a fulfilment of God's design *in* history. He has turned instead to Revelation for a vision of history corresponding to what is now his own.

The explicit use of New Testament names and symbols in *The Four Zoas* is almost entirely limited to Nights VIII and IX and to additions to the other Nights.[3] (We have already

---

[1] Quoted by Camus, *The Rebel*, p. 89.   [2] 4th ed. (1791), p. 122.
[3] See B 114–15.

mentioned the rule-proving exception on MS page 95. The
Revelation of St. John is a particularly important source
of these Christian references, as Blake acknowledges—
'John Saw these things Reveald in Heaven / On Patmos
Isle' (VIII. 111:4–5, E 371). At this point, despairing of
the revolutionary millenium he had once expected, Blake
turned to an apocalyptist who also saw history as outside
human control. In Revelation, the Wrath of the Lamb is
poured out on the world; Christ's thousand-year reign in
the New Jerusalem is anticipated, to be followed by war with
Satan, general resurrection, and Last Judgement. In Night
IX, as Frye complains, 'The Last Judgment simply starts
off with a bang. . . .'[1] Envisioning the destruction of history,
both of these apocalypses present eschatological doctrines
different from those of the Prophets and of the Lambeth books.
The distinction is between a Prophetic view of history promising a this-worldly fulfillment to God's design, and an apocalyptic view promising an other-worldly fulfillment.

. . . the Christian expectation of a new heaven and a new earth
is derived not from prophecy but from apocalyptic. The prophetic
expectation of a blessed future for the nation, however pure from an
ethical standpoint, was materialistic. Old Testament prophecy
looked forward to an eternal Messianic kingdom on the present
earth, which should be initiated by the final judgment, but in
apocalyptic this underwent a gradual transformation, till the hopes
of the righteous were transferrred from a kingdom of material
blessedness to a spiritual kingdom, in which they were to be as the
angels and become companions of the heavenly hosts. This trans-
ference of the hopes of the faithful from the material world, took
place about 100 B.C. At this period the earth had come to be regarded as wholly unfit for this kingdom, and thus new conceptions
of the kingdom arose, and it was taught by many that the Messianic Kingdom was to be merely of temporary duration, and that
the goal of the risen righteous was to be—not this temporary
kingdom or millennium—but heaven itself. This conception, combined with kindred apocalyptic beliefs, begat an attitude of detachment from this world. The faithful while in the world were not of it.
This temper of apocalyptic but not of prophecy finds expression in

---

[1] *Fearful Symmetry*, p. 308.

the New Testament in the words: 'Here we have no continuing city': 'We look for a city whose builder and maker is God.'[1]

After the failure of the French Revolution and the consolidation of Napoleonic tyranny, Blake turned in a similar way from a Prophetic to an apocalyptic model of history. As nothing was now to be hoped for from revolutionary energy, Orc became merely an encumbrance to be disposed of at the Last Judgement.

One of the notions which Blake derived from Boehme was that Wrath consumes itself as a prelude to regeneration. In order for this to take place, all restraint upon Orc must be removed: 'Let Luvah rage in the dark deep even to Consummation' (120:32, E 375). The errors of energy are still less reprehensible than those of repression, but both are now seen as linked in the juggernaut of modern war:

My anger against thee [Urizen] is greater than against this
    Luvah
For war is energy Enslavd but thy religion
The first author of this war & the distracting of honest minds[2]

Urizen repents of his empire building, 'anxious . . . To reassume the human . . .' 'Let Orc consume', he declares; 'Rage Orc Rage Tharmas Urizen no longer curbs your rage' (121:23, 26, E 376). With the impediment of the Urizenic 'Governor' removed, the Wrath of Orc begins to burn itself out. 'And now fierce Orc had quite consumd himself in Mental flames / Expending all his energy against the fuel of fire' (126:1–2, E 380). It is at this point that the 'Regenerate Man' (significantly altered from the 'Ancient Man') asserts his full identity and sends Luvah and Vala down to the place of seed. There follows the long, beautiful pastoral section in which the regained Beulah is evoked. The concluding action of the poem is the great harvest and vintage, the preparation of the sacramental meal at which 'the Regenerate Man / Sat at the feast rejoicing & the wine of Eternity / Was servd round by the flames of Luvah all Day & all the

---

[1] Charles, pp. 179–80.

[2] 120:41–3, E 375. The Eternal Man is the speaker. Blake first wrote 'For war is honest energy'; then changed it to 'For war is an energy Enslavd'; later deleted the 'an'. See B 127.

Night' (132:10–12, E 385). The epic concludes with the fulfilment of its new theme:

> . . . Urthona rises from the ruinous Walls
> In all his ancient strength to form the golden armour of science
> For intellectual War The war of swords departed now
> The dark Religions are departed & sweet Science reigns

5

In Night VIII, written after Blake had returned to London from
Felpham,[1] Blake's vision of history is given its most nightmarish expression. Erdman has shown how Blake incor-
porated the landscape of wartime London in the imagery of
this Night,[2] and there can be no doubt that the 'Endless
destruction never to be repelld' (101:31, E 359) is the re-
newed war with Napoleon. The dragon Urizen and the
serpent Orc, corporeal enemies but spiritually leagued in the
state called Satan, are seen 'Communing . . . in dark dissimulation.' The conjunction of Orc, Shadowy Female (Vala–
Rahab), and Tree of Mystery represent, as in VIIa, tyranny
and state religion. This time there is an interesting elabora-
tion: the jewels which are 'exuded round' Orc's limbs and
which link him with the Covering Cherub in *Milton*:

> A crest of fire rose on his forehead red as the carbuncle
> Beneath down to his eyelids scales of pearl then gold & silver
> Immingled with the ruby overspread his Visage down
> His furious neck writ[h]ing contortive in dire budding pains
> The scaly armour shot out. Stubborn down his back & bosom
> The Emerald Onyx Sapphire jasper beryl amethyst
> Strove in terrific emulation which should gain a place
> Upon the mighty Fiend the fruit of the mysterious tree
> Kneaded in Uveths kneading trough.[3]

The image is in part derived from Milton's Satan-as-serpent:

> . . . . on his reare,
> Circular base of rising foulds, that tour'd

---

[1] See M xxv; B 164. [2] *Blake*, pp. 368–72.
[3] 101:9–17, E 358–9. B prints 'writing' for 'writhing' in l.12 (p. 106), but
M also has 'writhing' (p. 84). 'Upon the mighty Fiend' was previously 'On the
immortal Fiend' (B 106).

Fould above fould a surging Maze, his Head
Crested aloft, and Carbuncle his Eyes;
With burnisht Neck of verdant Gold, erect
Amidst his circling Spires, that on the grass
Floted redundant . . .

(*P.L.* IX. 497–503)

The Covering Cherub is a symbol of tyranny in Ezekiel (28 : 13),
and the prophet depicts this prince of Tyrus similarly as covered
with gems:

> Thou hast been in Eden the garden of God; every precious stone
> was thy covering, the sardius, topaz, and the diamond, the beryl,
> the onyx, and the jasper, the sapphire, the emerald, and the car-
> buncle, and gold: the workmanship of thy tabrets and of thy pipes
> was prepared in thee in the day that thou wast created.[1]

What particular meaning attaches to the serpent Orc
covered with gems and gold? Why is Orc now equated with
the King of Tyrus and called 'a *King* of wrath & fury'?[2]
Perhaps the answer lies in the coronation of Napoleon on 2
December 1804 with the pope officiating, an event which
seemed to former partisans of the Revolution

> . . . the catastrophe (for so they dream,
> And nothing less), when finally, to close
> And rivet up the gains of France, a Pope
> Is summon'd in to crown an Emperor;
> This last opprobrium, when we see the dog
> Returning to his vomit, when the sun
> That rose in splendour, was alive, and moved
> In exultation among living clouds
> Hath put his function and his glory off,
> And, turned into a gewgaw, a machine,
> Sets like an opera phantom.[3]

The Covering Cherub in *Milton* is 'the Spectre of Luvah',
a symbol like the bejewelled Orc serpent of the Napoleonic
Empire, wrapped around the body of man, as the serpent in
Blake's *Paradise Lost* illustration.[4]

---

[1] Damon, *William Blake*, p. 408.   [2] 107:16, E 368, emphasis mine.
[3] Wordsworth, *Prelude* (1805), x. 931–41.
[4] An interesting analogue, linking jewels, serpent, and the Roman church

The Eternal Man sleeps in the Earth nor feels the vigrous sun
Nor silent moon nor all the hosts of heaven move in his body
His fiery halls are dark & round his limbs the Serpent Orc
Fold without fold encompasses him . . .   (108:23–6, E 369)

Once more in the words of Paracelsus: 'The man who is still
animal . . . . does not know himself and does not know how to
use the energies hidden in him, nor does he know that he
carries the stars within himself, that he is the microcosm, and
thus carries in him the whole firmament with all its influences.'[1] In Night IX, as we have seen, Albion, regenerate,
does learn to use the energies hidden within him, sends
Luvah and Vala to their paradise in the loins, and asserts
the supremacy of the whole human identity over its 'Gods'.

The folds of Orc, whether coiled around the body of fallen
man or looping 'a Serpent wondrous among the Constella-
tions of Urizen', represent the shape of history with its seven
'Eyes' and twenty-seven 'Churches'. We have already discussed the implications of this conception: combining the
cyclical and prophetic views of history, it shows history as
both a prison and a way out. Energy moves in circles
along the coils of Orc—revolutions are betrayed, despairing
victims bow down before equally despairing executioners. At
the same time, in Yeats's phrase, the gyre widens; the successive cycles open toward apocalypse. Thus, in the new beginning Blake wrote for Night IX, the serpent of history is

occurs in Paracelsus's *Book of Nymphs* (quoted in *Paracelsus: Magic into Science*
by Henry M. Pachter (New York, 1951), p. 73; the source is *Four Treatises
of Theophrastus von Hohenheim* (Baltimore, 1941), p. 246):

> Yet there are more *superstitiones* in the Roman Church than in all
> these women and witches. And so it may be a warning that if *superstitio* turns
> a man into a serpent, it also turns him into a devil. That is, if it happens
> to nymphs, it also happens to you in the Roman Church. That, is, you too
> will be transformed into such serpents, you who now are pretty and
> handsome, adorned with large diadems and jewels. In the end you will be a
> serpent and dragon. . .

Blake was not alone in his time in seeing a correspondence between Biblical
monsters and the Emperor: John Ashton reproduces a handbill 'as a sample of
one out of many' in which Napoleon is identified with the Beast of the Apocalypse (*English Caricature and Satire on Napoleon I*, i (New York, 1884), 9).
The handbill, dated June 1808, illustrates the tendency of English Dissenters
to regard contemporary events as corresponding to Biblical prototypes.

[1] *Selected Writings*, p. 228.

PLATE 1

Thus wept the Angel voice & as he wept the terrible blasts
Of trumpets, blew a loud alarm across the Atlantic deep.
No trumpets answer; no reply of clarions or of fifes,
Silent the Colonies remain and refuse the loud alarm.

On those vast shady hills between America & Albions shore;
Now barrd out by the Atlantic sea: calld Atlantean hills:
Because from their bright summits you may pass to the Golden world
An ancient palace, archetype of mighty Emperies.
Rears its immortal pinnacles, built in the forest of God
By Ariston the king of beauty for his stolen bride.

Here on their magic seats the thirteen Angels sat perturb'd
For clouds from the Atlantic hover oer the solemn roof.

Orc: Human Form (*America*, plate 10)

PLATE 2

Orc: Serpent Form (*Europe*, title page)

PLATE 3

The Spiritual Form of Nelson Guiding Leviathan

PLATE 4

Satan Smiting Job with Sore Boils (Engraving)

PLATE 5

The Dance of Albion

PLATE 6

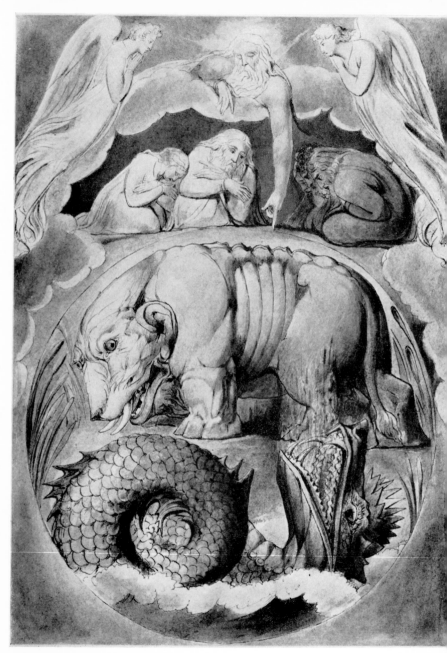

'Behold now Behemoth which I made with thee'
(Watercolour)

PLATE 7

Frontispiece to Hobbes' *Leviathan*

PLATE 8

Milton, plate 32
'But Milton entering my Foot; I saw in the nether Regions of the Imagination . . .'

itself destroyed, just as Boehme's Tree of Wrath is consumed at the Last Judgement:

> . . . Loud the Serpent Orc ragd thro his twenty Seven
> Folds. The tree of Mystery went up in folding flames

And the Tree of the fierce Quality . . . was kindled also, and burnt in the Fire of *God's Wrath* in a hellish Flame . . .[1]

As apocalypse breaks into history, as the Lamb of Revelation (8:1) opens the seventh seal, as the seventh Eye opens, history is itself destroyed. There is an analogy in the microcosm: it is the regeneration process that we have discussed. This takes place, according to Boehme, through seven dialectically related Forms. The tension of the first two, contraction and expansion, in the Wrath principle, produces the third; this propels man through the fourth Form, the 'Flash of Fire', into the upper triad of the Second Principle, which is Love.[2] At the crisis of the fourth form, man stands between two worlds. He can either enter a world of higher innocence by putting his imagination into it or be prisoned in Egoity, his Selfhood.

From the position of earthly man, from the lower ternary, the wrath is illusory, particularly if one looks at the *Angst* in the higher ternary, which appears to portray God as the angry creator of Evil. This Devil's view is man's lot because he fell out of the harmony of God into the *turba* and took all Nature with him: He has lost all perspective and cannot see *das Rad ganz*. Only by passing through the Fourth Form (Second Principle), where he must crucify his *eigene wille* to the Divine Will, can he enter the higher ternary and see the Wrath of God as the angels see it—a source of love. As Man passes through the Fourth Form amid *Schrack* and *Blitz*, the whirling Wheel of Nature becomes a cross, the cross of Christ. . . . Should Man, in the hour when this lightning strikes, 'imagine back into himself', the potential Wheel of Birth in the higher ternary would evade him and he would fall back into an eternal torture, an eternal darkness such as *Vernunft*.[3]

Blake conceives this process to be at the same time cosmogonic, historical, and psychological. The form of history is

---

[1] 119 : 3–4, E 373 (see Percival, p. 156, for analogies with the constellation Scorpio and the mythological serpent Midgard); Preface to *Aurora*, sec. 72, *Works*, i. 17.   [2] See Schorer, p. 127.
[3] Souders, *The Reappearance of Jacob Boehme*, pp. 19–20.

therefore perceived according to the spiritual condition of the beholder. To the Satanic will in the lower ternary, history appears cyclical—a succession of Orcs, as in 'The Mental Traveller'. By the regenerate will in the upper ternary, History is perceived as opening into apocalypse, a twenty-eighth 'Church' and an eighth 'Eye'. In *Milton* and *Jerusalem*, the works in which Blake's system is articulated in its final form, *both* these views are found in juxtaposition, as they are also found in Blake's 'Spiritual Portraits' of Pitt and Nelson.

7

The World Without Imagination:
Blake's Visions of Leviathan
and Behemoth

So that in the first place, I put for a general inclination of
all mankind, a perpetual and restless desire of power after
power, that ceaseth only in death.

HOBBES: *Leviathan*

IN the vision of history seen from the higher ternary, the
devolution of Energy to the will-to-power is perceived as
part of a larger apocalyptic scheme; seen from 'below',
without this imaginative perception, the same phenomenon
creates a demonic world in which human existence itself
is threatened: 'Desperate remorse swallows the present in
a quenchless rage' (VIII. 101:32, E 359). If the views from
these two different perspectives are focused in the same
image, the result is an ironic vision of history which satirizes
its own apparent meaning. This is the technique Blake employed in two major paintings he executed some time between 1805 and 1809, *The Spiritual Form of Nelson guiding
Leviathan* and *The Spiritual Form of Pitt guiding Behemoth*.
Because the ironic mode of their statements was not understood until recently, these paintings were subjected to literal
interpretations which obscured their true meanings, and
their place in Blake's mental universe remains to be discussed.

The Spiritual Forms of Nelson and Pitt were among the
sixteen paintings that Blake exhibited at the shop of his
brother James in 1809. This exhibition was the occasion of
a remarkably aggressive attack upon Blake, conjectured to
be by Robert Hunt, in the *Examiner*. Hunt had reviewed
Blake's designs for *The Grave* unfavourably in 1808, but

his vehemence seems to have a political motive now: 'If beside the stupid and mad-brained political project of their rulers, the sane part of the people of England required fresh proof of the alarming increase of the effects of insanity, they will be too well convinced from its having lately spread into the hitherto sober region of Art.'[1] The blame for such mis-understanding cannot be laid entirely to Hunt, for as Erdman says, 'On the face of it, to paint halos on Pitt and Nelson in the autumn of 1809 was to praise a policy that was wasting the flower of British manhood in the malarial swamps of Holland and the bleeding hills of Spain.'[2] Blake had even made such an interpretation more likely by wishing in his *Descriptive Catalogue* that he had a commission '. . . to execute these two Pictures on a scale that is suitable to the grandeur of the nation, who is the parent of his heroes, in high finished fresco . . .' (E 522). Yet Blake appears innocent of any suspicion that a liberal paper might resent his heroes and their haloes; to him this vicious attack was an example of the envy of his enemies and the character of editors:

> The manner in which my Character < has been blasted these thirty years > both as an artist & a Man may be seen particularly in a Sunday Paper cald the Examiner Publishd in Beaufort Buildings. < (We all know that Editors of Newspapers trouble their heads very little about art & science & that they are always paid for what they put in upon these ungracious Subjects > & the manner in which I have routed out the nest of villains will be seen in a Poem concerning my Three years < Herculean > Labours at Felpham which I will soon Publish. . . .   ('Public Address' (*c.* 1810), E 561)

Blake's revenge was, typically, to work the Hunts into his system. The names of the newspaper and its editors seemed to him ironically fitting: 'The Examiner whose very name is Hunt' (E 495). In a late addition to *Milton* and in *Jerusalem*, the three Hunts are represented as Hand, one of the giant sons of Albion who war against the divine image.[3] (Leigh

---

[1] *Examiner*, 17 September 1809; Mona Wilson, *The Life of William Blake* (London, 1948), pp. 224, 376.   [2] *Blake*, p. 419.
[3] References to Hand are scattered through *Jerusalem*, but see especially 70:1–9, E 222.

Hunt's editorial signature was a pointing hand.[1]) They also appear in *Jerusalem* as the three accusers of Socrates, an identification made explicitly in the 'Public Address' (E 567). The entire episode brings out the pathos of Blake's isolation as a poet and artist at this time. Even Blake's friend Allan Cunningham could only remark:

Of original designs, this singular exhibition contained sixteen— they were announced as chiefly 'of a spiritual and political nature' —but then the spiritual works and political feelings of Blake were unlike those of any other man. One piece represented 'The Spiritual Form of Nelson guiding Leviathan.' Another, 'The Spiritual Form of Pitt guiding Behemoth.' This, probably, confounded both divines and politicians; there is no doubt that plain men went wondering away.[2]

1

In creating his Spiritual Forms, Blake was working in a genre which his age called history painting, and which it valued as the highest and most poetic type of art. Jonathan Richardson expressed the common view when he wrote in 1715:

As to paint a history, a man ought to have the main qualities of a good historian, and something more; he must yet go higher, and have the talents requisite to a good poet; the rules for the conduct of a picture being much the same with those to be observed in writing a poem; and Painting, as well as poetry, requiring an elevation of genius beyond what pure historical narration does; the painter must imagine his figures to think, speak, and act, as a poet should do in a tragedy, or epic poem; especially if his subject be a fable, or an allegory.[3]

Sir Joshua Reynolds, in a passage annotated by Blake,

---

[1] See Erdman, *Blake*, p. 423; also his 'Blake's "Nest of Villains" ', *K-SJ*, ii (1953), 61–71.

[2] *The Lives of the Most Eminent British Painters and Sculptors* (New York, 1859), ii. 141.

[3] 'The Theory of Painting', *Works* (London, 1792), p. 12.

expresses the Academy's preference for idealized historical representation:

Agesilaus was low, lame, and of a mean appearance: none of these defects ought to appear in a piece of which he is the hero. In conformity to custom, I call this part of the art History Painting; it ought to be called Poetical, as in reality it is.

All this is not falsifying any fact; it is taking an allowed poetical licence. A painter of portraits retains the individual likeness; a painter of history shews the man by shewing his actions. . . . He cannot make his hero talk like a great man; he must make him look like one.[1]

To this Blake rejoins, 'A History Painter Paints The Hero, & not Man in General. but most minutely in Particular' (E 641). By this he means not a naturalistic depiction of a historical situation, but a rendering of the archetypal forces manifest in it; an interpretation of the 'hero' or event so as to bring out an underlying meaning. This same motive may be found in Blake's remarks on his Canterbury Pilgrims painting:

Of Chaucer's characters, as described in his Canterbury Tales, some of the names or titles are altered by time, but the characters themselves for ever remain unaltered, and consequently they are the physiognomies or lineaments of universal human life, beyond which Nature never steps.   (E 523–4)

The statement is meant to apply equally to imaginative fiction and history: Chaucer's Plowman 'is Hercules in his supreme eternal state' (E 527), while the *Pitt* and *Nelson* are 'compositions of a mythological cast' (E 521). In his prose writings and marginalia of 1808–10, Blake looks for a British renaissance as a result of anticipated public encouragement for this type of art:

To the Society for Encouragement of Arts I address myself with Respectful duty requesting their Consideration of my Plan as a Great Public [*deed*] means of advancing Fine Art in Protestant Communities Monuments to the dead Painted by Historical & Poetical Artists like Barry & Mortimer. I forbear to name living

---

[1] *Discourses on Art* (San Marino, Calif., 1959), p. 61.

Artists tho equally worthy I say Monuments so Painted must make England What Italy is an Envied Storehouse of Intellectual Riches.

(E 570)

James Barry, whose example Blake appeals to here, had urged a revival of history painting thirty years before in *An Inquiry into the Real and Imaginary Obstructions to the Acquisition of the Arts in England.*[1] Barry's hopes and, later, Blake's were founded upon the growing popularity of history painting in England.[2] Blake's younger contemporary Benjamin Robert Haydon also hoped for such a revival.

One of your own class has asserted that a historical picture of acknowledged merit, with a price proportioned to its skill, would be the longest unsold on the walls of the British Gallery, and would not he, as one of the patrons, be to blame? Certainly. He forgets he implicates himself. If the churches are not to be open (and why St. Paul's should not be open as well as Saint Peter's—why pictures should not be admitted as well as statues, no reason on earth can be given), let the public halls be adorned . . .[3]

Blake shared a sense of anticipation widely felt among English painters, yet again his definition of history painting—and of history—was not quite theirs.

The reasoning historian, [he wrote in his *Descriptive Catalogue*] turner and twister of causes and consequences, such as Hume, Gibbon and Voltaire; cannot with all their artifice, turn or twist one fact or disarrange self evident action and reality. . . . His

[1] London, 1775. On Barry's importance to Blake, see Erdman, *Blake,* pp. 37–43.

[2] See Edgar Wind, 'The Revolution of History Painting', *Journal of the Warburg Institute,* ii (1938), 116–27; Charles Mitchell, ' "Death of General Wolfe" and the Popular History Piece', *Journal of the Warburg and Courtauld Institutes,* vii (1944), 20–33.

[3] *The Autobiography and Memoirs of Benjamin Robert Haydon,* ed. Tom Taylor (New York, 1926), i. 148. The address is to 'representatives of the people of England'. After the death of Fuseli in March 1825, Haydon wrote: 'A historical painter dead is an irreparable loss; for, however unsuccessful, if living he is a perpetual reproach to the apathy, brutality and insincerity of the patrons. He keeps alive the complaint that historical painting is neglected— and thus, even in ruin, indirectly maintains a feeling which must die when he dies, for it can no longer be a subject of complaint that history is not supported when its professors are extinct' (i. 364).

opinions, who does not see spiritual agency, is not worth any man's reading. . . . (E 534)

Blake did see spiritual agency, and he undertook to paint this, and not what for him were mere circumstances. He rejected the realistic (yet still highly fictionalized) mode of Benjamin West as vehemently as he did the academic idealizations of Reynolds. Blake's pictures might be 'incorrect' literally but, he argues, they are true renderings of imaginatively perceived archetypes. Appropriating a point made earlier by Lessing,[1] he says of his 'ideal design' *The Bramins*: 'I understand that my Costume is incorrect, but in this I plead the authority of the ancients, who often deviated from the Habits, to preserve the Manners, as in the instance of Laocoon, who, though a priest, is represented naked' (E 539). Here Blake is in agreement with Reynolds (cf. *Discourses*, p. 128) and is attacking the practice, which West had popularized, of painting heroes in the costume of the day.

After Trafalgar, West painted an *Apotheosis of Nelson*. Joseph Farington noted in his diary for 29 November 1805[2] that it was to be considered a companion to West's *Death of General Wolfe*, a painting which had enjoyed enormous success more than thirty years before. The *Death of Wolfe*, engraved by Woollet in 1776, had an immense sale and completely overshadowed Barry's treatment of the same subject, first exhibited that year.[3] It seems reasonable to assume that Blake determined to reply to the *Apotheosis of Nelson* by painting 'Two Pictures, representing grand Apotheoses of NELSON and PITT' (E 517), in which he would communicate his perception of his subjects' significance as 'Spiritual Forms'.

---

[1] 'Some persons, it is said, find it very incongruous that a king's son and a priest should be thus represented at a sacrifice . . . . Conventionality was a matter of little value to the ancients. They felt that the highest aim of their art led to a total disregard of it. This highest aim is beauty. . . . There is also a certain beauty in drapery, but what is this as compared to the beauty of the human form?' G. E. Lessing, *The Laocoon and Other Prose Writings*, trans. and ed. W. B. Rönnfeldt (London, 1895), pp. 43–4.

[2] *The Farington Diary*, ed. James Greig (London, n.d.), iii. 127.

[3] See J. Clarence Webster, 'Pictures of the Death of Major-General James Wolfe', *Journal of the Society of Army Historical Research*, vi (1927), 30–6. The Barry painting is among those reproduced; the figures in it are *not* nude, although it is sometimes written that they are.

These, like the originals which the artist had seen in vision, would contain 'mythological and recondite meaning, where more is meant than meets the eye' (E 522).

> The two Pictures of Nelson and Pitt are compositions of a mytho-logical cast, similar to those Apotheoses of Persian, Hindoo, and Egyptian Antiquity, which are still preserved on rude monuments, being copies from some stupendous originals now lost or perhaps buried till some happier age. The Arist having been . . . taken in vision into the ancient republics, monarchies, and patriarchates of Asia, has seen those wonderful originals called in the Sacred Scriptures the Cherubim, which were sculptured and painted on walls of Temples, Towers, Cities, Palaces, and erected in the highly cultivated states of Egypt, Moab, Edom, Aram, among the Rivers of Paradise, being originals from which the Greeks and Hetrurians copied Hercules, Farnese, Venus of Medicis, Apollo Belvidere, and all the grand works of ancient art. They were executed in a very superior style to those justly admired copies, being with their accompaniments terrific and grand in the highest degree. The Artist has endeavoured to emulate the grandeur of those seen in his vision, and to apply it to modern Heroes, on a smaller scale.
>
> (E 521–2)

Here Blake again follows Barry, who had speculated on 'those coloured, basso-rilievo, historical representations, which were vitrified, or enamelled on the brick walls of Babylon', and who had suggested that the cherubim were the sculpture of the ancient Jews.[1] According to Barry, too, ancient art was antediluvian in origin:

> These royal, deified personages, so important in the history of Egypt, and which appear to have given a beginning to that history, were not of Egyptian but of Titanic origin, and were part of the wrecks of that Atlantic people, whose country (according to the Egyptian account mentioned in Plato) was submerged by an inun-dation of that ocean, which, probably from the circumstance, was called the Atlantic.[2]

Yet, as the Flood had washed away the original meanings of the ancient mythologies, it was up to the artist to re-establish them; and it must be said that Blake gave his audience little

---

[1] *Lectures on Painting by the Royal Academicians*, ed. Ralph N. Wornum (London, 1848), pp. 58 n. and 67 n.   [2] Ibid., p. 64 n.

to go on. We 'Children of the future Age', familiar with the symbolism of his other works, are in a more fortunate position.

In the Bible, Leviathan is a primitive water monster overcome by Jahweh in ancient times.

Thou didst divide the sea by thy strength: thou brakest the heads of the dragons in the waters.

Thou brakest the heads of leviathan in pieces, and gavest him to be meat to the people inhabiting the wilderness.

Thou didst cleave the fountain and the flood: thou driedst up mighty rivers. (Ps. 74:13–15)

There is a similar or identical myth about a sea dragon called Rahab:

Awake, awake, put on strength, O arm of the LORD; awake, as in the ancient days, in the generations of old. Art thou not it that hath cut Rahab, and wounded the dragon?

Art thou not it which hath dried the sea, the waters of the great deep; that hath made the depths of the sea a way for the ransomed to pass over? (Isa. 51:9–10)

These variants of a single myth are, as Frye observes,[1] used by the Prophets as metaphors of the eventual destruction of the enemies surrounding the Hebrews.

Son of man, set thy face against Pharaoh king of Egypt, and prophesy against him, and against all Egypt:

Speak, and say, Thus saith the Lord GOD; Behold, I am against thee, Pharaoh king of Egypt, the great dragon that lieth in the midst of his rivers, which hath said, My river is mine own, and I have made it for myself.

But I will put hooks in thy jaws, and I will cause the fish of thy rivers to stick unto thy scales, and I will bring thee up out of the midst of thy rivers, and all the fish of thy rivers shall stick unto thy scales. (Ezek. 29:2–4)

In that day the LORD with his sore and great and strong sword shall punish leviathan the piercing serpent, even leviathan that crooked serpent; and he shall slay the dragon that is in the sea.

(Isa. 27:1)

---

[1] *Fearful Symmetry*, p. 209.

Blake's use of the Leviathan symbol changes, along with the meaning of Satan, as his view of Energy changes. In *The Marriage*, where 'Energy is the only life', Satan is the true Messiah, and Leviathan turns out to be an innocuous fantasy. In *America*, where the conception of Energy is more ambiguous, Orc's serpent form is associated with the dragon of Revelation:

> . . . . Art thou not Orc; who serpent-form'd
> Stands at the gate of Enitharmon to devour her children . . .?
>
> (7:3–4, E 52)

> . . . and the dragon stood before the woman which was ready to be delivered, for to devour her child as soon as it was born.
>
> (Rev. 12:4)

The red dragon whose tail 'drew the third part of the stars of heaven, and did cast them to the earth' (ibid.) is Rahab–Satan, but we must remember that the question addressed to Orc comes from Albion's Angel, who can only perceive the destructive aspect of revolutionary energy. However, in *Vala*, as we have seen, this is all that remains of Orc by Night VIIa. (A similar Leviathan may be found in *Night Thoughts* Illustration 349, guided by a scaly merman who wields the symbols of Church and State, sword and crozier.) Vala herself becomes Rahab, now identified with 'the great whore that sitteth on many waters' (Rev. 17:1); Night VIIb shows her as 'the deluded harlot of the Kings of Earth' (91:15, E 395), embracing the Orc serpent.[1] The situation is analogous to *Purgatorio* xxxii, where Dante sees the harlot of corrupt religion in the arms of a giant who represents

---

[1] Harold Bloom, *Blake's Apocalypse* (New York, 1963), points out that Blake purposely changes the traditional meaning of Rahab to 'the unredeemable harlot of Babylon, the Mystery of the book of Revelation. Blake departs quite deliberately from the figurative or typological reading of Rahab in the Bible of Heaven, and presents us with his Bible of Hell's most sinister female. For Rahab is an orthodox type of the Church, identified by traditional commentary (and Dante) with the bride of the Song of Songs. . . . Blake identifies the Rahab of Jerico with the other Rahab of the Old Testament, the sea monster associated with Egypt and Babylon in the Psalms and Isaiah, and therefore a type of Job's Leviathan. This Rahab Blake identifies also with the Covering Cherub of Ezekiel, once an inhabitant of Eden, but now a demon blocking man's way back to Paradise' (pp. 259–60).

the French monarchy (lines 148–56). In the Apocalypse this conjunction represents the Roman Empire and its gods; in Dante it is Philip the Fair and the 'Babylonian Captivity' of the papacy at Avignon.[1] For Blake, the prototypical situation is again repeated with the pope's coronation of Napoleon.

> . . . . John Saw these things Reveald in Heaven
> On Patmos Isle & heard the Souls cry out to be deliverd
> He saw the Harlot of the Kings of Earth & saw her Cup
> Of fornication food of Orc & Satan pressd from the fruit of
>   Mystery[2]

The conjunction of Rahab and the dragon produces war, as the Satanic will of the State seeks to aggrandize itself. Rahab in *Milton* is called 'Religion hidden in War' (40:20, E 140). In *Jerusalem* the Spectre creates

> . . . . Leviathan
> And Behemoth: the War by Sea enormous & the War
> By Land astounding . . .   (91:38–40, E 249)

In choosing Leviathan and Behemoth for his spiritual portraits, Blake was drawing upon meanings he had established in his poetry, although the public of his time could not be aware of this.

2

> Blake is as great a warrior as Nelson the one was honoured with titles the other not.   JOHN CLARE

> England expects that every man should do his duty, in Arts, as well as in Arms, or in the Senate.
>
>   BLAKE: *Descriptive Catalogue*

Miscomprehension of the Pitt and Nelson paintings did not come to an end with the *Examiner* article. One was

---

[1] *Dante's Purgatorio*, Temple Classics (London, 1956), p. 417. In Blake, the configuration also occurs in *Night Thoughts* Illus. 345. This is the frontispiece to Night VIII, 'Virtue's Apology'. Rahab is seated on the back of the monster, which Blake has given seven wonderfully grotesque heads, including those of a king, a priest, a pope, a judge, and a warrior.

[2] 111:4–7, E 371. A late addition.

exhibited at the Royal Academy sixty-five years after Blake's exhibition as 'The Right Hon. William Pitt'![1] The *Pitt* is referred to in the catalogue of the 1876 Blake exhibition at the Burlington Fine Arts Club as 'This surprising but inexplicable invention' (p. 53). A writer in *MacMillan's Magazine*, H. H. Statham, took exception to the charge of obscurity: 'No one expects allegory to be as legible as A, B, C', he wrote of the *Pitt*. 'Blake's remarks upon some general art-topics *à propos* of it are wild and excursive enough, but his heading contains the whole gist of the subject, and tells us in plain words, what any one who bears a brain might conclude for himself—that "Behemoth" represents "the people" guided by Pitt, whose form, of course, loomed very large in those days to his contemporaries both English and foreign.'[2] We are not favoured with his view of the *Nelson*, but after another Blake exhibition, one 'M.A.' wrote of this picture in the *Burlington Magazine*: 'The significance at the present moment of the idea which Blake expresses in this picture is plain to all who know that symbolism of scripture, and the same idea is unmistakeably stated in James Thompson's prosaic line, "Rule Britannia, rule the waves!" '[3]

Blake had, indeed, written lines on the 'Rule Britannia' theme, but their sentiment might have surprised M.A.

> Spirit who lovst Brittannias Isle
> Round which the Fiends of Commerce smile   (E 471)

In the period of the war against France, Blake links Britain's militarism with her foreign trade; when Urizen, whose naval preparations are described in Night VIII of *The Four Zoas*, repents, he regrets 'burdning with my Ships the angry deep' (121:8, E 375). Blake's vision of naval glory was an ironical one, and the *Nelson* is a dark satire upon Corporeal War. The first to recognize this was Mark Schorer, and it is now

---

[1] See Samuel Palmer's letter to George Richmond dated 1 June 1874, in A. H. Palmer, *The Life and Letters of Samuel Palmer* (London, 1892), p. 347.

[2] 'The Blake Drawings at the Burlington Fine Arts Club', *MacMillan's*, xxxiv (1876), 60–1.

[3] 'William Blake's "Nelson" ', *The Burlington Magazine*, xxvi (1914–15), 139.

agreed that both paintings are symbolical in 'a way designed to conceal and deceive'.[1] Perhaps their meanings would have become clear sooner had their companion piece, *The Spiritual Form of Napoleon*, not been lost; for, judging from the description that has been left of it, its symbolism was less obscure than that of the others.

The Spiritual Form of Napoleon was last exhibited in the Burlington show of 1876. The Catalogue lists it as No. 90, a tempera, $25'' \times 31''$, lent by Samuel Palmer. It is noted as not appearing in the *Descriptive Catalogue* of 1809 but is conjecturally dated as 'evidently painted about that year, along with the "Spiritual Forms" of Nelson and Pitt'. (Erdman, in the other hand, assumes that it must have been painted in 1822, after Napoleon's death.[2]) Both the exhibition Catalogue and the Catalogue compiled by William Michael Rossetti for Gilchrist's *Life* call the *Napoleon* 'A very powerful example of effect.'[3] H. H. Statham described this Spiritual Form as a 'strong energetic figure grasping at the sun and moon with his hands . . . with a pavement of dead bodies. . .in the foreground'.[4] There are 'angelic figures on either side of the Napoleon', as in the *Pitt*; the former is 'the most striking conception of the two' but 'not the finest in execution'.

The meaning of the *Napoleon* as described above is quite clear and reflects on the meanings of the other two paintings. Napoleon is a 'hero'—that is to say, a monster of energy, an Orc in Luvah descended into the state called Satan. In his *hybris* this personification of the will-to-power grasps at the sun and moon, but the dead bodies in the foreground attest his true nature: 'war is energy Enslavd' (*Four Zoas*, 120: 42, E 375). 'What do these Knaves mean by Virtue', Blake asked in his annotations to Bacon. 'Do they mean War & its horrors & its Heroic Villains' (E 612) Hung together, Nelson, Pitt, and Napoleon would have formed a political

---

[1] *William Blake*, p. 174. See also Erdman, *Blake*, pp. 415–20; Sir Anthony Blunt, *The Art of William Blake* (New York, 1959), pp. 97–100. Blunt views the two paintings as apocalyptic in meaning, but his interpretation becomes confused when he associates Pitt with Los.

[2] *Blake*, p. 455. Harold Bloom, 'Napoleon and Prometheus: The Romantic Myth of Organic Energy', *YFS*, no. 26 (1960–1), p. 79, also assumes this.

[3] 2nd ed. (1880), ii. 254.   [4] *MacMillan's*, xxxiv, 61.

complement to Blake's other unholy trinities—Bacon, Newton, and Locke; Hume, Gibbon, and Voltaire; the brothers Hunt; the accusers of Socrates. But even if Blake had painted Napoleon's Spiritual Form some fourteen years before his death, it is unlikely that he would have shown it beside the *Pitt* and *Nelson*: it might have made their meanings too clear for the artist's good. Instead, Blake did his best to obscure his intention when he described these two pictures in his exhibition catalogue.

In the *Descriptive Catalogue* Blake twice refers to his subjects as 'heroes' but says nothing about the peculiar sense in which he uses the word. It is true that at times he employs it literally: 'The Knight is a true Hero, a good, great, and wise man; his whole length portrait on horseback, as written by Chaucer, cannot be surpassed. He has spent his life in the field; has ever been a conqueror, and is that species of character which in every age stands as the guardian of man against the oppressor' (E 524). In his copy of Lavater's *Aphorisms*, Blake had found similar definitions of the hero: 'every genius, every hero, is a prophet'; 'The disinterested defender of oppressed humanity against an usurping tyrant— is a royal hero . . .'; and 'He, who has frequent moments of complete existence, is a hero, though not laurelled. . . .'[1] '. . . I have the happiness of seeing the Divine countenance', Blake wrote to Hayley, 'in such men as Cowper and Milton more distinctly than in any prince or hero' (28 May 1804, K 845). More trenchantly, he wrote in the Laocoön aphorisms, 'Satans Wife The Goddess Nature is War & Misery & Heroism a Miser' (E 270). Blake's use of the word 'hero' in the *Descriptive Catalogue* is ironical, much like Fielding's in *Jonathan Wild*. Wild, Fielding declares, achieved unsurpassed greatness,

though it must be allowed that there have been some few heroes who have done greater mischiefs to mankind, such as those who have betrayed the liberty of their country to others, or who have undermined and overpowered it themselves; or conquerors who have impoverished, pillaged, sacked, burnt, and destroyed the

---

[1] *Aphorisms on Man* (London, 1788), pp. 140, 93, 170 resp. Two of these were marked by Blake; see E 582, 584.

countries and cities of their fellow-creatures, from no other provocation than that of glory. . . .[1]

To many Englishmen Nelson was a Happy Warrior 'That every man in arms should wish to be'. To Blake the military hero was merely an heroic villain.

Britain's naval glory is the subject of some lines by a poet who called himself Birmingham J., lines which Blake liked enough to copy into his Notebook. Their subject is the English bombardment of neutral Copenhagen in 1807, as a result of which 2,000 people were killed and the cathedral and the university destroyed. (Nelson himself had been in command of a previous bombardment in 1801.) The poem begins 'The Glory of Albion is tarnishd with Shame' and concludes

> For the triumph which Liberty hallowd is fled
> And the might of the Tyrant has raged in its stead
> And changd is the radiance that streamd oer the heath
> To the warning of Nations. the meteor of Death.[2]

Blake's own comment on naval glory may be found in this chorus of impressed seamen, from *Jerusalem*:

> We were carried away in thousands from London; & in tens
> Of thousands from Westminster & Marybone in ships closd up:
> Chaind hand & foot, compelld to fight under the iron whips
> Of our captains; fearing our officers more than the enemy.
>
> (65:33–6, E 214)

In the Nelson painting itself, we find human forms—the 'Nations of the Earth'—enfolded in the coils of the monster, crushed by Power. A Negro slave lies prone in the foreground. Struggling in the jaws of Leviathan is a figure clutching the hilt of a sword. He is crowned with lilies, symbolic of innocence as in Milton's *Comus*, where Sabrina is pictured "In twisted braids of Lillie knitting . . . thy amber-dropping hair" (*Works*, I, pt. 1, 117). In his right hand Nelson flourishes the streaming hair plucked from a female figure which Erdman identifies as 'France, shorn of sea-power at

---

[1] *The Complete Works of Henry Fielding, Esq.* (London, 1903), ii. 204.

[2] See Erdman, 'Blake's Transcript of Bisset's "Lines Written on hearing the surrender of Copenhagen"', *BNYPL*, lxxii (1968), 519.

Trafalgar.'[1] His other hand guides the War by Sea enormous by means of a halter round Leviathan's neck, explicitly defying God's word to Job:

> Canst thou draw out leviathan with an hook? or his tongue with a cord which thou lettest down?
> Canst thou put an hook into his nose? or bore his jaw through with a thorn?
>
> .   .   .   .
>
> Who can discover the face of his garment? or who can come to him with his double bridle?   (Job 41:1-2, 13)

Lightnings of divine wrath converge on him; flames of naval bombardment stream around his figure; his halo and his placid expression contrast ironically with the violence around him.

Blake's other 'modern hero', Pitt, has previously appeared in Blake's political symbolism as Rintrah,[2] the 'red limb'd Angel' of *Europe* who prepares for war against Orc. On Plate 8 of *Europe*, Rintrah appears as a scaly crowned figure with a sword; beneath this picture in the British Museum copy, Damon found the following quotation from *2 Henry VI* written in a hand other than Blake's:

> O War! thou Son of Hell,
> Whom angry heavens do make
> their minister.[3]

Blake chose Pitt to guide Behemoth, 'the War by land astounding', because he regarded him as the architect of Britain's war policy. Pitt, 'minister' under an angry heaven, becomes in the *Catalogue* 'that Angel who, pleased to perform the Almighty's orders, rides on the whirlwind, directing the storms of war' (E 521). We can perhaps capture something of the meaning of this by taking a Blake's-eye view of Pitt's speeches to Parliament during the war years.

---

[1] *Blake.*, p. 417.

[2] Jacob Bronowski, *William Blake, A Man Without a Mask* (London, 1944), p. 80; Erdman, *Blake*, pp. 193, 195, 201-7, 355, 360.

[3] Damon, *William Blake*, p. 349, found a number of such quotations written in the B.M. copy. He conjectured them to have been inscribed by the original owner with Blake's knowledge and, perhaps, help. G. E. Bentley, Jr., has identified the hand as that of Blake's friend George Cumberland. See Jean H. Hagstrum, *William Blake, Poet and Painter* (Chicago, 1964), p. 91 n.

On 1 February 1793, Pitt moved an ultimatum to France before the House; on the same day, as it happened, France declared war. Blake might well have written his 'Fiends of Commerce' fragment in the margin of Pitt's war speech of 12 February:

If, said Mr. Pitt, you entertain a sense of the many blessings which you enjoy, if you value the continuance and safety of that commerce which is a source of so much opulence, if you wish to preserve and render permanent that high state of prosperity by which this country has for some years past been so eminently distinguished, you hazard all these advantages more, and are more likely to forfeit them, by submitting to a precarious and disgraceful peace, than by a timely and vigorous interposition of your arms.[1]

Pitt delivered the first of many speeches against motions for peace on 17 June, declaring that Fox's motion was 'only calculated to amuse and delude the people' (p. 93). After the First Coalition failed in 1794, Pitt continued to press his war policy. To Fox's question of whether he was never to make peace with the Jacobins, Pitt replied: '. . . the moment will never come, when I shall not think any alternative preferable to that of making peace with France, upon the system of its present rulers' (p. 108). After a series of extraordinary French military successes in the autumn and winter of 1794, there was again a motion for peace, this time by Wilberforce. Pitt expressed astonishment that an opponent of the slave-trade could advocate abandoning the West Indies to Jacobinism, 'their government of anarchy, the horrors of which are even more dreadful than those of slavery' (p. 127). The French victories were the work of 'inscrutable Providence' (p. 119). But France's resources were overstrained; she would soon collapse economically. Despite this prediction, the French continued their conquest of the Netherlands in the spring of 1795, and in 1796 occupied Nice, Savoy, and parts of Italy. Pitt entered into informal negotiations with the Directory, a government which he

---

[1] *The War Speeches of William Pitt the Younger*, selected by R. Coupland (Oxford, 1940), p. 58. Subsequent quotations from Pitt's speeches are from this source.

declared more stable than its predecessor, but he was unable to obtain satisfactory terms of peace.

Blake responded to the domestic effects of the war in *The Four Zoas* as taxes rose, grain became scarce, and there were mutinies in the Fleet.[1] In these circumstances he could have seen a particularly sinister meaning in Pitt's linking of heroism and commerce at the end of 1798: '. . . in the memorable era of the past year Great Britain has exhibited the glorious example of a nation showing the most universal spirit of military heroism at a time when she had acquired the most flourishing degree of national commerce' (pp. 239–40). (In the same speech, Nelson, who had destroyed Napoleon's fleet in the Battle of the Nile, is singled out in a tribute to 'the heroism, zeal, patriotism, and devotion of our transcendent commanders' as 'that great commander whose services fill every bosom with rapturous emotion . . .' (p. 238).) The shortage of grain, Blake's 'bread of sorrow', was not in Pitt's opinion a legitimate subject of debate. In 1800 he rebuked his opponents for contributing to popular unrest by blaming the scarcity on the war.

> God forbid I should question the freedom of thought or the liberty of speech! But I cannot see how gentlemen can justify a language and a conduct which can have no tendency but to disarm our exertions and to defeat our hopes in the prosecution of the contest. . . . Above all, nothing can be more unfair in reasoning, than to ally the present scarcity with the war, or to insinuate that its prosecution will interfere with those supplies which we may require. (p. 287)

War abroad and dearth at home—these were to Blake the accomplishments of Pitt's ministry. On 11 September 1801, he wrote to Thomas Butts:

> Bacon & Newton would prescribe ways of making the world heavier to me, & Pitt would prescribe distress for a medicinal potion; but as none on Earth can give me Mental Distress, & I know that all Distress inflicted by Heaven is a Mercy, a Fig for all Corporeal! (K 809)

---

[1] See Erdman, *Blake*, pp. 317, 340.

Little more than a month later (19 October), Blake was writing in a very different tone, for peace had broken out in the interim:

Dear Flaxman,

I rejoice to hear that your Great Work is accomplish'd. Peace opens the way to greater still. The Kingdoms of this World are now become the Kingdoms of God & his Christ, & we shall reign with him for ever & ever. The Reign of Literature & the Arts Commences. Blessed are those who are found studious of Literature & Humane & polite accomplishments. Such have their lamps burning & such shall shine as the stars.   (K 810)

Pitt, out of office at the time,[1] supported the Treaty of Amiens, for the collapse of the Second Coalition in February had left England alone at war with France. But the Peace turned out to be a truce; war was resumed in May 1803. Blake's despair about the renewal of the war is recorded in in Night VIII:

> . . . . All futurity
> Seems teeming with Endless destruction never to be repelld
> Desperate remorse swallows the present in a quenchless rage
>
> (*Four Zoas*, 101:30–2, E 359)

Although Pitt did not return to power until the spring of 1804, he took an active part in proposing measures against the invasion that was expected from France during the autumn of 1803. The army was enlarged and militiamen conscripted to defend the coast. It was in an atmosphere of public fear and apprehension that Blake was accused of making seditious utterances by Private John Schofield in the town of Felpham by the sea.

The story of Blake's trial for sedition is well known.[2] Blake turned Schofield out of his garden and, after the soldier had threatened to knock out his eyes, took him by the elbows and carried him down the road to the inn where he was

---

[1] Pitt had resigned over the King's unwillingness to approve a removal of Catholic civil disabilities.

[2] See Blake's Memorandum, E 700–2, and his letter to Thomas Butts, 16 August 1803; Wilson, *Life of William Blake*, pp. 151–6; Alexander Gilchrist, *Life of William Blake*, 2nd ed. (London, 1880), i. 190–9.

quartered. Subsequently Schofield and one Private Cock deposed that Blake had uttered treasonable words, including 'that the French Knew our Strength very well, and if Bonaparte should come he would be Master of Europe in an Hour's Time, that England might depend upon it, that when he set his Foot on English Ground that every Englishman would have his choice whether to have his Throat cut, or join the French, and that he was a strong Man, and would certainly begin to cut Throats. . . .' Especially amusing is Schofield's assertion that Mrs. Blake had declared 'altho' she was but a Woman, she would fight as long as she had a drop of blood in her.'[1] That such a complaint was made the basis of a prosecution is an indication of what effect the fear of invasion had had in England. Blake himself wrote of the incident to Thomas Butts: 'I have been before a Bench of Justices at Chichester this morning; but they, as the Lawyer who wrote down the Accusation told me in private, are compell'd by the Military to suffer a prosecution to be enter'd into: altho' they must know, & it is manifest, that the whole is a Fabricated Perjury' (K 827).

Blake was acquitted in January 1804, but he must have suffered great anxiety in the five months that elapsed between accusation and trial. It must have occurred to him that someone might bring in his past association with the radicals of Joseph Johnson's circle as support for Schofield's charge. Although the Lambeth books were perhaps safely obscure, what would a jury have made of *The French Revolution?*[2] Fortunately, nothing of this sort happened, and Blake's lawyer had merely to demonstrate the unlikelihood of Blake's using the language attributed to him.[3] Yet the event troubled Blake deeply, as we can see from the interpretation he makes of it in the symbolism of *Milton* and *Jerusalem*. Schofield and several others connected with the trial are enlisted, with

[1] From Schofield's Information and Complaint, cited by Wilson, *Life of William Blake*, pp. 154–5.

[2] According to Gilchrist, i. 199, Blake believed that the soldier had been employed in a government plot to entrap him. But even had Blake believed this, he could hardly have continued to do so when no evidence of his acquaintanceship with radicals was produced at the trial.

[3] See Erdman, *Blake*, p. 377 n.

'Hand', among the twelve giant sons of Albion who war against the unity of man.

> . . . . all his Sons,
> Hand, Hyle & Coban, Guantok, Peachey, Brereton, Slayd & Hutton,
> Scofeld, Kox, Kotope & Bowen; his Twelve Sons: Satanic Mill![1]

At times these twelve compose a monstrous jury which is at the same time accuser, sentencing judge, and executioner; opposing Love with Law and Mercy with Justice.[2] Schofield represents War in its Corporeal aspect—the war against France, the inner divisions of society and of man. In *Milton* (19:59) and again in Jerusalem (11:21), 'Schofield is bound in iron armour' (compare 'Auguries of Innocence': 'Nought can deform the Human Race / Like to the Armours iron brace').[3] On Plate 51 of *Jerusalem*, Schofield—or, rather, his spiritual state—is pictured chained and in flames. In his conflict with Schofield, Blake, whose habit of mind was to look for the universal in the particulars of his experience, saw the aggression of warrior against visionary; and the fact that Schofield's charge was entertained became another symptom of the disease of war in the members of Albion.

Pitt himself was not one of the warriors and mighty hunters of mankind; he was a man who pleaded his desire for peace while urging the necessity of war. His Spiritual Form is therefore quite different from, although complementary to, Nelson's. As the painting has darkened, obscuring its detail, reproductions of it are not very useful and a lengthy description of it is therefore necessary. The following account, by A. G. B. Russell, is from the Catalogue of the Tate Gallery exhibition of 1913:

In the midst, 'riding upon the whirlwind,' is the young angelic

---

[1] *Jerusalem*, 19:17–19, E 162. Kox is Private Cock; Guantok or Quantock the Justice of the Peace who signed a recognizance to ensure the two soldiers' presence at the trial; Peachey and Brereton two other Justices; Bowen the prosecutor; Hutton the Lt. Hulton who was made responsible for the soldiers' appearing. Hyle is Hayley. Coban, Kotope, and Lloyd have not been identified. See Geoffrey Keynes, 'Blake's Trial at Chichester', *N & Q*, iv (November 1957), 484–5.   [2] See Damon, *William Blake*, p. 436.

[3] E 483. Written *c.* 1800–3.

form of Pitt,[1] calm and inexorable, clothed in a robe of greenish grey heightened with gold, holding in his right hand a crimson thong for the guiding of Behemoth's neck, and with his left 'directing the storm of war'; about his head is a triple fiery aureole: within the outer circle of which there revolve a company of the ancient spirits of the wisdom from on high, and in its centre a ring of angels, the innermost circle being one of pure light. Arising from the earth and crouching upon the ground beneath his feet is Behemoth or 'the War by Land' (cf. 'Jerusalem,' 91, 39), a vast and darkly transparent greenish shape, with many hued shaggy head and long pointed snout, upturned and curling backwards, and armed with terrible tusks. His jaws are open, disclosing a blood-red tongue to devour the crop of human bodies (some living and transfixing others with spears as they fall) which are being dropped into them by the Reaper, who is seen in the half-naked giant figure kneeling at Pitt's right hand, upon a mountain above, with his sickle uplifted for the reaping of the vine of the earth. By the beast's forepaws and at his flanks, upon the ground, are others of his victims, in agony and supplication awaiting their end; and through his transparent hide can be seen four monstrous heads, two of them encircled with crowns and a third thrown back with gaping mouth and protruding tongue. To the right of Pitt, corresponding to the Reaper, is the Plowman, with one foot upon a mountain and the other upon the plain below, dealing destruction with a vast plough-share ('the plow to go over the nations'. 'Jerusalem,' 34, 13), wreathed about with black flames leaping from the gulf beneath. A group of three figures will be seen, fleeing in terror before it. In the foreground to the right beneath the point of the share a woman is driving a poniard into an aged man from behind,—an act of mercy, it may be. In the background at the foot of the mountain is a huge domed building behind which a conflagration arises; and in the plain before it are two belching guns. In the heaven above are six planetary globes (the reddish one to r. being probably Mars), in each of which is a spiritual body of human form, since each, according to Blake, has its human and personal existence; and in the interstices, the stars and (l.) a brilliant rushing comet; all these, together with the earth below, representing the Universe, throughout the whole of which the operation of war extends (cf. 'Vala,' IX, 307–311 and 574–579).[2]

[1] Here Russell cites in a footnote six lines of Addison's *Campaign* discussed below.

[2] Quoted in full from 'M. A.', *Burlington Magazine*, xxvi. 140. I have been unable to find some of the details which Russell saw, but it may be that the painting has deteriorated further in the intervening fifty years.

Although he saw correlations between the imagery of this painting and the symbolism of Blake's poetry, Russell evidently did not perceive the irony of the former. Yet the six lines which he quoted from Addison's *Campaign* should have made the ironic contrast apparent. Blake described his subject in the *Pitt* as 'that Angel who, pleased to perform the Almighty's orders, rides on the whirlwind, directing the storms of war: He is ordering the Reaper to reap the Vine of the Earth, and the Plowman to plow up the Cities and Towers' (E 521). The ultimate source of this is Revelation 14 : 19 : 'And the angel thrust in his sickle into the earth, and gathered the vine of the earth, and cast it into the great winepress of the wrath of God.'[1] There is also very likely an allusion to *The Campaign*, where Marlborough, '*England's* Heroe' and 'Our God-like Leader', is described as 'Plunging thro' Seas of Blood his fiery Steed', and likened to an angel as he directs the battle.

> So when an Angel, by Divine Command,
> With rising Tempests shakes a guilty Land,
> Such as of late o'er pale *Britannia* past,
> Calm and Serene he drives the furious Blast;
> And pleas'd th' Almighty's Orders to perform,
> Rides in the Whirl-wind, and directs the Storm.[2]

This was sure to be recognized by Addison's contemporaries as a sublime simile, while Blake's typical imagery of warfare is not sublime but grotesque:

Troop by troop the beastial droves rend one another sounding loud
The instruments of sound & troop by troop in human forms they urge
The dire confusion till the battle faints those that remain
Return in pangs & horrible convulsions to their beastial state
For the monsters of the Elements Lions or Tygers or Wolves
Sound loud the howling music Inspird by Los & Enitharmon
    Sounding loud terrific men
They seem to one another laughing terrible among the banners
              (*Four Zoas*, 101:47–8; 102:1–5, E 360)

---

[1] See Blunt, *Art of William Blake*, p. 98.

[2] London, 1710, p. 11. This passage (with the third quoted line omitted) is in Edward Bysshe's anthology, *The Art of English Poetry* (London, 1775), p. 213, an edition of which Blake owned.

The winepress of the wrath of God also appears in *Milton* (27:8, E 123) as the Wine-press of Los, 'call'd War on Earth', symbolizing the destruction which precedes the Last Judgement. This Wine-press which crushes 'human grapes' was assigned to Luvah in *The Four Zoas*, IX, but has been transferred to Los because it is through his imaginative perception that war and oppression are seen as the final definition of Wrath in history:

> The Wine-press on the Rhine groans loud, but all its central beams
> Act more terrific in the central Cities of the Nations
> Where Human Thought is crushd beneath the iron hand of Power.
> There Los puts all into the Press, the Opressor & the Opressed
> Together, ripe for the Harvest & Vintage & ready for the Loom.[1]

Pitt's function is, then, similar to that of the 'mighty Spirit' named Newton in *Europe*: each brings about a manifestation of error in some final form and so, inadvertently, brings on the Last Judgement. (Pitt's priestly vestment and his Buddhist halo[2] contribute further to the irony—he remains in saintly detachment from the results of his action.) The reaper and ploughman whom this Angel orders have been identified as Rintrah and Palamabron, the sons of Los who gather the human harvest in *Milton*. There were also such angelic figures on either side of the Spiritual Form of Napoleon. The destructive sword and the Wine-press of Los are portions of eternity too great for the eye of man, but they are indifferent to the identity of the hero who wields them.

---

[1] *Milton*, 25:3–7, E 120. The winepress of Luvah is described in Night IX, 135:28–39; 136:1–40; 137:1–4, E 389–90. The crushing of the 'Human Grapes' stands for the deaths of soldiers in the enormous wars which Blake regards as bringing about a consummation of history. 'They howl & writhe in shoals of torment in fierce flames consuming . . .' (136:22). Yet in the 'upper' world where this is seen as part of, or at least prelude to, the regeneration of Albion, there is joy and music. 'The ultimate world-war foretold in all Apocalypses', Damon remarks, 'seems to the Eternals like a village festival' (*William Blake*, p. 395). Blake thought the wars of his time were these ultimate world wars, which is why the symbol of the winepress of the wrath of God in Revelation seemed to him appropriate.

[2] Blunt, *Art of William Blake*, p. 38, calls attention to this.

The heroes who unknowingly serve the divine will are therefore depicted as parodies of the sublime, and so are their symbolic beasts. This will be made clear when we compare the *Pitt* and *Nelson* with several of Blake's other designs. We must first explain why the language of the *Descriptive Catalogue* leads the reader away from such a view.

'Blake's language in his description of these pictures', writes Schorer, '. . . is exactly as equivocal as the pictures themselves, and the equivocation is now so shrewd that probably he alone perceived the irony' (p. 174). The problem may be solved if we regard the equivocation of the *Catalogue* as distinct from the irony of the paintings. In wishing for a national commission to execute enormous frescoes of his heroes, Blake was not writing ironically. He did wish he could paint a companion monument to the then projected Naval Column, and he actually did engrave three designs for John Flaxman's *Letter To the Committee For Raising the Naval Pillar or Monument* (London, 1799), in which Flaxman proposed that

A statue might be raised like the Minerva in the Athenian citadel, whose aspect and size should represent the Genius of the Empire: its magnitude should equal the Colossus of Rhodes; its character should be Britannia Triumphant; it should be mounted on a suitable pedestal and basement; the pedestal might be decorated with the Heroes and Trophies of the Country, and the History of its Prowess inscribed upon the basement.   (pp. 7–8)

But Blake's own 'grand Apotheoses' would have one meaning to 'the nation, who is the parent of his heroes', while to the initiate few they would reveal their 'mythological and recondite meanings, where more is meant than meets the eye'.[1] The failure of communication between Blake and the public had been such that he could consider such a recourse. Even in his private correspondence, as Schorer has shown (pp. 171–2), Blake frequently employed veiled and private meanings which conveyed one impression to the correspondent while reserving another in the privacy of Blake's thought. In this manner Blake avoided trying the limits of his friend Butts

---

[1] 'Advertisement', E 517; *Descriptive Catalogue*, E 522.

and played the role of a harmless enthusiast for William Hayley. The fury of Blake's epigrams about Hayley is doubtless in reaction to the saccharine, pietistic tone Blake felt constrained to employ in the letters. (At the same time he recorded the 'eternal' nature of his previous difficulties with the Hermit of Felpham, but even if Hayley read *Milton* it is unlikely that he recognized himself as Satan trying to do the work of the true artist.) The *Descriptive Catalogue* only extends to the public the mode of communication, if it can be called that, which Blake frequently employed in his correspondence. The *Catalogue* turns the irony of the paintings it describes into equivocation.

3

I have suggested that the Pitt and Nelson paintings are parodies of the sublime. It will be useful to regard them as examples of one of the literary categories in Northrop Frye's *Anatomy of Criticism*—'demonic parody'.[1] A demonic parody caricatures the nature of the celestial world as, for example, the three-headed Satan at the centre of Dante's Hell caricatures the Trinity. The demonic could also be regarded as a grotesque imitation of the sublime.

We can bring out the element of parody in the *Nelson* by setting it beside two other well-known Blake designs. One of these is 'The Dance of Albion' (also known as 'Glad Day'), the other Plate 6 of the *Job* illustrations, showing Satan smiting Job with boils. The similarities among these three compositions can easily be seen. Each has at its centre a naked male figure with a halo, arms outstretched. The differences are significant. Albion represents the sublime of the human body, that 'human form divine' to which Blake attached so much artistic and religious importance. The limbs are taut, the right leg rises from the ground and seems about to bring the rest of the body with it. A halo of white radiance streams from and around the upper part of the figure. Nelson's bodily attitude is limp by comparison, the muscles undefined; the arms give an impression of passivity. Although

---

[1] Princeton, 1957, pp. 147–50.

the right leg is off to the side like Albion's, it is not in the
air but rests on a fold of Leviathan. The halo is rigidly
circular and emits flame rather than light. Most important,
perhaps, the genitals are discreetly veiled by a wisp of smoke
or cloud, in contrast to the complete nakedness of Albion:
'The head Sublime, the heart Pathos, the genitals Beauty,
the hands & feet Proportion.'[1]

'Art can never exist without Naked Beauty displayed.'[2]
Nelson is a parody of the sublime; Satan, a grotesque caricature, has scales, a circular halo, both feet on Job's supine
body, and no genitals at all. The texts for the first two
pictures brings out a further contrast between them. Albion's
reads:

> Albion rose from where he labourd at the Mill with Slaves
> Giving himself for the Nations he danc'd the dance of
> Eternal Death[3]   (E 660)

'Eternal Death' means the death of Selfhood that must precede regeneration—'I go to Eternal Death!' declares Blake's
Milton as he begins the symbolic journey that is to redeem
his past errors. In Blake's visionary conception, Albion rises
from the prison of Selfhood or mill of Satan to become part
of a regenerate human community. The opposite of Albion
'giving himself for the Nations' is Nelson guiding the monster
'in whose wreathings are infolded the Nations of the Earth'
(E 521). Crushed by British sea power, the nations will be
forced to give themselves for Albion. Just as Corporeal War
is to Blake a perversion of Mental War, man's occupations
in Eternity being 'War and Hunting',[4] and the spear and the
arrow symbols of thought and desire, so the 'hero' is a
demonic parody of a completely realized human identity.

Leviathan and Behemoth themselves are demonic parodies
of the sublime of energy. They are created by the Spectre of
Los in *Jerusalem* and are represented as grotesque caricatures in the *Job* series. The Lord's answer to Job with its
ultimate evocation of the two beasts was regarded as an

---

[1] 'Proverbs of Hell', E 37.   [2] 'The Laocoön', E 272.
[3] Cf. Milton's Samson, who also leaves the mill of slavery for a willing
sacrifice of self. (See Frye, *Fearful Symmetry*, pp. 362–3.)
[4] See *Milton*, 35:1–3, E 134.

expression of unequalled sublimity in the eighteenth century,
but Blake wrote his own commentary on Job in pictorial form,
and the fifteenth illustration has as its subject the limitations
of natural energy. Leviathan and Behemoth are seen enclosed in the mundane shell like goldfish in a bowl. They
appear to grin—'sharers', writes Milton O. Percival, 'in
the colossal joke of their success as realities'.[1] Somewhere
between such caricature and parody are two other designs:
the grinning Orc serpent of *Europe* and the quadrupedal
Nebuchadnezzar of *The Marriage*. Somewhere behind all
these is the innocuous-looking illustration to 'The Tyger.'[2]
Once more we have a spectrum of designs which shades from
the sublime of energy through ironic parody into grotesque
caricature, complementing the transitions of Blake's thought
regarding the nature of energy itself.

*   *   *

If Blake knew the engraved title-page of Hobbes's
Leviathan—and as he was a professional engraver, it is at
least likely that he did—he must have recognized it too as a
parody of the sublime. The illustration depicts Charles II as
a giant towering over a peaceful countryside; his outstretched
arms wield sword and crozier, and his body is made up of a
mass of tiny men. Over his head is written in Latin a verse
from Job: '*Non est potestas Super Terram quae Comparetur ei.*'
This king over all the children of pride is ironically analogous
to Blake's Christ, who is One and yet Many, comprising the
imaginations of all believers. Albion, too, is a composite of
humanity. The Leviathan giant, in contrast, is a Covering
Cherub—the Law which changes figurative significance to
corporeal command. While Blake conceives of mankind as a
single organism, Albion, Hobbes calls the state 'but an
artificial man'. Hobbes's definition of the imagination as
'decaying sense' is also peculiarly opposite to Blake's; in
fact, what Hobbes terms 'imagination' is what Blake calls
'Memory' or 'Phantasy' (for the producers of recollection and

---

[1] *Circle of Destiny*, p. 270.
[2] See John E. Grant, 'The Art and Argument of "The Tyger"', in *Discussions of William Blake*, ed. Grant (Boston, 1961), p. 75.

illusion, respectively).[1] 'Of Commonwealth', Part II of
Leviathan, is flanked by 'Of Man' and 'Of a Christian Commonwealth.' Thus the political philosophy proper is pre-
ceded by a definition of man which rests upon a mechanical
view of the imagination; and it is followed by a discussion of
political and religious institutions in the Bible which is
largely taken up with limiting the claims of prophecy. Post-
Biblical prophecy is denied any validity whatever. As can be
seen in his history of the English Civil Wars, entitled *Behemoth*, Hobbes distrusted modern prophets because some of
the seventeenth-century Dissenters had claimed the authority
of prophecy in disrupting the power of the Crown and its
Established Church. Even Biblical prophets had to pass two
tests: were their predictions proved authentic, and did they
adhere to the established religion? As Jonah would have
failed the first test, Hobbes declared:

> The book of Jonah is not properly a register of his prophecy;
> for that is contained in these few words, *Forty days and Nineveh
> shall be destroyed*; but a history, or narration of his frowardness and
> disputing God's commandments. . . .[2]

Blake's belief is again exactly the opposite, and the passage
on prophecy from his marginalia to Watson's *Apology* seems
once more appropriate:

> Prophets in the modern sense of the word have never existed
> Jonah was no prophet in the modern sense for his prophecy of
> Nineveh failed Every honest man is a Prophet he utters his opinion
> both of private & public matters Thus If you go on So the result is
> So He never says such a thing Shall happen let you do what you
> will. a Prophet is a Seer not an Arbitrary Dictator. . . .   (E 606–7)

Hobbes's politics depends upon a view of the world without
imagination, a world in which power must provide the sanc-
tions which truth cannot. Both he and Blake use the Leviathan
as a symbol of such a world, though with completely

---

[1] Frye observes that ' "Mental" and "intellectual" . . . are exact synonyms
of "imaginative" everywhere in Blake's work', while ' "fantasy" . . . relates
to the memory and its "spectres" ' (*Fearful Symmetry*, p. 19).

[2] *Leviathan*, ed. Michael Oakeshott, Blackwell's Political Texts (Oxford,
1946), p. 251.

different intentions. This lowest level of existence is called Ulro in the later prophecies; the *Pitt* and *Nelson* paintings are terrible visions of its demonic forces, cruel parodies of the sublime, of that integrated physical-spiritual existence Blake calls Eden. Life in the Leviathan world would become impossible were it not seen, as it were, from above as a phase preceding the regeneration of the human community. The organ of this prophetic perception which redeems man from seeing himself as entrapped in the coils of Leviathan is the Imagination, which has succeeded Energy in Blake's thought as the true sublime.

8

The Sublime of Imagination

However, phantasy [imagination] retains the structure and the tendencies of the psyche prior to its organization by the reality, prior to its becoming an 'individual' set off against other individuals. And by the same token, like the id to which it remains committed, imagination preserves the 'memory' of the subhistorical past when the life of the individual was the life of the genus, the image of the immediate unity between the universal and the particular under the rule of the pleasure principle. In contrast, the entire subsequent history of man is characterized by the destruction of this original unity. . . .

HERBERT MARCUSE: *Eros and Civilization*

The Nature of my Work is Visionary or Imaginative it is an Endeavour to Restore < what the Ancients calld > the Golden Age

Blake's Notebook (1810)

HAVING explored the lower world of Blake's symbolism, we now turn to that part of his universe which corresponds to Boehme's Higher Ternary, the Spiritual or Light-World, the Imagination. We have previously seen that Blake's concept of Imagination as symbolized by Los in the Lambeth books and in *Vala* is different from the conception we find in *The Four Zoas*. According to this later idea of Imagination, elaborated in *Milton* and *Jerusalem*, Los is not merely one of four faculties but is the creator of all human realities, just as in Coleridge's *Biographia* the primary Imagination is called 'the living Power and prime Agent of all human Perception' and 'a repetition in the finite mind of the eternal act of creation in the infinite I AM' (i. 202). Blake wrote: 'The Imagination is not a State: it is the Human Existence itself' (*Milton*, 32: 32). This Imagination is intuitive, and its knowing is grounded not in materials of sensation but in innate ideas.

It is constructive of Time and Space.[1] It receives in the form of prophetic vision messages, words, and images, from the unfallen Paradise within. The poet's 'great task' is

> To open the Eternal Worlds, to open the immortal Eyes
> Of Man inwards into the Worlds of Thought: into Eternity
> Ever expanding in the Bosom of God. the Human Imagination
>
>   (*Jerusalem*, 5 : 18–20, E 146)

Our study of the development of Blake's thought will conclude with an exposition of the symbolism of the Imagination in *Milton* and *Jerusalem*. Before this, we will trace the history of the concept of Imagination and will attempt to indicate the relation of Blake's concept to its most important or most representative antecedents. And, as Blake was not a formal philosopher but a poet and artist, we will begin with a discussion of 'Vision' in his imaginative experience.

1

From all that has been written about Blake's visions,[2] one fact emerges clearly: these visions were not hallucinations but neither were they fantasies—they were *seen*, but were not believed to be 'there' in the sense that physical objects are. 'The Prophets', wrote Blake, 'describe what they saw in Vision as real and existing men whom they saw with their imaginative and immortal organs; the Apostles the same; the clearer the organ the more distinct the object' (*Descriptive Catalogue*, E 532). Blake went on to say of his painting

---

[1] 'Demonstration Similitude & Harmony are Objects of Reasoning Invention Identity & Melody are Objects of Intuition' (Annotations to Reynolds, E 648). 'Creating Space, Creating Time according to the wonders Divine / Of Human Imagination . . .' (*Jerusalem*, 98 : 31–2, E 255).

[2] The best account is Damon's chapter ' "Spirits" and Their "Dictation" ', in *William Blake*, pp. 196–211. See also Mona Wilson, *The Life of William Blake*, pp. 65–71. I have purposely not drawn on Gilchrist in this part of the discussion because in many cases there is no way of distinguishing history from anecdote from folklore in Gilchrist's delightful accounts (see, e.g., i. 7 and 18). Attention should be called, however, to Gilchrist's extremely interesting chapter on the drawing of the Visionary Heads (i. 298–304) and to contemporary accounts by J. T. Smith, Allan Cunningham, Crabb Robinson, and others, all conveniently gathered in the Appendices to Symons's *William Blake*.

The Bard, from Gray: 'The painter of this work asserts that all his imaginations appear to him infinitely more perfect and more minutely organized than any thing seen by his mortal eye.' Blake's first biographer, Frederick Tatham, wrote that 'He always asserted that he had the power of bringing his imaginations before his mind's eye, so completely organized, and so perfectly formed . . . that while he copied the vision (as he called it) upon his plate or canvas, he could not err.'[1] Yet among all the friends and associates of Blake's later years, none doubted his sanity with the single exception of Henry Crabb Robinson, who appears to have been too literal-minded to understand Blake's mode of reference.[2] The others, including the young painters who gathered around him, seem never to have doubted Blake's claim that he really saw what he painted.[3] Blake himself clearly distinguished between such perception and memory:

> The spirit of Titian was particularly active, in raising doubts concerning the possibility of executing without a model, and when once he had raised the doubt, it became easy for him to snatch away the vision time after time, for when the Artist took his pencil, to execute his ideas, his power of imagination weakened so much, and darkened, that memory of nature and of Pictures of the various Schools possessed his mind, instead of appropriate execution, resulting from the inventions . . .   (E 537–8)

It is clear from this and other statements by Blake that he had a highly developed capacity for what is now called eidetic imagery, a capacity which a number of other artists and poets

---

[1] 'The Life of William Blake', in *The Letters of William Blake*, ed. Archibald G. B. Russell (London, 1906), p. 18.

[2] For example, consider the following remarks by Blake set down in Robinson's Diary: 'I have conversed with the Spiritual Sun. I saw him on Primrose-hill. He said "Do you take me for the Greek Apollo?" No I said that [& Blake pointed to the sky] that is the Greek Apollo. He is Satan' (*Blake, Coleridge, Wordsworth, Lamb, Etc.*, ed. Edith J. Morley (Manchester, 1922), p. 7). A few sentences later, Robinson remarks, '& when he is not referring to his Visions he talks sensibly & acutely.' Now, there was a sensible and acute meaning in what Blake had said—he was warning against the error of taking symbols literally—but he was also having fun at the expense of a literal-minded man. Robinson misses not only the meaning of the story but also the wit of it.

[3] See A. H. Palmer, *The Life and Letters of Samuel Palmer* (London, 1892), pp. 22–6.

have manifested. Longinus, for example, wrote of a line in Euripides: 'The Poet here actually saw the Furies with the Eyes of his Imagination, and has compell'd his Audience to see what he beheld himself.'[1] Henry Fuseli, defending the artist's right to invent from his own mind, speaks of 'that intuition into the sudden movements of nature, which the Greeks called φαντασίας, the Romans *visiones*, and we might circumscribe by the phrase of 'unpremeditated conceptions" the reproduction of associated ideas'.[2] Blake would of course have rejected Fuseli's associationist vocabulary, but the phenomenon described is a similar one.

Eidetic images are defined in E. R. Jaensch's classic monograph on the subject as

phenomena that take up an intermediate position between sensations and images. Like ordinary physiological after-images, they are always *seen* in the literal sense. They have this property of necessity and under all conditions, and share it with sensations. In other respects they can also exhibit the properties of images (*Vorstellungen*). In those cases in which the imagination has little influence, they are merely modified after-images, deviating from the norm in a definite way. . . . In the other limiting case, when the influence of the imagination is at its maximum, they are ideas that, like after-images, are projected outward and literally *seen*.[3]

Gardner Murphy writes of Blake and Goethe as eidetics who cultivated their imagery and lived largely in an eidetic world.[4] Wordsworth provides another obvious example. Coleridge, too, had this capacity, and it may be that the 'Vision in a Dream' of *Kubla Khan* was actually of the type we have been discussing, especially as such doubt has been cast on Coleridge's own account.[5] I introduce the term here not to invest Blake with the mantle of psychological prestige,

---

[1] *On the Sublime*, p. 40.
[2] *The Life and Writings of Henry Fuseli*, ed. John Knowles (London, 1831), ii. 145.
[3] *Eidetic Imagery* (New York, 1930), pp. 1–2.
[4] *Personality: a Biosocial Approach to Origins and Structure* (New York, 1947), pp. 393–4.
[5] See Elisabeth Schneider, *Coleridge, Opium, and Kubla Khan* (Chicago, 1953). For an interpretation of Coleridge's poetry which brings out his affinities to Blake, see John Beer, *Coleridge the Visionary* (London, 1959).

but because it serves three useful purposes. It reaffirms the fact that Blake was not speaking figuratively when he said he saw visions. It makes us aware of resemblances between Blake's concept of Imagination and those of Wordsworth and other poets who habitually employ a different kind of vocabulary. Most important, perhaps, it suggests that Blake's visions are related to other characteristics of his art—such as the analogical structure of *Jerusalem* and the counterpoint of text and image in this work—in being examples of 'autistic thinking', a mode of thought different from the rational processes of conscious life.

In his extremely interesting study *Imagination and Thinking*, Peter McKellar distinguishes between the two modes of thought as follows:

R-thinking ['reality-adjusted thinking'] characterizes sanity and waking consciousness in their more logical, realistic and prejudice-free moments. Crawshay-Williams (1947, p. 7) provides a useful definition of these processes as 'thinking specially adapted to the specific purpose of enabling us to deal successfully with the objective world and its phenomena, by forming correct opinions about these phenomena and about their causes and effects.' By contrast, A-thinking is characteristic of sleep and the hypnagogic state rather than waking consciousness; it is dependent upon mere association of ideas rather than upon logical connection and testing against reality. A-thinking is subject to intrusions of fantasy rather than to correction by accurate perceptual observation.[1]

A-thinking is characteristically metaphorical. It is the typical mode of thought among young children, primitive men, psychotics, and Romantic and symbolist poets in their poetry. What this has to teach us is *not* that poetry is atavistic, regressive, or mentally disturbed. Rather, A-thinking runs in a spectrum through all individuals[2] and all cultures; to attempt to rule it out completely would be as insane as to

[1] London, 1957, p. 5. McKellar later points out that the writer of the 'image-provoking words' of 'The Tyger' was himself subject to 'vivid visual experiences' (pp. 67–8).

[2] More than half the University of Aberdeen students interviewed by McKellar (p. 54) had experienced either a sense of *déjà vu* or hypnagogic images (perceived just before falling asleep). Over 21 per cent had experienced either hypnopompic imagery (between sleep and waking) or synaesthesia.

reject R-thinking. As Northrop Frye remarked in a lecture to the American Psychiatric Association, 'The world outside us, or physical nature, is a blind and mechanical order, hence if we merely accept its conditions we find ourselves setting up blind and mechanistic patterns of behaviour';[1] in this sense, a whole culture might be 'mad'. The crisis of John Stuart Mill could be taken as an example of the desiccation of a great mind by the unique concentration of its powers upon R-thinking; in Wordsworth's poetry he found the balm of thought as feeling.

The development of the capacity for eidetic imagery and other autistic powers in a person is at least in part a function of culture. Jaensch (pp. 9–10), observing a very high discrepancy in the incidence of eidetic imagery among German school children in different localities, discovered he could account for this according to whether a town had the traditional type of *Lernschule* or the new *Arbeitsschule*, in which much attention was given over to 'object lessons' involving the senses. The newer schools 'yielded an incomparably larger percentage of eidetics'—sometimes as many as 85–90 per cent. of the children tested in some *Arbeitsschule* classes had marked eidetic abilities. British schools in Blake's time were certainly of the *Lernschule* type, but fortunately he was sent to a drawing-school, then apprenticed to an engraver who set him to work sketching the sculptured tombs in Westminster Abbey. Thus his particular type of artistic ability was allowed to develop. Still, there was little place for A-thinking in the culture of Blake's day; hence Blake's 'madness'. It is at this point that Blake confronts the dominant philosophies of the eighteenth century. His conception of Imagination was derived from his own experience and not from reasoning about the subject, but he found that the reasoning of his time denied his experience.[2] 'They mock

---

[1] 'The Imaginative and the Imaginary', *American Journal of Psychiatry*, cxix (1962), 296.

[2] McKellar found that those subjects who had not experienced autistic phenomena tended to deny its very possibility in others. The writer, having experienced both hypnagogic and hypnopompic imagery, can confirm this. Those who do not immediately understand from their own experience what these images are like will frequently insist that 'it must have been a dream',

Inspiration & Vision', he wrote of Bacon, Newton, Locke, Burke, and Reynolds. 'Inspiration & Vision was then & now is & I hope will always Remain my Element my Eternal Dwelling place. how can I then hear it Contemnd without returning Scorn for Scorn—' (Annotations to Reynolds's *Discourses*, E 650).

2

The last remark we have quoted reminds us that Blake was an unschooled but not an unlearned man. He was aware that his view of the Imagination did not square with the philosophies dominant in his day, and he recognized the need for defining an alternative tradition. Although his convictions about the Imagination derived from experience and practice, they were not expressed in an intellectual vacuum. Blake almost certainly had read the major works of Plato and some of those of Aristotle; he had some familiarity with the Neoplatonists (via Taylor's translations) and probably with the Cambridge Platonists as well. In addition to the English works mentioned in the note, we know he read Bacon's *Essays* and Berkeley's *Siris*; among works on the arts, besides Reynolds's *Discourses*, works by Winckelmann, Gilpin, Barry, and Cennini.[1] This is, moreover, a minimal list, limited by our still fragmentary knowledge of Blake. The man who annotated Reynolds's *Discourses* so voluminously was not indifferent to ideas. Before turning to the theme of Imagination within Blake's later works, we ought to consider what, for our purposes, the most important conceptions of the Imagination have been—important either in that Blake found them so, or in that they are so representative of a given era or style of thought that any conception of the Imagination would have to be affected by them. In this survey, we will leave aside for the moment conceptions of prophetic Imagination, as these constitute a special category and should be discussed together.

despite one's assurance of the distinctly different type of imagery involved. Raising such a situation to the nth power will perhaps convey something of Blake's dilemma in arguing for the Realities of Imagination.

[1] On books owned by Blake, see Keynes, 'Blake's Library', *TLS*, 6 November 1959, p. 648; and Bentley and Nurmi, *A Blake Bibliography*, pp. 195–212.

Plato's general view of Imagination is described by G. S. Brett in his *History of Psychology* (London, 1912):

> Imagination is a mental activity in a sensuous form; sensation, memory, and opinion are all accompanied by an imagination. The word Phantasy (φαντασία) in Plato suggests the unreal as opposed to the real; the art of phantastic (ἡ φανταστική) is the art of producing appearances; so, being concerned more with the cognitive value of mental processes than their intrinsic characteristics, Plato pays little attention to this power of producing unreal appearances. There is a science of imitations called 'representation' (ἡ εἰκαστική) which aims at truth more than the art of fantastic: to this the preference is given, and among the cognitive faculties we shall find conjectural representation (εἰκασία) included. (i. 78)

Phantasy is usually considered by Plato to be irrational and untrustworthy, while in the Divided Line of the *Republic* 'representation' is the lowest form of cognition, having to do with images of images. The highest form of cognition here is intellection, which apprehends Form. Such apprehension may seize on an 'intellectual image', but what Plato has in mind here are mathematical entities.[1] Blake gives the notion of the intellectual apprehension of Form his own characteristic expression when he writes '. . . the Oak dies as well as the Lettuce but Its Eternal Image & Individuality never dies. but renews by its seed. just [*as*] ⟨so⟩ the Imaginative Image returns [*according to*] ⟨by⟩ the seed of Contemplative Thought' (E 545). 'Although he finds fault with the Platonic method,' comments Peter Fisher, 'he [Blake] is in agreement with what he is convinced Plato is actually talking about: the forms or ideas of eternal existence.'[2]

The Neoplatonist attitude towards imagination is ambivalent. For Plotinus, the imagination is the meeting-place of the higher and lower parts of the soul. 'Thought is apprehended by the imagination; the notion (νόημα) at first indivisible and implicit being conveyed to it by an explicit discourse (λόγος). . . . That which apprehends thought apprehends

---

[1] See Livingston Welch, *Imagination and Human Nature* (London, 1935), p. 28.

[2] *Valley of Vision*, p. 50; see also Harper, *The Neoplatonism of William Blake*, p. 108.

perceptions also.'[1] This is a psychological conception of consciousness, and in this sense could be compared to Blake's idea of Imagination as 'Human Existence Itself'. But the comparison would be only that, as for Plotinus, consciousness is not the highest form of thought, being above sense but below pure intellect, and the creative power of the artist lies in Reason, not Phantasy. Still, in Plotinus's mysticism of Beauty there is, latently, a constructive or creative view of Imagination; and this view anticipates a good deal of Romantic poetic theory and practice. Blake could have come across it in Thomas Taylor's *Restoration of the Platonic Theology*:

... those who are totally filled with the intoxicating nectar of divine contemplation, since beauty diffuses itself through every part of their souls do not become spectators alone. For in this case the spectator is no longer external to the spectacle: but he who acutely perceives, contains the object of his perception in the depths of his own essence; though while possessing, he is often ignorant that he possesses. For he who beholds any thing as external, beholds it as something visible, and because he wishes to perceive it attended with distance. . . . . It is requisite we should transfer the divine spectacle into ourselves, and behold it as one, and as the same with our essence: just as if any one hurried away by the vigorous impulse of some god, whether Apollo or one of the Muses, should procure in himself the intuition of the god; since in the secret recesses of his own essence, he will behold the divinity himself. . . . But it is requisite that the soul which is about to perceive a divinity of this kind, should possess a certain figure of his nature, and assiduously persevere, while it endeavours perspicuously to know him; and thus well understanding the importance of its pursuit, and trusting it is about to enter on the most blessed vision, should profoundly merge itself in contemplation, till instead of a spectator, it may become another specimen of the object of its intuition; such as it came from thence, abundantly shining with intellectual conceptions.[2]

Here, although the term 'imagination' is not used, is an antecedent of that Romantic extension of consciousness by

[1] Thomas Whittaker, *The Neo-Platonists*, 2nd ed. (Cambridge, 1918), p. 51.

[2] *The Philosophical and Mathematical Commentaries of Proclus on the First Book of Euclid's Elements* (London, 1792 (1788–9)), ii. 262.

which, as in Keats's 'Nightingale', we become what we behold
and our perceptions are temporarily raised to another
level of existence. This other level, in both Keats and Blake,
is the realm of Art. However, the Neoplatonists do not
usually take such a view toward art itself, owing to their
equivocal attitude toward imagination, which they have
situated between the senses and the intellect. An exception
is Synesius, who conceives of a possibility of intuitive perception through the imagination (see Taylor, *Restoration*,
pp. 269–70). Augustine, who argued against Synesius's
view of phantasy, made a distinction between the sensory
image and the reproductive imagination.[1] The imagination
could make new combinations from fragments of memory,
but it could not create. This is a view very much in accord
with the Aristotelian one which dominated the later Middle
Ages.

Aristotle in *De Anima* defines imagination as 'the process
by which an image is presented to us'. Though different from
perception and thought, imagination 'does not occur without
perception, and without imagination there is no belief'.[2]
We may also construct a single image from a number of
perceptual phantasms. The imagination is therefore important epistemologically and psychologically, but it is a passive
and reproductive function, producing images from sensation
or memory and combining these materials into new images.
This latter function was by some medieval philosophers
distinguished as phantasy.[3] Aquinas gives both terms the
meaning of a power which retains sensible forms: 'Phantasy
or imagination is as it were a storehouse of forms received
through the senses.'[4] This is, with some few exceptions,[5]

---

[1] See Murray Wright Bundy, *The Theory of Imagination in Classical and Medieval Thought*, Univ. of Ill. Stud. in Lang. and Lit., xii (1927), 158–9.

[2] *Aristotle On the Soul, Parva Naturalia, On Breath*, ed. W. S. Hett (Cambridge, Mass., 1957), pp. 159, 157 resp.

[3] See Bundy, p. 194.   [4] Ibid., p. 217.

[5] One exception is the instruction of Will by 'Imaginatif' in Passus XII of *Piers the Plowman*, on which see Morton W. Bloomfield,*Piers Plowman as a Fourteenth-century Apocalypse* (New Brunswick, N.J., 1961), pp. 170–4. Another, notes Bundy (p. 205), is in the *Benjamin Minor* of Richard of St. Victor. In Richard's allegory of the mind, Rachel (Reason) keeps contact with the outer world through her handmaid, Bilhah (Imagination). Bilhah has

the typical medieval view whether or not a distinction is made between the two terms. In *The Divine Comedy*, however, we find a view of Imagination (*alta fantasia*) which transcends Aristotelian psychology. Blake read and annotated Dante from a Protestant and republican point of view, complaining that 'the Goddess Nature ⟨Memory⟩ ⟨is⟩ his Inspirer & not ⟨Imagination⟩ the Holy Ghost' (E 668); but in the symbolism of his illustrations to Dante, particularly in the figures of Virgil and St. John the Evangelist,[1] Blake shows an awareness that embedded in the dreams, visions, and symbolism of the *Comedy* is a concept of Imagination similar to his own.

Renaissance theory did not build on what elements of a constructive view of imagination there were in medieval thought, but instead developed the synthesis of Neo-Aristotelian and Neoplatonist psychology which we have already sketched out in Chapter 4. A standard treatise on the subject is *On the Imagination* (1500) by Gianfrancesco Pico della Mirandola. Pico defines imagination as a

motion of the soul which actual sensation generates . . . a power of the soul which out of itself produces forms . . . a force related to all the powers . . . a faculty of assimilating all other things to itself—all or a very great part of which has been thoroughly investigated and ascertained by the Peripatetic philosophers and by the Platonic also.[2]

Imagination is necessary to man because it connects the lower soul with the higher:

What communication would the rational part have with the irrational, if there were not phantasy intermediate, somehow to prepare for reason the inferior nature, and to set up this nature to be cognized? For when the imagination has received the impressions

---

two children—Dan, who 'knows nothing save through the corporeal', and Naphtalim, who 'rises through visible forms to the intelligence of the invisible'. Bundy calls Naphtalim 'the first allegorical embodiment in literature of the symbolic imagination'.

[1] See Albert S. Roe, *Blake's Illustrations to the Divine Comedy* (Princeton, 1953), pp. 185–6.

[2] Trans. Harry Caplan, Cornell Studies in English, xvi (New Haven, 1930), p. 33.

of objects from the senses, it retains them within itself, and, having rendered them more pure, furnishes them to the active intellect. . . . the potential intellect later is informed and perfected by means of these intelligible images. (p. 41)

But this very intermediacy, as in the Neoplatonist tradition, makes the imagination suspect: Pico's seventh chapter is 'On the numerous Evils which come from the Imagination'. These evils result from Imagination's getting out of the control of reason and being carried away by the senses and irrational appetites. 'As for the beasts, it is not from any fault in them that they are brutes, but because of their proper form; while it is from his phantasy, which he has set up to be his princess and mistress, that man becomes a brute in life and character. . .' (p. 45). The only exception to Pico's distrust of imaginative activity independent of reason is to be found in the single paragraph (p. 57) he devotes to true (Biblical) prophecy. He does not discuss the Imagination as a source of artistic creativity.

Another typical Renaissance view of Imagination, this time with the artistic role of the faculty considered, may be found in Act V of *A Midsummer Night's Dream*. Duke Theseus' speech is a congeries of Renaissance commonplaces about the Imagination. This power, here synonymous with fantasy, is a producer of chimeras which have no relation to reality.

> Lovers and madmen have such seething brains,
> Such shaping fantasies, that apprehend
> More than cool reason ever comprehends. (i. 4–6)

According to Renaissance psychology, Reason 'comprehends' concepts abstracted from sensation; fantasy 'apprehends'— draws into the mind's eye—images of desire or fear.

> Such tricks hath strong imagination,
> That, if it would apprehend some joy,
> It comprehends some bringer of that joy;
> Or in the night, imagining some fear,
> How easy is a bush supposed a bear! (18–22)

This Renaissance view is merely an extension of medieval descriptive psychology, of which Bundy writes:

When the analytical tendency of the Middle Ages encloses imagination or phantasy within the confines of a cell or compartment of the brain, there is a tendency to ignore the participation of this faculty in the higher processes of cognition, and to confine it to a lower sphere quite as rigidly as did the Platonic dualism. It is little wonder that the common contrast was between imagination and reason, phantasy and intellect.   (p. 180)

So to Theseus poetry is something very much like Bacon's 'feigned history': the poets may deliver a golden world out of Nature's brazen one, but this provides only the illusory pleasures of wish-fulfilment fantasy:

> And as imagination bodies forth
> The forms of things unknown, the poet's pen
> Turns them to shapes and gives to airy nothing
> A local habitation and a name.   (14–17)

Blake objected to the argument of this passage; says Gilchrist:

> Blake saw spiritual appearances by the exercise of a special faculty—that of imagination—using the word in the then unusual, but true sense, of a faculty which busies itself with the subtler realities, *not* with fictions. He, on this ground, objected even to Shakespeare's expression—'And gives to airy *nothing* | A local habitation and a name.' He said the things imagination saw were as much realities as were gross and tangible facts.   (i. 364)

Where someone had inscribed the Shakespeare passage in a copy of Swedenborg's *Heaven and Hell*, Blake remarked: 'Thus Fools quote Shakespeare The Above is Theseus's opinion Not Shakespeares You might as well quote Satans blasphemies from Milton & give them as Miltons Opinions' (E 590). In *Milton*, Blake gives his own, corrected version of the passage:

> Some Sons of Los surround the Passions with porches of iron & silver
> Creating form & beauty around the dark regions of sorrow,
> Giving to airy nothing a name and a habitation
> Delightful! with bounds to the Infinite putting off the Indefinite
> Into most holy forms of Thought: (such is the power of inspiration)
> They labour incessant; with many tears & afflictions:
> Creating the beautiful House for the piteous sufferer.[1]

---

[1] 28:1–7, E 124. See Damon, *William Blake*, pp. 421–2.

It might well be argued that the view Shakespeare's *play* takes is closer to Blake's than to Theseus's, as indicated by Hippolyta's reply to the Duke and the stage direction that follows it:

> But all the story of the night told over,
> And all their minds transfigured so together,
> More witnesseth than fancy's images
> And grows to something of great constancy;
> But, howsoever, strange and admirable.   (23–7)

As if in proof of her words, the lovers enter. Still, the transfiguration they have undergone in the soft moony night that Blake calls Beulah cannot be explained in terms of 'fancy's images'. The imagination cannot as yet be compared with Adam's dream. Lacking a constructive view of Imagination and of art, Renaissance psychology must leave it a mystery.

Milton, the last great poet to use the Renaissance synthesis, already anachronistic in his day, has a view of imagination similar to Theseus's, as can be seen in Adam's explanation of Eve's dream in Book V of *Paradise Lost*:

> . . . . But know that in the Soule
> Are many lesser Faculties that serve
> Reason as chief; among these Fansie next
> Her office holds; of all external things,
> Which the five watchful Senses represent,
> She forms Imaginations, Aerie shapes,
> Which Reason joyning or disjoyning, frames
> All what we affirm or what deny, and call
> Our knowledge or opinion; then retires
> Into her private Cell when Nature rests.
> Oft in her absence mimic Fansie wakes
> To imitate her; but misjoyning shapes,
> Wilde work produces oft, and most in dreams,
> Ill matching words and deeds long past or late.
> (100–13)

Once more fancy is distrusted because of its freedom. Milton gives to Reason the functions Blake will assign Imagination, including intuition. In the Renaissance, the imagination is still being judged by moral and not by aesthetic standards. However, it is interesting that here, too, the poem undermines the orthodox explanation of the speech—Satan did, after all, visit Eve in form of a toad.

If we turn from the exponents of the Renaissance synthesis to those of the New Philosophy, we find a conception of imagination different in some respects from the previous one, but for Blake's purposes no more useful. Livingston Welch writes: 'Both the theorists of art and the rationalistic inter-preters of the new science repeat Platonic estimates of the role of imagination; and the latter in exploring its dangers are even more hostile than the medieval Augustinians, who had largely compromised with Aristotle on sense-experi-ence and its mechanisms' (p. 47). One such Platonic estimate may be found in a passage of Bacon's which Blake quotes with seeming approval in his letter to Dr. Trusler: ' "Sense sends over to Imagination before Reason have judged, & Reason sends over to Imagination before the Decree can be acted." See Advancem^t of Learning, Part 2, P. 47 of first Edition.'[1] Such a description might have done well enough for the faculty psychology of *Vala*, but it is hardly adequate to Blake's later concept of Imagination, which is in fact alluded to for the first time in this very letter:

But to the Eyes of the Man of Imagination, Nature is Imagination itself. As a man is, So he Sees. As the Eye is formed, such are its Powers. You certainly Mistake, when you say that the Visions of Fancy are not to be found in This World. To Me This World is all One continued Vision of Fancy or Imagination, & I feel Flatter'd when I am told so. What is it sets Homer, Virgil & Milton in so high a rank of Art? Why is the Bible more Entertaining & In-structive than any other book? Is it not because they are addressed to the Imagination, which is Spiritual Sensation, & but mediately to the Understanding or Reason? Such is True Painting, and such was alone valued by the Greeks & the best modern Artists.   (K 793–4)

The quotation from Bacon, so incongruous with this notion of intuitive Imagination, 'Spiritual Sensation', follows. Blake

---

[1] K 794. The Revd. Dr. Trusler, author of *The Way to Be Rich and Respect-able*, had not been satisfied with Blake's execution of an artistic commission (according to K 926, the water-colour 'Malevolence'). This letter is Blake's defence of his art. Perhaps he thought that a quotation from Bacon would be appropriate to the spiritual condition of the recipient.

must have known this, for in the same paragraph of the *Advancement* that he quotes from, Bacon says: 'And again, in all persuasions that are wrought by eloquence, and other impressions of like nature, which do paint and disguise the true appearance of things, the chief recommendation unto Reason is from the Imagination.'[1] Here we are back to the untrustworthiness of imagination as a means of knowledge. Later, in discussing the function of imagination in rhetoric, Bacon makes plain his conception of it as a potential ally of reason in a war against feeling:

> Reason would become captive and servile, if eloquence of persuasions did not practise and win the imagination from the affections' part, and contract a confederacy between the reason and imagination against the affections; for the affections themselves carry ever an appetite to good, as reason doth. The difference is, . . . reason beholdeth the future and sum of time. And therefore the present filling the imagination more, reason is commonly vanquished; but after that force of eloquence and persuasion hath made things future and remote appear as present, then upon the revolt of the imagination reason prevaileth.[2]

The model for this functional analysis is of course the tripartite soul of Plato's *Republic*, with imagination corresponding to the 'spirited' part that must be enlisted, in the self as in the State, in the service of reason against desire.

By Descartes and his followers imagination is considered an aid to understanding but decidedly subordinate to it. 'The understanding is indeed alone capable of perceiving the truth, but yet it ought to be aided by imagination, sense and memory, lest perchance we omit any expedient that lies within our power.'[3] As in the older view, imagination is a useful power only as it contributes to reasoning, but with the difference that reasoning itself has become in its highest form mathematical. Independent imaginative activity is as much mistrusted by the Cartesians as it was by the Aristotelians and Neoplatonists: '. . . Neither our imagination nor our senses

[1] *Advancement of Learning*, ed. G. W. Kitchin (London, 1958), p. 121.
[2] Ibid., pp. 147–8.
[3] *The Direction of the Mind*, Rule xii, in *Descartes Selections*, ed. Ralph M. Eaton (New York, 1927), p. 82.

can ever assure us of anything, if our understanding does not intervene.'[1]

Descartes [writes Ernst Cassirer] exerts himself to the utmost to free it [geometrical method] from the limitations of intuition and to make it independent of the obstacles which beset the 'imagination.' The result of this philosophical exertion was analytical geometry, whose essential accomplishment consists in its discovery of a method by which all intuitive relations among figures can be represented and exhaustively determined in exact numerical relationships. Thus Descartes reduces 'matter' to 'extension' and physical body to pure space; however, space in Cartesian epistemology is not subject to the conditions of sensory experience and of the 'imagination' but to the conditions of pure reason, to the conditions of logic and arithmetic. This criticism of the faculties of sense and imagination, which is introduced by Descartes, is taken up and extended by Malebranche. The entire first part of his chief work *Inquiry concerning Truth* . . . is devoted to this task. Here again the imagination appears not as a way to the truth but as the source of all the delusions to which the human mind is exposed. . . . To keep the imagination in check and to regulate it deliberately, is the highest goal of all philosophical criticism.[2]

The limits of imagination are emphasized in such a way by Robert Boyle in his controversy with Henry More on the subject of spirit:

When I say that spirit is incorporeal substance . . . if he should answer, that when he hears the words incorporeal substance, he imagines some aerial or other very thin, subtil, transparent body, I shall reply, that this comes from a vicious custom he has brought himself to, of imagining something whenever he will conceive anything, though of a nature incapable of being truly represented by any image in the fancy. . . . Because the use of imagining, whenever we would conceive things, is so stubborn an impediment to the free actings of the mind, in cases that require pure intellection, it will be very useful, if not necessary, to accustom ourselves not to be startled or frighted with every thing that exceeds or confounds the imagination, but by degrees to train up the mind to consider notions that surpass the imagination and yet are demonstrable by reason.[3]

---

[1] *On Method*, in *Selections*, p. 34.

[2] *The Philosophy of the Enlightenment* (Boston, 1962), pp. 282–3.

[3] Quoted by Burtt in *Metaphysical Foundations of Modern Physical Science*, pp. 176–7.

Despite what Boyle implies, More had no higher notion of imagination than he did; their dispute was about the nature of spirit, which More had argued could be extended. More's conception of imagination (phantasie), as bodied forth in the form of almost unreadable Spenserians, is merely the familiar Renaissance one, now about to be eclipsed by both the rationalistic and the associationist psychologies:

> Phansy's th'impression of those forms that flit
> In this low life: They oft continue long,
> Whenas our spright more potently is hit
> By their incursions and appulses strong,
> Like heated water, though a while but hung
> On fiercer fire, an hot impression
> Long time retains; so forms more stoutly flung
> Against our spright make deep insculption;
> Long time it is till their clear abolition.
>
> Hence springeth that which men call memory,
> When outward object doth characterize
> Our inward *common spright*; or when that we
> From our own soul stir up clear phantasies
> Which be our own elicited *Idees*,
> Springing from our own centrall life, by might
> Of our strong *Fiat* as oft as we please.
> With these we seal that under grosser spright,
> Make that our note-book, there our choisest notions write.[1]

To the Cambridge Platonist, the deep truth is imageless:

> All the five senses, Phansie, Memorie,
> We feel their work, distinguish and compare,
> Find out their natures by the subtiltie
> Of sifting reason. Then they objects are
> Of th'understanding, bear no greater share
> In this same act then objects wont to do.
> They are two realties distinguish'd clear
> One from the other, as I erst did show.
> She knows that spright, that spright our soul can never know.[2]

[1] *Psychathanasia, or The Immortality of the Soul*, in *The Complete Poems of Dr. Henry More*, ed. Alexander B. Grosart (Edinburgh, 1878), p. 74.
[2] Ibid., p. 75.

Again, Cudworth writes:

> . . . the Atheists pretend, that there is a feigning power in the soul, whereby it can make ideas and conceptions of nonentities; as of a golden mountain, or a centaur: and that by this an idea of God might be framed, though there be no such thing. Answer: that all the feigning power of the soul consisteth only in compounding ideas of things, that really exist apart, but not in that conjunction. The mind cannot make any new conceptive cogitation which was not before; as the painter or limner cannot feign foreign colours.[1]

What he and his like called the 'Imagination' [writes Basil Willey of John Smith and the other Cambridge Platonists] is the image-making faculty—a thing of earthly rather than heavenly affinity—which continually throws up a stream of phantoms which come between the mind and the object of contemplation. Here on earth we see but in a glass darkly, not *in speculo lucido*: 'Our own *Imaginative Powers*, which are perpetually attending the highest acts of our Souls, will be breathing a gross dew upon the pure Glass of our Understandings, and so sully and besmear it, that we cannot see the Image of the Divinity sincerely in it.' Imagination, according to this view, is a weakness incident to the flesh; it must be transcended as far as may be, or used, if at all, only to body forth what eye hath not seen, nor ear heard.[2]

Hobbes, at variance both with the dualism of the Cartesians and with the Cambridge Platonists' notion of 'plastic spirit'— to him mind, too, is *res extensa*—has a view of imagination which at times seems more negative than either of theirs:

> But for those idols of the brain, which represent bodies to us, where they are not, as in a looking-glass, in a dream, or to a distempered brain waking, they are, as the apostle saith generally of all idols, nothing; nothing at all, I say, there where they seem to be; and in the brain itself, nothing but tumult, proceeding either from the action of the objects, or from the disorderly agitation of the organs of our sense. And men, that are otherwise employed, than to search into their causes, know not of themselves, what to call them. . . .
>
> (*Leviathan*, p. 256)

In his *Human Nature*, Hobbes defines imagination as '*conception remaining, and by little and little decaying from and*

---

[1] *The True Intellectual System of the Universe* (London, 1820), iv. 498.
[2] *The Seventeenth Century Background*, p. 141.

after the act of sense'.[1] The imagination is a creator of dreams, 'phantasms' (after-images), and 'fictions', but all of these are 'idols' with no relation to reality.

As when the *water*, or any liquid thing moved at once by *divers* movements, receiveth *one* motion compounded of them all; so also the *brain* or spirit therein... composeth an imagination of *divers* conceptions that appeared single to the sense. As for example, the sense sheweth at one time the figure of a *mountain*, and at another time the colour of *gold*; but the imagination afterwards hath them both at once in a *golden mountain*. From the same cause it is, there appear unto us *castles* in the *air*, *chimeras*, and other monsters which are *not* in *rerum natura*, *but* have been conceived by the sense in pieces at several times. And this composition is that which we commonly call *fiction* of the mind. (*Works*, iv. 11)

Yet in Hobbes's 'Answer to the Preface to *Gondibert*' there is a different emphasis. Here Hobbes asserts that Fancy in the service of 'true philosophy' has produced great benefits to mankind, and has even taken the place of philosophy where it was wanting:

All that is beautiful or defensible in building; or marvellous in engines and instruments of motion; whatsoever commodity men receive from the observations of the heavens, from the description of the earth, from the account of time, from walking on the seas; and whatsoever distinguisheth the civility of Europe, from the barbarity of the American savages; is the workmanship of fancy, but guided by the precepts of true philosophy. But where these precepts fail, as they have hitherto failed in the doctrine of moral virtue, there the architect Fancy must take the philosopher's part upon herself. (*Works*, iv. 449–50)

This high view of fancy appears somewhat different from Hobbes's usual one, which we find elsewhere in the same essay: 'Time and education beget experience; experience begets memory; memory begets judgment and fancy; judgment begets the strength and structure, and fancy begets the ornaments of a poem. The ancients therefore fabled not absurdly, in making Memory the mother of the Muses' (p. 449). It is this more characteristic definition of Hobbes's that

[1] *The English Works of Thomas Hobbes*, ed. Sir William Molesworth (London, 1840) (hereafter cited as *Works*), iv. 9.

we find echoed in Dryden's famous characterization of 'Wit writing' as

the faculty of imagination in the writer, which, like a nimble spaniel, beats over and ranges through the field of memory, till it springs the quarry it hunted after; or, without metaphor, which searches over all the memory for the species or ideas of those things which it designs to represent.[1]

Though Hobbes praises Davenant for not having invoked the Muse as do other poets, he insinuates that he does so because the notion of inspiration is a false and foolish one 'by which a man enabled to speak wisely from the principles of nature, and his own meditation, loves rather to be thought to speak by inspiration, like a bagpipe' (*Works*, iv. 448). An exception is made, as in *Leviathan*, for Biblical prophecy, but equivocally.[2] Blake, in contrast, holds Milton's view that 'A work of Genius is a Work "Not to be obtain'd by the Invocation of Memory & her Syren Daughters. but by Devout prayer to that Eternal Spirit. who can enrich with all utterance & knowledge & sends out his Seraphim with the hallowed fire of his Altar to touch & purify the lips of whom he pleases"'.[3]

3

Locke sank into a swoon;
The Garden died;
God took the spinning-jenny
Out of his side.

These four gnomic lines by Yeats[4] epitomize Blake's own arguments against the dominant world-view of the eighteenth

---

[1] Preface to *Annus Mirabilis*, in *Essays of John Dryden*, ed. W. P. Ker (Oxford, 1900), p. 14.

[2] Hobbes says he will not condemn the 'heathen custom' of invoking the Muse, 'For their poets were their divines; had the name of prophets; excercised amongst the people a kind of spiritual authority; would be thought to speak by a divine spirit; have their works which they writ in verse (the divine style) pass for the word of God, and not of man, and to be hearkened to with reverence. Do not the divines, excepting the style, do the same, and by us that are of the same religion cannot justly be reprehended for it?' (*Works*, iv. 447–8).

[3] Annotations to Reynolds, E 635.

[4] 'Fragments', *Collected Poems*, p. 240.

century. In a demonic parody of the creation of Eve, the universe-as-machine comes into being, and man awakes to find not Truth as in Keats's simile, but 'dark Satanic Mills'— what Owen Barfield has called 'the mechanomorphic collective representations which constitute the Western world to-day'.[1] In Blake's own words,

> I turn my eyes to the Schools & Universities of Europe
> And there behold the Loom of Locke whose Woof rages dire
> Washd by the Water-wheels of Newton. black the cloth
> In heavy wreathes folds over every Nation; cruel Works
> Of many Wheels I view, wheel without wheel, with cogs tyrannic
> Moving by compulsion each other: not as those in Eden: which
> Wheel within Wheel, in freedom revolve in harmony & peace.[2]

The cloth spun by this great textile mill is the garment of Generation, the Philosophy of Five Senses that covers up spiritual vision or Imagination. The Lockian epistemology may have in some ways prepared the way for an aesthetic of imagination by transferring the locus of reality to the perceiving mind,[3] but Blake saw in Locke's model of the mind as a camera obscura and in Newton's idea of the universe as God's sensorium images of hell, Ulro; 'The same dull round even of a univer[s]e would soon become a mill with complicated wheels.'[4]

Much more congenial to Blake's thought is the philosophy of Berkeley, with its attack upon the universe as mechanism and its refutation of the notions of absolute space and time. Yet Berkeley's concept of imagination is much like the Neoplatonists' and Bacon's. 'Sense supplies images to memory. These become subjects for fancy to work upon. Reason considers and judges of the imaginations. And these acts of reason become new objects to the understanding. In this scale, each lower faculty is a step that leads to one above it.'[5] Blake's marginalia on *Siris* have a curious relation to

---

[1] *Saving the Appearances* (London, 1957), p. 52.

[2] *Jerusalem*, 15:14–20, E 157. The contrasting wheels are of course the visionary ones of Ezek. 1:15–21.

[3] See Ernest Lee Tuveson, *Imagination as a Means of Grace* (Berkeley and Los Angeles, 1960), p. 165.

[4] *There Is No Natural Religion* [b] (*c.* 1788), E 2.

[5] *Siris*, par. 303, *The Works of George Berkeley Bishop of Cloyne*, eds. A. A. and T. E. Jessop (London, 1953), v. 140. The date given by Keynes for Blake's

Berkeley's text—he is not attacking Berkeley as he does Bacon or Reynolds—but, rather, is carrying the thought to a point where the Bishop does not wish to go. 'God knoweth all things as pure mind or intellect', Berkeley wrote, 'but nothing by sense, nor in nor through a sensory. Therefore to suppose a sensory of any kind—whether space or any other— in God, would be very wrong, and lead us into false conceptions of His nature' (pp. 134–5). 'Imagination', adds Blake, 'or the Human Eternal Body in Every Man', and to Berkeley's assertion that God has no body, Blake adds 'Imagination or the Divine Body in Every Man' (E 652). The rest of his annotations to *Siris* are similar in content to these. Perhaps the most interesting is Blake's comment on paragraph 292 (pp. 135–6), where Berkeley says,

> Natural phenomena are only natural appearances. They are, therefore, such as we see and perceive them. Their real and objective natures are, therefore, the same—passive without anything active, fluent and changing without anything permanent in them. However, as these make the first impressions, and the mind takes her first flight and spring, as it were, by resting her foot on these objects, they are not only first considered by all men, but most considered by most men. They and the phantoms that result from those appearances, the children of imagination grafted upon sense— such for example as pure space (Sect. 270)—are thought by many the very first in existence and stability, and to embrace and comprehend all other beings.

Blake himself held a similar doctrine—that the phenomena are dependent upon Mind active in perception—but for him the expression 'children of imagination' had a meaning other than it did for Berkeley. To show this, he underlined these words in Berkeley's text and added:

> The All in Man The Divine Image or Imagination
> The Four Senses are the Four Faces of Man & the Four Rivers
> of the Water of Life   (E 653)

annotations to this work is 1820, but the reason given is merely the coincidence of the opinions expressed with those of the Laocoon aphorisms (K 923). Blackstone (*English Blake*, p. 337) has argued that Blake may have read *Siris* much earlier than this, pointing out that 'Newton', 'particles of light', and 'Democritus', occur on a single page of Berkeley's book and are also conflated in Blake's Notebook poem 'Mock on Mock on Voltaire Rousseau' (E 468–9).

What Blake is saying here is that if you were to take Berkeley as far as Berkeley took Locke, and in the same direction, you would arrive at an analogy between the world as an idea in the mind of God and the work of art as an image in the mind of the artist. Artistic activity would then become a form of intuitive perception. But

> Berkeley [Yeats wrote] deliberately refused to define personality, and dared not say that Man in so far as he is himself, in so far as he is a personality, reflects the whole act of God; his God and Man seem cut off from one another. It was the next step, and because he did not take it Blake violently annotated *Siris*, and because he himself did take it, certain heads—'Christ Blessing'—in Mona Wilson's *Life* for instance—have an incredible still energy.[1]

We have already discussed certain affinities between Blake's earlier view of the Imagination and David Hume's (Ch. 1, pp. 26–7), although recognizing that for Hume, the constructions of the imagination are not cognitive, as they are for Blake. Although the associationist psychology was based on mechanical principles, it did leave room for a constructive view of Imagination in a limited sense.[2] The aesthetic consequences of such a view are the subject of a celebrated series of *Spectator* essays on the pleasures of the imagination (Nos. 411–21, 1712). Addison takes fancy and imagination as synonymous, locates their pleasures in the realm of sight, and divides these pleasures into primary ('which entirely proceed from such objects as are before our eyes') and secondary ('called up into our memories, or formed into agreeable visions of things that are either absent or fictitious') —No. 411.[3] The pleasures of art are 'secondary': 'It is sufficient that we have seen places, persons, or actions, in general, which bear a resemblance, or at least some remote analogy, with what we find represented. Since it is in the power of the imagination, when it is once stocked with particular ideas, to enlarge, compound, and vary them at her own pleasure' (No. 416, p. 375). Nothing is in the imagination

---

[1] 'Bishop Berkeley', *Essays and Introductions* (New York, 1961), p. 408 n.
[2] See Welch, pp. 69–73, 76; Tuveson, op. cit. (above, p. 221, n. 3).
[3] *The Works of the Right Honourable Joseph Addison*, collected by Mr. Tickell (London, 1804), ii. 355–6.

that was not first in the senses, though fancy is free to recombine sensations. Once more, this brings us back to the equivocal nature of the power, 'for the imagination is as liable to pain as pleasure. When the brain is hurt by any accident, or the mind disordered by dreams or sickness, the fancy is over-run with wild dismal ideas, and terrified with a thousand hideous monsters of its own framing' (No. 421, p. 396). Even the pleasures which imagination gives are not 'so refined as those of the understanding' (No. 411, p. 356). Nor are these pleasures a means of knowing; they merely provide the soul with agreeable illusions:

Things would make but a poor appearance to the eye, if we saw them only in their proper figures and motions: and what reason can we assign for their exciting in us many of those ideas which are different from any thing that exists in the objects themselves, (for such are light and colours,) were it not to add supernumerary ornaments to the universe, and make it more agreeable to the imagination? We are every where entertained with pleasing shows and apparitions; we discover imaginary glories in the heavens, and in the earth, and see some of this visionary beauty poured out upon the whole creation; but what a rough unsightly sketch of nature should we be entertained with, did all her colouring disappear, and the several distinctions of light and shade vanish!   (No. 413, p. 364)

The imagination enables us to mistake the place of secondary qualities as in the objects and not in our senses, and so restores to us a prelapsarian—or at least pre-Cartesian—world in which, through his senses, man participates in the objects of his perception. But as to Addision this is merely a pleasing illusion, there must come an expulsion from the false paradise that the mind has created. Addison's metaphor for this is an interesting anticipation of those Blake will use in 'The Crystal Cabinet' and Keats in 'La Belle Dame Sans Merci':

In short, our souls are at present delightfully lost and bewildered in a pleasing delusion, and we walk about like the inchanted hero of a romance, who sees beautiful castles, woods, and meadows; and at the same time hears the warbling of birds, and the purling of streams; but upon the finishing of some secret spell, the fantastic scene breaks up, and the disconsolate knight finds himself on a barren heath, or in a solitary desert.   (pp. 364–5)

The difference in theme is that the two poems we have mentioned are about false imaginative experiences and the necessary expulsion from the false paradises they create, while for Addison, the imagination is *necessarily* false, or to use Hobbes's term, a creator of 'fictions'. To leave no doubts about the matter, Addison directs his English reader to 'the eighth chapter of the second book of Mr. Locke's Essay on Human Understanding' (p. 365).

Before Addison, John Dennis had already brought together the concepts of the imagination and the sublime.[1] The very supposition that had made imagination suspect to the Neoplatonists—that of its proximity to the senses—became for Dennis, interested in explaining the effects of poetry, the psychological basis for the sublime of terror. 'The Soul never takes the Alarm from any thing so soon as it does from the Senses, especially those two noble ones of the Eye and the Ear, by reason of the strict Affinity which they have with the Imagination. . . .'[2] Addison linked the sublime and the imagination in his discussion of Milton's greatness in *The Spectator*, No. 279:

> Milton's chief talent, and indeed his distinguishing excellence, lies in the sublimity of his thoughts. There are others of the moderns who rival him in every other part of poetry; but in the greatness of his sentiments he triumphs over all the poets both modern and ancient, Homer only excepted. It is impossible for the imagination of man to distend itself with greater ideas, than those which he has laid together in his first, second, and sixth books. . . . Let the judicious reader compare what Longinus has observed on several passages in Homer, and he will find parallels for most of them in the Paradise Lost. (p. 103)

Addison echoes the notion of his contemporary Shaftesbury that the experience of the sublime comes from the mind's contemplating objects too grand for imagination to comprehend. In *The Moralists* Shaftesbury's enthusiastic spokesman, Theocles, addresses the Deity who created Nature as follows:

> 'Thy being is boundless, unsearchable, impenetrable. In thy

---

[1] See Hooker, Introduction to *Critical Works*, ii. xci–xcix.
[2] *Critical Works*, i. 362.

immensity all thought is lost, fancy gives over its flight, and wearied imagination spends itself in vain, finding no coast nor limit of this ocean, nor, in the widest tract through which it soars, one point yet nearer the circumference than the first centre whence it parted. Thus having oft essayed, thus sallied forth into the wide expanse, when I return again within myself, struck with the sense of this so narrow being and of the fulness of that immense one, I dare no more behold the amazing depths nor sound the abyss of Deity.[1]

This is quite different from Blake's view, and it may be that Blake's 'One thought. fills immensity' in the Proverbs of Hell (E 36) is in reply to Shaftesbury. Yet Shaftesbury anticipates Blake in connecting the sublime with the infinite, in rejecting the Lockian epistemology, and in defending innate ideas. In a letter to Michael Ainsworth, Shaftesbury wrote:

'Twas Mr. Locke, that struck the home blow: for Mr. Hobbes's character and base slavish principles in government took off the poyson of his philosophy. 'Twas Mr. Locke that struck at all fundamentals, threw all *order* and *virtue* out of the world, and made the very *ideas* of these (which are the same as those of God) *unnatural*, and without foundation in our minds. *Innate* is a word he poorly plays upon: the right word, tho' less used, is *con-natural*, for what has *birth* or *progress* of the *foetus* out of the womb to do in this case? the question is not about the *time* the ideas enter'd, or the moment that one body came out of the other: but whether the constitution of man be such, that sooner or later (no matter when) the idea and sense of *order*, *administration*, and a God will not infallibly, inevitably, necessarily spring up in him.[2]

(Compare Blake, E 637: 'Knowledge of Ideal Beauty. is Not to be Acquired It is Born with us Innate Ideas. are in Every Man Born with him. they are < truly > Himself. The Man who says that we have No Innate Ideas must be a Fool & Knave. Having No Con-Science <or Innate Science >.'[3]) 'Having rescued nature from the mechanists,' writes R. L. Brett (p. 68), 'Shaftesbury developed his theory along neo-Platonic lines. The natural world, if, indeed, it were a work

---

[1] *Characteristics* (Gloucester, Mass., 1963), ii. 98.

[2] Quoted in R. L. Brett, *The Third Earl of Shaftesbury* (London, 1951), pp. 84–5. Shaftesbury's letters to Ainsworth were published in 1716.

[3] Annotations to Reynolds. See also E 635: 'I say These Principles could never be found out by the Study of Nature with Con or Innate Science.'

of art, could now be viewed as symbolical of a world lying behind sense appearances, just as a poem expresses imperfectly the incommunicable conception which exists in the poet's mind. God is the great artist and this world is the imperfect manifestation of what exists in a perfect form only in His mind.' This takes us toward Wordsworth's perception in Nature of 'Types and symbols of Eternity', Coleridge's demand for a symbolical meaning in the moon dim-glimmering through the window pane, and Blake's characterization of the world as 'One Continual Vision of Fancy or Imagination.'

This development of the sublime tradition towards an idea of a symbol-making constructive Imagination was continued in Mark Akenside's *The Pleasures of Imagination*, first published in 1744. Akenside, amalgamating elements of Addison and Shaftesbury[1] with a diffuse Neoplatonism, produced a poem which is both a summary of the aesthetic of the sublime and a forerunner of the romanticism to come. Akenside described his aim as

not so much to give formal precepts, or enter into the way of direct argumentation, as, by exhibiting the most engaging prospects of nature, to enlarge and harmonise the imagination, and by that means insensibly dispose the minds of men to a similar taste and habit of thinking in religion, morals, and civil life.[2]

Shelley was to advance a similar programme in his *Defence of Poetry*, but while Shelley actually does try to embody mental processes in the symbolism and structure of *Prometheus Unbound*, Akenside does exactly what he says he will not do: he writes a didactic poem in discursive language, the inflated language, what is more, of the 'sublime poem'.[3] The theory was there, but the mode of symbolism that was to characterize the elaborated mythopoeic structures of Blake, Shelley, and Keats had yet to be developed. As Professor Nicolson says in *Newton Demands the Muse*,

The poets of the eighteenth century were conditioned more than they knew by their response to the metaphysics of Locke and

---

[1] See Brett, p. 117.

[2] *The Pleasures of Imagination*, in *Akenside's Poetical Works*, ed. G. Gilfannan (Edinburgh, 1857), p. 3.   [3] See Miles, pp. 56–7; Tuveson, p. 156.

Newton, their subconscious acceptance of the dualism of Descartes. The world 'out there', the mind 'in here', remained to many of them separate and distinct; try as they would, they could not bridge the gap. Even 'Imagination', of which they made so much, was unable to go far, 'cabin'd, cribb'd, confined, bound in' to one part of man's 'soul'; passive rather than active, its place was predetermined, its functions limited.[1]

In 1756, nine years after Hartley's *Observations on Man*, Burke published his *Enquiry*, the book that stirred Blake's 'Contempt & Abhorrence' because of its attempt to discover a physiological basis for the sublime. Burke's view of Imagination results from applying Hartleian associational psychology to aesthetic experience.

The mind of man possesses a sort of creative power of its own; either in representing at pleasure the images of things in the order and manner in which they were received by the senses, or in combining those images in a new manner, and according to a different order. This power is called Imagination; and to this belongs whatever is called wit, fancy, invention, and the like. But it must be observed, that this power of the imagination is incapable of producing any thing absolutely new; it can only vary the disposition of those ideas which it has received from the senses. Now the imagination is the most extensive province of pleasure and pain, as it is the region of our fears and our hopes, and of all our passions that are connected with them; and whatever is calculated to affect the imagination with these commanding ideas, by force of any original natural impression, must have the same power pretty equally over all men. For since the imagination is only the representative of the senses, it can only be pleased or displeased with the images from the same principle on which the sense is pleased or displeased with the realities; and consequently there must be just as close an agreement in the imaginations as in the senses of men. (pp. 16–17)

Given such a view, the Imagination must be considered as inferior to the understanding though at times more powerful. Burke gives the example of two rooms: one well-proportioned and bare, the second worse-proportioned and decorated: the second 'will make the imagination revolt against the reason; it will please much more than the naked

[1] Princeton, N.J., 1946, pp. 163–4.

proportion of the first room which the understanding has so much approved' (p. 109).

In his Annotations to Reynolds, Blake says that 'Burke's Treatise on the Sublime & Beautiful is founded on the Opinions of Newton & Locke on this Treatise Reynolds has grounded many of his assertions. in all his Discourses' (E 650). Against Reynolds, Blake maintains the reality of inspiration (647); defends enthusiasm (636); expresses his his admiration for the sublime painters Barry (631), Fuseli (631), and Mortimer (635); affirms his belief in innate ideas (637); and delivers at various points in Reynolds's margins what amounts to his own manifesto of the sublime:

> Minute Discrimination is Not Accidental All Sublimity is founded on Minute Discrimination (632)
>
> Without Minute Neatness of Execution. The. Sublime cannot Exist! Grandeur of Ideas is founded on Precision of Ideas (636)
>
> Broken Colours & Broken Lines & Broken Masses are Equally Subversive of the Sublime (641)

The source of the Sublime to Blake is the Imagination, but not as Reynolds conceives it. '. . . He Thinks Mind & Imagination not to be above the Mortal & Perishing Nature' (649). Blake thinks 'All Forms are Perfect in the Poets Mind. but these are not Abstracted nor Compounded from Nature < but are from Imagination >' (637). The highest exemplars of imaginative art are Michelangelo and Raphael; Salvator Rosa is their opposite ('As to Imagination he was totally without Any.' 644). One of the few instances in which Blake can agree with Sir Joshua is on Poussin, whom Reynolds praised for his 'dry manner' and because his subjects were 'Ancient Fables.'[1] Rubens and the Venetian school Blake sees as blurrers of distinctions, visually and therefore philosophically, as indeed he sees Sir Joshua:

> The obligations Reynolds has laid on Bad Artists of all Classes will at all times make them his Admirers but most especially for

[1] E 644. In Winckelmann's *Reflections on the Painting and Sculpture of the Greeks*, which Blake owned in the translation by his friend Henry Fuseli (London, 1765), Poussin is praised as an allegorical painter (p. 230). In this book Raphael is called 'this Apollo of painters' and Michelangelo 'this Phidias of latter times' (pp. 183, 46 resp.).

this Discourse in which it is proved that the Stupid are born with Faculties Equal to other Men Only they have not Cultivated them because they thought it not worth the trouble   (E 647)

Blake's Wordsworth marginalia are similar in substance but different in tone and emphasis, for in Wordsworth Blake sees a great imaginative poet hampered by what Blake considers to be a mechanistic philosophy. The associationism of Locke and Hartley had provided Wordsworth with a terminology which Blake could not accept because of its metaphysical implications ('to Educate a Fool how to build a Universe with Farthing Balls').[1] It is probably Wordsworth's Hartleian vocabulary that caused Blake to say, 'I do not know who wrote these Prefaces they are very mischievous & direct contrary to Wordsworths own Practise' (E 655). Wordsworth's practice Blake considers to be at times 'in the highest degree Imaginative & equal to any Poet. . . .'[2] When Crabb Robinson read him the Immortality Ode, Blake was moved to tears.[3] But against Wordsworth's Hartleian topic heading 'Influence of Natural Objects in calling forth and strengthening the Imagination in Boyhood and early Youth', Blake set Wordsworth's own translation from Michelangelo:

> Heaven born the Soul a Heavenward Course must hold
> For what delights the Sense is False & Weak
> Beyond the Visible World she soars to Seek
> Ideal Form, The Universal Mold[4]

[1] 'Public Address', E 568. Where Bishop Watson, about to quote a passage from the *Observations on Man*, refers to Hartley as a man of judgement, Blake breaks in: 'Hartley a Man of Judgment then Judgment was a Fool what nonsense' (E 608). According to K 905, Blake engraved a portrait of Hartley in 1791 for a new edition of the *Observations*! Sometimes it is easy to see why Blake identifies the Spectre with his work as an engraver.

[2] E 654, From note to 'To H. C. Six Years Old', in the *Poems* of 1815. This book was annotated by Blake in 1826, as was *The Excursion* (K 782, 784).

[3] By the passage beginning 'But there's a tree, of many one', which Robinson admits he was in the habit of omitting when reading the poem to friends 'lest I shd. be rendered ridiculous. . . .' See *Blake, Coleridge, Wordsworth, Lamb, Etc.*, p. 23.

[4] In the marginalia Blake merely directed the reader to the poem, but he wrote the lines out in William Upcott's autograph album that same year (E 675). K 925 notes that lines 2 and 3 are transposed.

4

We have left undiscussed so far the conceptions of visionary or prophetic imagination to be found in philosophy from Plato to Blake's day. Often such conceptions are unrelated to a writer's general doctrine of imagination, for philosophers, whatever their persuasion, often reserved a special compartment of their thought for Scripture—the visions in the Bible had to be explained in terms of a mental power that could apprehend 'true' and, often, symbolically significant forms. The *Timaeus* seemed to offer a parallel and a precedent for this: here was a view of prophetic imagination as a special case, different from Plato's more typical distrust of the faculty. In the eighteenth century, some of the sublime aestheticians conjoined the notion of imagination as a producer of poetry with the ancient tradition of prophetic imagination, though no one went quite as far in this direction as William Blake was to go.

In tracing the history of prophetic imagination, let us not omit the obvious, though we need not dwell on it: the prophets of the Old Testament *were* both poets and visionaries:

In the year that King Uzziah died I saw also the Lord sitting upon a throne, high and lifted up, and his train filled the temple.

Above it stood the seraphims: each one had six wings; with twain he covered his face, and with twain he covered his feet, and with twain he did fly.

And one cried unto another, and said, Holy, holy, holy, is the LORD of hosts: the whole earth is full of his glory. (Isa. 6 : 1–3)

It was in this tradition that Blake placed himself as seer of visions and prophet–poet. 'It ought to be understood that the Persons Moses & Abraham are not here meant but the States Signified by those Names the Individuals being representatives or Visions of those States as they were reveald to Mortal Man in the Series of Divine Revelations. as they are written in the Bible these various States I have seen in my Imagination' (E 546). The New Testament figure with whom he feels most closely identified is John of Patmos, also a seer of visions. The 'States' which Blake speaks of as apprehended by the prophetic Imagination are figural symbols[1] to which, in their aggregate, Blake gives the name of Vision. 'The Hebrew Bible & the Gospel of Jesus are not Allegory but Eternal Vision or Imagination of All that Exists' (E 544). Such a view of the prophetic imagination was in part anticipated by classical and later philosophers, though they did not arrogate the power to themselves.

The description of prophetic imagination in the *Timaeus* has often been taken as a parallel to the prophetic visions in the Bible. Plato's view is somewhat more equivocal than the Bible's, however, in that he places the seat of divination in the liver, the appetitive and irrational part of the soul:

> However, as the Divinity perceived that this part would not be obedient to reason, but that it would naturally reject its authority in consequence of every sensible impression, and would be animastically hurried away by images and phantasms both by day and night—considering this, he constituted the form of the liver, and placed it in the habitation of this desiderative part . . . by employing the innate sweetness of the liver, and rendering all its parts properly disposed, smooth, and free . . . so that it might even refrain from excess in the night, and employ prophetic energies in sleep: since it does not participate of reason and prudence. For those who composed us, calling to mind the mandate of their father, that they should render the mortal race as far as possible the best, so constituted the depraved part of our nature that it might become connected with truth; establishing in this part a prophetic knowledge of future events. But that Divinity assigned divination to human madness may be . . . inferred from hence; that no one while endued with intellect becomes connected with a divine and true prophecy; but this alone takes place either when the power of prudence is fettered by sleep, or suffers some mutation through disease, or a certain enthusiastic energy: it being in this case the employment of prudence to understand what was asserted either sleeping or waking by a prophetic and enthusiastic nature. . . .[2]

Blake's attitude towards this equivocal notion of the prophetic

---

[1] In the sense in which Erich Auerbach uses the term *figura*. 'An event taken as a figure preserves its literal and historical meaning. It remains an event, does not become a mere sign.' Auerbach speaks of the 'figural realism' of the High Middle Ages 'which can be observed in full bloom in sermons, the plastic arts, and mystery plays . . .' (*Mimesis, The Representation of Reality in Western Literature* (Princeton, N.J., 1953), pp. 195–6).

[2] *The Works of Plato*, trans. Floyer Sydenham and Thomas Taylor (London, 1804) ,ii. 546–7.

imagination was equivocal. In the Reynolds Annotations he wrote: 'The Ancients did not mean to Impose when they affirmd their belief in Vision & Revelation Plato was in Earnest. Milton was in Earnest. They believd that God did Visit Man Really & Truly & not as Reynolds pretends' (E 647). Yet two years later he wrote in his Notebook: 'Plato has made Socrates say that Poets & Prophets do not know or Understand what they write or Utter this is a most Pernicious Falshood. If they do not pray is an inferior Kind to be calld Knowing Plato confutes himself'.[1]

An affirmative view of the prophetic imagination is often found in medieval and Renaissance philosophers who were otherwise mistrustful of the imaginative faculty. Maimonides, whose view of imagination is generally Aristotelian, regards the visions of the Prophets as symbolism presented through the imagination; and Thomas Aquinas considers such visions as implanted directly in the mind by angels.[2] Pico also makes a special category for the imagination exercised in Scriptural prophecy:

Prophecy flows into the intellect, whenever God, as it were, engraves therein the signs of the future. And again, by the splendour of heavenly light, the prophets discern portents from contemplating the images of things presented to their eyes from without; yet, when we turn the pages of Holy Writ, we find but few things thus divinely revealed to the prophets in comparison with those disclosed to them by imaginative vision. For—to pass over the books of Amos, Zechariah, and other ancient prophets, all abounding in imaginative visions—the Apocalypse of John is imaginative, including the career of the whole Church, even to the punishments of the damned and the glory of the blessed; and many imaginative visions are described by Luke in the Acts of the Apostles.

(*On the Imagination*, p. 57)

---

[1] E 544. Erdman discovered that on Plate 73 of *Jerusalem* Los created not only 'Adam Noah Abraham Moses Samuel David Ezekiel' but also 'Pythagoras Socrates Euripedes Virgil Dante Milton' (E 226, lines 41–2). The latter line was at some time deleted. No doubt Blake would have at least kept Milton had not his mode of publishing—etching—subjected him to certain limitations as far as deletions and revisions were concerned. See Erdman, 'Suppressed and Altered Passages', *SB*, xvii (1964), 28.

[2] See Bundy, pp. 216, 221–2.

The spiritual alchemists went further than this, for they believed that the imagination was physically as well as intellectually productive. Both Paracelsus and Cornelius Agrippa believe that the mother's imagination shapes the foetus in her body, and that the physician can effect cures through the imagination.[1] Agrippa remarks, 'How much imagination can affect the soul no man is ignorant, for it is nearer to the substance of the soul than the sense is, and therefore acts more upon the soul than the sense doth' (p. 200). He also explains the stigmata of St. Francis as produced by the imagination (p. 199), a supposition noted in Robert Burton's *Anatomy of Melancholy*[2] and in Bacon's *Advancement of Learning*. Bacon derides 'the school of Paracelsus' for having 'exalted the power of imagination to be much one with the power of miracle-working faith' (p. 119). Yet the alchemists, whatever the insufficiencies of their theory, had at least tried to account for miracles according to human knowledge. Bacon brings in the division of knowledge and faith which was to become more and more pronounced in his century. A special category, which Blake calls Mystery, will be set up for things religious; these things will not be open to question, but neither will they be allowed to intrude upon the real business of life. We see this again in Bacon's view of Imagination. He too has a special view of the role of Imagination in revelation, but cautions against its application to, for example, poetry:

> For we see that, in matters of Faith and Religion, we raise our Imagination above our Reason; which is the cause why Religion sought ever access to the mind by similitude, types, parables, visions, dreams. And again, in all persuasions that are wrought by eloquence, and other impressions of like nature, which do paint and disguise the true appearance of things, the chief recommendation unto Reason is from the Imagination. Nevertheless, because I find

---

[1] Paracelsus, 'Concerning the Nature of Things', *Hermetic and Alchemical Writings*, i. 122; Agrippa, *Three Books of Occult Philosophy*, ed. Willis F. Whitehead (Chicago, 1898), p. 204. Both Paracelsus and Agrippa identify imagination with the sun, as Blake does (*Hermetic and Alchemical Writings*, i. 7 n; *Three Books*, p. 88).

[2] Ed. Floyd Dell and Paul Jordan-Smith (New York, 1955), p. 221. Burton's own view is the typical 'Renaissance' one delightfully exaggerated and extended. See also pp. 139–40.

not any science that doth properly or fitly pertain to the Imagination, I see no cause to alter the former division. For as for poesy, it is rather a pleasure or play of Imagination, than a work or duty thereof. (p. 121)

He defers the subject, therefore, until he gets to Rhetoric; but when he does so, it is only to emphasize the power of Imagination to stir the irrational appetites.

In Hobbes the gap between the two kinds of Imagination is even more obvious. How are we to square the associative train of imaginations, decaying sense, with Hobbes's statement that

generally the prophets extraordinary in the Old Testament took notice of the word of God no otherwise than from their dreams, or visions; that is to say, from the imaginations which they had in their sleep, or in an extasy: which imaginations in every true prophet were supernatural: but in false prophets were either natural or feigned. (*Leviathan*, p. 279)

(As we have seen in our discussion of *Leviathan*, true prophets may be distinguished from false by the orthodoxy of their beliefs and the accuracy of their predictions; and the power of prophecy ceased with the end of Scripture.) The angels addressed by Lot were 'images of men, supernaturally formed in the fancy'; Gabriel in Daniel 12 : 1 'was nothing but a supernatural phantasm' (p. 258). In the next century, David Hartley found the visions of the Prophets genuine *because* absurd:

As the prophecies were, many of them, communicated in the way of divine visions, trances, or dreams, so they bear many of the foregoing marks of dreams. Thus they deal chiefly in visible imagery; they abound with apparent impossibilities, and deviations from common life, of which yet the prophets take not the least notice: they speak of new things as of familiar ones; they are carried in the spirit from place to place; things requiring a long series of time in real life, are transacted in the prophetical visions, as soon as seen; they ascribe to themselves and others new names, offices, &c.; every thing has a real existence conferred upon it; there are singular combinations of fragments of visible appearances; and God himself is represented in a visible shape, which of all other things must be most offensive to a pious *Jew*. And it seems to me, that these, and such like criterions might establish the genuineness of the prophecies, exclusively of all other evidences.

Earlier in the same chapter ('Of Imagination, Reveries and Dreams'), Hartley defines dreams as 'nothing but the imaginations, fancies, or reveries of a sleeping man . . . deducible from the three following causes viz. first, The impressions and ideas lately received . . . Secondly, the state of the body . . . And, thirdly, association'.[1] This view of imagination lets vision in through the back door, as it were, assigning it the same mechanical operation as dreams, and accounting in no way for the supposed difference in validity.

Hobbes's opponents, the Cambridge Platonists, were no more consistent about the imagination than he. John Smith called imagination 'a gross dew on the glass of our understandings', but like so many others he made a special case of visions in Scripture: 'The Prophetical scene or Stage upon which all apparitions were made to the Prophet, was his Imagination . . . there all those things which God would have revealed to him were acted over Symbolically, as in a Masque, in which divers persons are brought in, amongst which the prophet himself bears a part'.[2] This conception, once more, was not meant to apply to anything outside the Bible. Neither was Spinoza's assertion that the prophets perceived God through the imagination,[3] but by insisting on the imaginative nature of prophecy, such views prepared the way for literary criticism of the Bible as sublime poetry. It then remained for William Blake to argue that all scriptures were sublime poems, including Milton's and his own.

5

The first complete work which Blake built around his new concept of the Imagination is *Milton*, which was written

---

[1] *Hartley's Theory of the Human Mind*, 2nd ed. (London, 1790), pp. 223, 218 resp.

[2] Quoted by Willey, pp. 148–9.

[3] *Theological-Political Treatise*, pp. 24–6. An exception is made for Moses (p. 18), who saw God face to face. John Smith also recognized a *gradus Mosaicus* different from the visions of prophecy, by which God was directly perceived (see Willey, pp. 147, 150–1).

after *The Four Zoas* (with the possible exception of Night VIII).[1] My purpose here is not to write another commentary on the poem,[2] but to demonstrate its essential unity as a symbolic account of the regeneration process, and to explain the only flaw in that unity, the unresolved prophecy concerning Orc. The poem as a whole is an example of what Blake calls 'Allegory address'd to the Intellectual powers, while it is altogether hidden from the Corporeal Understanding'; this is 'My Definition of the Most Sublime Poetry . . .' (K 825). (Although Blake does not give the title of the poem he is describing, the 'Sublime Allegory' can only be *Milton*, for its subject is 'all our three years' trouble' at Felpham.) It has been suggested that the source of Blake's distinction between two types of allegory may be Winckelmann's *Reflections*:

> Perhaps the allegory of the ancients might be divided, like painting and poetry in general, into two classes, *viz.* the *sublime*, and the *more vulgar*. Symbols of the one might be those by which some mythological or philosophical allusion, or even some unknown or mysterious rite, is expressed.
>
> Such as are more commonly understood, *viz.* personified virtues, vices, &c. might be referred to the other.[3]

'Allegory address'd to the Intellectual Powers' is what Blake later calls 'Vision' and opposes to 'Fable or Allegory':

> The Last Judgment is not Fable or Allegory but Vision Fable or Allegory are a totally distinct & inferior kind of Poetry. Vision or Imagination is a Representation of what Eternally Exists. Really & Unchangeably. Fable or Allegory is Formd by the daughters of Memory. Imagination is Surrounded by the daughters of Inspiration who in the aggregate are calld Jerusalem . . . < Fable is Allegory but what Critics call The Fable is Vision itself > . . . The Hebrew Bible & the Gospel of Jesus are not Allegory but

---

[1] The date on the title-page is 1804, but this may refer only to that page or to the beginning of the poem. Bentley believes that *Milton* was largely written in 1804 and partly engraved in that year, though it was added to for several years afterwards (B 163–4). Erdman, however, suggests that it was not completed until 1809–10 (E 728).

[2] For commentary, see Damon, William Blake, pp. 172–82, 403–32; Frye, 'Notes for a Commentary on *Milton*', in *The Divine Vision*, pp. 97–138.

[3] *Reflections*, pp. 201–2. See Harper, p. 116.

Eternal Vision or Imagination of All that Exists < Note here that Fable or Allgory is Seldom without some Vision Pilgrims Progress is full of it the Greek Poets the same but [*Fable [or]* < & > *Allegory*] < Allegory & Vision > [< & *Visions of Imagination* >] ought to be known as Two Distinct Things & so calld for the Sake of Eternal Life . . . >

('A Vision of the Last Judgment', E 544)

Vision is perceived directly by the poet's or artist's Imagination and rendered into works of art whose symbolic meaning is apprehended directly by the reader or spectator. There is no intermediacy of translation from the abstract picture-language of allegory into discursive terms. The symbols of Vision may be taken allegorically, as Bacon interpreted myth, but then only Fable remains. 'Such is the Mighty difference between Allegoric Fable & Spiritual Mystery Let it. here be Noted that the Greek Fables originated in Spiritual Mystery & Real Vision and Real Visions Which are lost & clouded in Fable & Alegory . . . the Hebrew Bible & the Greek Gospel are Genuine Preservd by the Saviours Mercy' (E 545). Blake's own work 'is Visionary or Imaginative it is an Endeavour to Restore < what the Ancients calld > the Golden Age'.

Milton, being 'Vision', does not attempt to sustain a plot as *Vala* had attempted to do. Its structure is more thematic than narrative. The secret of understanding the poem is to realize that it all takes place in a moment of time and that there is therefore no real sequence of events.[1] Instead, the poem displays the kind of form which Joseph Frank, writing about modern poetry, has called 'spatial', defining this as 'meaning-relationship . . . completed only by the simultaneous perception in space of word-groups that have no comprehensible relation to each other when read consecutively in time'.[2] *Milton* is not a narrative with allegorical meaning; it is a series of figural events embedded in a myth, events which are not sequential but which should be apprehended simultaneously. The myth is the quarrel of Satan and Palamabron

---

[1] See Damon, *William Blake*, p. 179.

[2] 'Spatial Form in Modern Literature', *The Widening Gyre* (New Brunswick, N.J., 1963), p. 13.

related in the 'Bards prophetic Song'; the events are the descent of Milton to the fallen world, his struggle with Urizen, his entrance as a falling star into William Blake's left foot, Blake's becoming one with Los and going with him 'to his supreme abode', and Milton's combining with his own emanation, the Virgin Ololon. All these are symbolically phases in the process of regeneration.

The quarrel between Satan and Palamabron represents, as is widely recognized, Blake's struggle to preserve the integrity of his art against the temptations of fashionable success, as, for example, in portrait painting, held out by his patron Hayley. Blake regarded Hayley's successful career as a poet as an ironical counterpart to his own failure—the essentially prosaic man had assumed the function of the inspired artist, and was trying to get the true artist, Blake, to subordinate his genius to trivial pursuits. This creates a breach in the order of the universe, in an echo of the Phaethon myth and of the *Gita's* doctrine that the worst thing a man can do is to try to assume another's *karma*. Satan is 'Newtons Pantocrator[1] weaving the Woof of Locke' (4:11). He has no place in poetry, yet 'To Mortals thy Mills seem every thing . . .' (4:11–12, E 97). Satan, furious at being put in his rightful place by a solemn assembly of Eternals, makes the Great Withdrawal of the *principium individuationis*:

. . . . I am God alone
There is no other! let all obey my principles of moral individuality
I have brought them from the uppermost innermost recesses
Of my Eternal Mind, transgressors I will rend off for ever,
As now I rend this accursed Family from my covering.

(9:25–9, E 102)

This action precipitates the fall of Satan into Ulro, Blake's hell, the delusion of mechanism. So ends the Bard's song, delivered 'According to the inspiration of the Poetic Genius' (14:1, E 107).

Milton, symbol of the inspired poet, is led by the Bard's song to recognize the Satan in himself: he had not given full

---

[1] Newton used this Greek term ('almighty') with reference to God in the *Principia* (Blackstone, *English Blake*, p. 333 n.).

expression to his emanation, at once his inspiration, the feminine portion of himself and, historically, his three wives and three daughters.[1]

> What do I here before the Judgment? without my Emanation?
> With the daughters of memory, & not with the daughters of inspiration[?]
> I in my Selfhood am that Satan: I am that Evil One!
> He is my Spectre! in my obedience to loose him from my Hells
> To claim the Hells, my Furnaces, I go to Eternal Death.
>
> (14 : 28–32, E 107)

Having acknowledged the Satanic Selfhood within him, Milton 'descends' to the world of generation to redeem the errors it had made him commit.[2] His mission will be to cast out error in philosophy, literature, and art:

> To bathe in the Waters of Life; to wash off the Not Human
> I come in Self-annihilation & the grandeur of Inspiration
> To cast off Rational Demonstration by Faith in the Saviour
> To cast off the rotten rags of Memory by Inspiration
> To cast off Bacon, Locke & Newton from Albions covering
> To take off his filthy garments, & clothe him with Imagination
> To cast aside from Poetry, all that is not Inspiration
> That it no longer shall dare to mock with the aspersion of Madness
> Cast on the Inspired, by the tame high finisher of paltry Blots,
> Indefinite, or paltry Rhymes; or paltry Harmonies.
>
> (41 : 1–10, E 141)

A diagram on Plate 33 shows the path of his descent: the four Zoas are intersecting circles surrounded by the flames of the fallen world; in the centre is the Mundane Egg, inside whose blue shell we live, with its two 'limits', Satan and Adam. Adam, appropriately is entirely in the circle of Urthona,

---

[1] On Milton's wives and daughters, see Damon, *William Blake*, p. 413.

[2] Crabb Robinson wrote that Blake told him, 'I saw Milton in Imagination And he told me to beware of being misled by his Paradise Lost'. I think it more likely that Robinson than Blake was in error in saying 'In particular he wished me to shew the falsehood of his doctrine that the pleasures of *sex* arose from the fall. The fall could not produce any pleasure' (*Blake, Coleridge, Wordsworth, Lamb, Etc.*, p. 9). Milton is as diligent as Blake in confuting this 'falsehood'; 'as Blake', Frye points out, 'who made at least four illustrations of Satan watching the love-play of the unfallen Adam and Eve, knew very well' ('Notes for a Commentary', p. 101 n.).

for man is capable of being regenerated through the indwelling Christ of Imagination; while Satan straddles the
other three Zoas, the ruined world created by the fall. The
line labelled 'Miltons Track' passes through the intersecting
circles of Luvah and Urizen to join Adam in Urthona:
Milton, here a type or figural representation of Christ,
passes through the domains of repressive Law and the will-to-
power to become incarnate in regenerate man. The Seven
Angels of the Presence and the Shadowy Eighth (his own
sleeping body) attend him, indicating that man need not wait
for the consummation of history that is to occur with the
opening of the Eighth Eye, but may himself become an
epitome of history, passing through all Seven Eyes to a
regenerate life. This, again, is the symbolic 'way out' of the
bound circle of recurrence, represented in *Milton* by the
twenty-seven Churches and the twenty-seven heavens through
which the Lark of inspiration mounts. Therefore Milton,
entering his shadow, *becomes* history:

> . . . . he enterd into it
> In direful pain for the dread shadow, twenty-seven-fold
> Reachd to the depths of dirast Hell, & thence to Albions land:
> Which is this earth of vegetation on which now I write.
> (14 : 38–41, E 108)

The historical Milton had, Blake thought, in part subordi-
nated his Imagination to the repressive Urizen-principle;
and so he is depicted as, in his former existence, Moses
delivering the Law:

> He saw the Cruelties of Ulro, and he wrote them down
> In iron tablets: and his Wives & Daughters names were these
> Rahab and Tirzah, & Milcah & Malah & Noah & Hoglah.
> They sat rang'd round him as the rocks of Horeb round the land
> Of Canaan: and they wrote in thunder smoke and fire
> His dictate; and his body was the Rock Sinai; that body,
> Which was on earth born to corruption: & the six Females
> Are Hor & Peor & Bashan & Abarim & Lebanon & Hermon
> Seven rocky masses terrible in the Desarts of Midian.
> (17 : 9–17, E 109)

Rahab is already familiar to us; Milton's other women are

named after the five brotherless daughters of Zelophehad in Numbers: they 'represent the five senses, and particularly Man fallen into a purely sensorial existence'.[1] Milton is described as a mountain in a desert surrounded by mountains, all symbols of 'opacity', of the dead letter of the law. He *is* Urizen. Therefore in the course of his descent he must encounter and subdue Urizen.

The literary prototypes of this battle of Man against Monster, such as those we find in *Beowulf* or in Book I of *The Faerie Queene*, usually present the conflict as between two completely opposite natures, one of which must be destroyed so that the other may triumph. 'Good' must conquer 'Evil', the dragon be slain, the dragon-principle denied. Reading these poems or myths analytically, we may perhaps conclude that the antagonists really represent two parts of the same nature, but it is the intention of the poem or myth to destroy one at the expense of the other.[2] It was Blake's method to undercut such dualisms with the perception that the demonic masks we create are as much part of ourselves as our noumenal heroes. Milton's struggle, as it is beautifully described in Plate 19, is not to destroy Urizen but to make him part of a whole human identity:

Silent they met, and silent strove among the streams, of Arnon
Even to Mahanaim, when with cold hand Urizen stoop'd down
And took up water from the river Jordan: pouring on
To Miltons brain the icy fluid from his broad cold palm.
But Milton took of the red clay of Succoth, moulding it with care
Between his palms; and filling up the furrows of many years
Beginning at the feet of Urizen, and on the bones
Creating new flesh on the Demon cold, and building him,
As with new clay a Human form in the Valley of Beth Peor.

(6–14, E 111)

Arnon is 'the river of space' where the Spectres put on their garments of flesh, and Mahanaim is where Jacob wrestled.[3]

---

[1] Damon, *William Blake*, p. 386; see also p. 413.

[2] An important exception is the great fourteenth-century poem *Sir Gawain and the Green Knight*, where Gawain (culture) and the Green Knight (the energies of Nature) are in the end reconciled. See Francis Berry, 'Sir Gawayne and the Grene Knight', in *The Age of Chaucer*, ed. John Speirs (Harmondsworth, Middlesex, 1954), pp. 148–58.

[3] *Four Zoas*, VIII. 113 : 14–15; see Damon, *William Blake*, pp. 414, 415.

For Blake, Jacob's victory is a victory of man over a Urizenic God and a prototype of his own struggle against a Church which 'Crucifies Christ with the Head Downwards', which permits and even blesses social injustices and war. Urizen attempts to baptize Milton into this 'Druidical' religion with the icy waters of abstraction and materialism, but Milton struggles to flesh his skeletal opponent with the red clay of a new Adam, to turn the ossified literalism of religion back into material to be shaped by art.

> . . . . Silent Milton stood before
> The darkend Urizen; as the sculptor silent stands before
> His forming image; he walks round it patient labouring.
> (20:7-9, E 113)

On Plate 40, near the end of the poem, this struggle is still going on, bringing out once more the non-sequential, non-temporal nature of the events.

Descending to earth, Milton enters William Blake's left foot (15:49, E 108; 21:4, E 114), investing him with the imaginative power of the prophet–poet. This is analogous to Boehme's 'Flash of Fire', the point at which Imagination is thrust into the 'upper' world of Light, the Second Principle. Thus, at the apocalyptic conclusion of the poem, the poet whirls through the Seven Forms of psychic regeneration:

> Suddenly around Milton on my Path, the Starry Seven
> Burnd terrible! my Path became a solid fire, as bright
> As the clear Sun & Milton silent came down on my Path.
> And there went forth from the Starry limbs of the Seven: Forms
> Human; with Trumpets innumerable, sounding articulate
> As the Seven spake; and they stood in a mighty Column of Fire
> Surrounding Felphams Vale, reaching to the Mundane Shell,
>   Saying
>
> Awake Albion awake! reclaim thy Reasoning Spectre. Subdue
> Him to the Divine Mercy, Cast him down into the Lake
> Of Los, that ever burneth with fire, ever & ever Amen!
> Let the Four Zoa's awake from Slumbers of Six Thousand Years[1]

---

[1] 39:3-13, E 139. Cf. Paracelsus, *Aurora* (in *Hermetic and Alchemical Writings*, i. 52): 'Magic, it is true, had its origin in the Divine Ternary and arose from the Trinity of God. For God marked all His creatures with this Ternary and engraved its hieroglyph on them with His own finger. . . . This

The 'Starry Seven' are also the Seven Eyes of history. Apocalypse in history has as its psychological equivalent regeneration in the individual: Man himself becomes the Eighth Eye in the great vision with which the poem concludes:

Terror struck in the Vale I stood at that immortal sound
My bones trembled. I fell outstretchd upon the path
A moment, & my Soul returnd into its mortal state
To Resurrection & Judgment in the Vegetable Body
And my sweet Shadow of Delight stood trembling by my side

Immediately the Lark mounted with a loud trill from Felphams
   Vale
And the Wild Thyme from Wimbletons green & impurpled Hills
And Los & Enitharmon rose over the Hills of Surrey . . .[1]

Blake's description of his moment of illumination in the garden at Felpham recalls the account of Boehme's vision in the fields, given in the preface to the 'Law edition':

After this, about the Year 1600, in the twenty-fifth Year of his Age, he was again surrounded by the divine Light, and replenished with the heavenly Knowledge; insomuch, as going abroad into the Fields, to a Green before *Neys-Gate*, at *Gorlitz*, he there sat down, and viewing the Herbs and Grass of the Field, in his inward Light he saw into their Essences, Use and Properties, which were discovered to him by their Lineaments, Figures, and Signatures.

(*Works*, i. xiii)

In Boehme's own words:

For I saw and knew the Being of all Beings, the Byss and the Abyss, and the eternal Generation of the *Holy Trinity*, the Descent and Original of the World, and of all Creatures through the Divine Wisdom: I knew and saw in myself all the three Worlds, namely, *The Divine*, angelical and paradisical; and *The dark World*, the Original of the Nature to the Fire; and then, thirdly, the *external* and *visible World*, being a Procreation or external Birth from both

covenant of the Divine Ternary, diffused throughout the whole substance of things, is indissoluble. By this, also, we have the secrets of all Nature from the four elements. For the Ternary, with the magical Quaternary, produces a perfect Septenary. . . . When the Quaternary rests in the Ternary, then arises the Light of the World on the horizon of eternity, and by the assistance of God gives us the whole bond. . . .'

[1] 42 : 24–31, E 142. The 'immortal sound' is that of the Four Zoas' trumpets. Blake's 'sweet Shadow of Delight' is his wife, Catherine.

the internal and spiritual Worlds. And I saw and knew the whole
working Essence, in the Evil and the Good, and the Original and
Existence of each of them; and likewise how the fruitful-bearing
Womb of Eternity brought forth. . . . I saw it as in a great Deep in
the Internal.   (Ibid. xv)

Blake's own vision of the three worlds is rendered in the
central part of *Milton*, a magnificent section 243 lines long,[1]
beautifully embodying Blake's model of this world of Time
and Space seen as a construct of the Imagination.

> Such is the World of Los the labour of six thousand years.
> Thus Nature is a Vision of the Science of the Elohim.
>
> > (29: 64–5, E 127)

The union of Blake with Milton's prophetic Imagination
is also a union with Los, the archetypal poet–prophet, an
event prefigured in the verses Blake sent to Thomas Butts
in his letter of 22 November 1802 (K 818; see above, p. 142).

> . . . . Los descended to me:
> And Los behind me stood; a terrible flaming Sun: just close
> Behind my back; I turned round in terror, and behold.
> Los stood in that fierce glowing fire . . .
>
> . . . .
>
> And I became One Man with him arising in my strength:
> Twas too late now to recede. Los had enterd into my soul:
> His terrors now possess'd me whole! I arose in fury & strength.
>
> > (22: 5–8, 12–14, E 116)

In the lines sent to Butts, the apparition of Los was followed
by Blake's achieving a fourfold perception of the human world:

> > Now I a fourfold vision see,
> > And a fourfold vision is given to me;
> > 'Tis fourfold in my supreme delight
> > And threefold in soft Beulah's night
> > And twofold Always. May God us keep
> > From Single vision & Newton's sleep!

In *Milton* the equivalent perception is rendered as a trip to
Los's 'supreme abode', Golgonooza, 'namd Art & Manufac-
ture by mortal men'. (24 : 50). Here Blake sees Los's Furnaces,

---

[1] 25 : 66–29 : 65, E 120–7 (the end of Book I). See Damon, *William Blake*,
p. 421.

his Bellows, Hammers, and Anvils—all symbols of creative Imagination—and his Winepress, 'call'd War on Earth' but in actuality 'the Printing-Press of Los' (27:8–9). Blake recognizes Los himself as 'the Spirit of Prophecy the ever apparent Elias' (24:71). Los and his fellow labourers ('All the Gods of the Kingdoms of Earth', each 'a fallen Son of the Spirit of Prophecy') are at work preparing for the Great Harvest and Vintage which is to come. Los instructs them to bind men into Sheaves 'not by Nations or Families' but according to three classes.

> . . . . .The Elect is one Class: You
> Shall bind them separate: they cannot Believe in Eternal Life
> Except by Miracle & a New Birth. The other two Classes;
> The Reprobate who never cease to Believe, and the Redeemd,
> Who live in doubts & fears perpetually tormented by the Elect
> These you shall bind in a twin-bundle for the Consummation—
> But the Elect must be saved [from] fires of Eternal Death,
> To be formed into the Churches of Beulah that they destroy not
>   the Earth   (25: 32–9, E 121)

The Elect are to be bound back into the cycle of history in order to protect them from the Satanic condition into which they have precipitated themselves. The Reprobate—prophetic figures—and the Redeemd—common, perplexed men —will have their errors purged by the fires of the Last Judgement until only truth remains. The function of the prophet–poet in bringing on the Judgement is to identify each class.[1]

Rintrah, a son of Los who now represents wrath, warns his father against Blake–Milton, whom he mistakes for the former, Elect Milton. Sketching out the image of a world in torment,[2] Rintrah declares: 'Miltons Religion is the cause: there is no end to destruction!' (22:39). Rintrah pleads with

---

[1] For a full discussion of this theme in Blake's work, see Fisher.

[2] As Frye summarizes it, 'a crisis in history with the Napoleonic wars, a crisis in religion with the collapse of Swedenborg and the failure of anyone to make a genuinely imaginative development out of the challenge of the Methodist movement, a crisis in philosophy with the dogmatic formulation of natural religion in contemporary Deism, and a crisis in art with the domination of "the tame high finisher of paltry Blots" '. "Notes . . . on *Milton*", pp. 135–6.)

his father to punish and not forgive, but Los points to the results of wrath in history:

> Remember how Calvin and Luther in fury premature
> Sow'd War and stern division between Papists & Protestants
> Let it not be so now! . . .   (23 : 47–9, E 118)

His function, Los says, is 'to circumscribe this dark Satanic death . . . that the Seven Eyes of God may have space for Redemption' (51–2). Wrath will only cause a repetition of the fall of the Zoas and its terrible consequences. 'Break not forth in your wrath', Los warns, 'lest you also are vegetated by Tirzah' (25 : 57–8). Tirzah, binder of spirit into flesh, the Woman Old of 'The Mental Traveller', has a way of turning even honest wrath into endless destruction. Therefore, as in Night VIIa of *The Four Zoas* where Los modulates his fires, the poet must devote himself to his art until he and his fellow labourers have brought about that definition and casting-out of error which Blake calls the Last Judgement.

The work of regeneration cannot be accomplished unless Milton unites with his Emanation ('the total form of all the things a man loves and creates'[1]), Ololon, she whom as Eve Milton expelled from Paradise.

> There is in Eden a sweet River, of milk & liquid pearl.
> Namd Ololon; on whose mild banks dwelt those who Milton
>   drove
> Down into Ulro . . .   (21 : 15–17, E 114)

She in turn has descended from Eternity in search of Milton. Very much like another Thel, she views the Polypus of human hearts (34: 24–5) and the 'Couches of the Dead' which are the lives of those in the lower world. But unlike Thel's, hers is not a cloistered and neglected virtue: she continues on into the world of Experience in search of her male counterpart. Blake, walking in his garden, encounters her as a child of twelve and addresses her as a 'Virgin of Providence'. At this point in the poem she is very reminiscent

---

[1] Frye, *Fearful Symmetry*, p. 73. Sloss and Wallis (*Prophetic Writings*, ii. 153) note that the term 'Emanation' first occurs in added passages of *The Four Zoas*. They suggest that the source of the term may have been Jacob Bryant's *New System*, i. 18.

of Boehme's Sophia, the maiden Wisdom ('a maiden who stands, in the dawn of eternity, before the God who gives Himself up to Self-manifestation, and who, so to speak, allures Him to manifest Himself, by showing Him the exceeding riches of His glory').[1]

> . . . . nor time nor space was
> To the perception of the Virgin Ololon but as the
> Flash of lightning but more quick the Virgin in my Garden
> Before my Cottage stood, for the Satanic Space is delusion
> (36 : 17–20, E 136)

Ololon's union with Milton occurs in the moment of psychic transformation, the 'Moment in each Day that Satan cannot find' (35: 42, E 135) and with which Blake associates the wild thyme, the lark, and the dawn. The dawn is particularly important as a time of spiritual illumination in visionary literature (both Paracelsus and Boehme wrote books called *Aurora*); the thyme is the first flower to shed its perfume,[2] as the lark is the first bird to sing. Blake may have seen a symbolic meaning in Shakespeare's lark which 'at heaven's gate sings'; his own

> . . . Lark is Los's Messenger thro the Twenty-seven Churches
> That the Seven Eyes of God who walk even to Satans Seat
> Thro all the Twenty-seven Heavens may not slumber nor sleep
> But the Larks Nest is at the Gate of Los, at the eastern
> Gate of wide Golgonooza & the Lark is Los's Messenger
> (35 : 63–7, E 135)

Twenty-seven Larks represent the presence of inspiration and of potential regeneration in every 'Church' of the cycle of history. The twenty-eighth Lark, outside the scheme of history (like the Eighth Eye), is the Eternal Now:

> Thus are the Messengers dispatchd till they reach the Earth again
> In the East Gate of Golgonooza, & the Twenty-eighth bright
> Lark. met the Female Ololon descending into my Garden

---

[1] Hans L. Martensen, *Jacob Boehme (1575–1624)*, trans. T. Rhys Evans, with Notes and Appendices by Stephen Hobhouse, rev. ed. (London, 1949), p. 41.

[2] See Damon, *William Blake*, pp. 425, 204 n., and 426 resp.

Thus it appears to Mortal eyes & those of the Ulro Heavens
But not thus to Immortals, the Lark is a mighty Angel.

> (36 : 8–12, E 135)

At the end of the poem, as Milton and Ololon unite in the
illumination of dawn and the Lark mounts 'with a loud trill
from Felpham's Vale', the Eight Eyes combine as Jesus, and
Blake glimpses Eternity.

Milton is a symbolic epic unified by the theme of regeneration through the Imagination. There is only one flaw in this
unity, and that is the inclusion of a prophecy concerning Orc
which is neither fulfilled nor otherwise accounted for. The
reason for this must be that when Blake began *Milton* he had
not yet made his final disposition of the Orc symbol in *The
Four Zoas*. He still hoped somehow to reconcile Orc's
revolutionary energy with the regenerative Imagination
symbolized by Jesus, Milton, and the inspired Los. Some of
the plates of *Milton* must have been etched before Blake
decided that there was no place for Orc in this vision of
regeneration, and once material was etched it was very
difficult to change it. Thus we have an 'old Prophecy' remembered by Los at two points in the poem:

> At last when desperation almost tore his heart in twain
> He recollected an old Prophecy in Eden recorded,
> And often sung to the loud harp at the immortal feasts
> That Milton of the Land of Albion should up ascend
> Forwards from Ulro from the Vale of Felpham; and set free
> Orc from his Chain of Jealousy . . .   (20 : 56–61, E 114)

> I recollect an old Prophecy in Eden recorded in gold; and oft
> Sung to the harp: That Milton of the land of Albion
> Should up ascend forward from Felphams Vale & break the Chain
> Of Jealousy from all its roots . . . [1]   (23 : 35–8, E 118)

The Imagination of the regenerate Milton was to free revolutionary energy from the chains of its commitment to
domination or power. But the prophecy is never fulfilled in
Milton, for its fulfilment would have had no relation to

---

[1] Rintrah and Palamabron fear that Blake–Milton 'Will unchain Orc &
let loose Satan, Og, Sihon & Anak, / Upon the Body of Albion' (22 : 33–4).
Damon identifies the three Old Testament giants as 'natural forces' (*William
Blake*, p. 418).

reality. The references to Orc in *Milton* therefore remain scattered and unorganized. There is a glimpse of the revolutionary Orc of the Lambeth period: 'Lo Orc arises on the Atlantic. Lo his blood and fire / Glow on Americas shore . . .' (23 : 6–7). There is the Orc of *Vala*, a 'generated form' of Luvah: '. . . Urizen beheld the immortal Man, / And Tharmas Demon of the Waters, & Orc, who is Luvah' (17 : 36–18 : 1, E 110). And there is the Satanic Orc of *The Four Zoas*: 'Satan is the Spectre of Orc & Orc is the generate Luvah',[1] a line which relates the Orc symbol to the doctrine of Individuals and States. The Seven Angels of the Presence tell Milton:

> The Imagination is not a State: it is the Human Existence itself
> Affection or Love becomes a State, when divided from Imagination
> The Memory is a State always, & the Reason is a State
> Created to be Annihilated & a new Ratio Created
>
> (32 : 32–5, E 131)

Luvah is Love divided from Imagination, and Orc as the fallen form of Eros is domination and the will-to-power. The further division represented by the existence of a Spectre of Orc suggests that these qualities present themselves in both passional and reasoning forms, in a Rousseau aspect and a Voltaire aspect. The Spectre of Energy is equivalent, socially and psychologically, to the repressive principle of the old order, for 'Satan is Urizen, Drawn down by Orc and the Shadowy Female into Generation'. But Blake never joins Wordsworth and Coleridge in mistaking the chartered rights of the old order for freedom.[2]

Throughout *Milton* Orc remains chained in Entuthon

---

[1] 29 : 34. Damon's gloss is 'Error is the Reason of Revolution; and Revolution is the god of Passions in the world of Generation' (ibid., p. 423).

[2] In reading Reynolds's *Discourses* in or about 1808, Blake came to a reference to 'the ferocious and enslaved Republick of France' followed by a quotation from Dryden which terminated, 'They led their wild desires to woods and caves, / And thought that all but SAVAGES were slaves'. Blake then wrote his own couplet: 'When France got free Europe, 'twixt Fools & Knaves / Were Savage first to France, & after; Slaves' (E 630). (On the source couplet, formerly thought to be by Pope, see Note by Robert P. Kolker, *Blake Newsletter*, no. 1 (1967), p. 7.)

Benython, which in *Jerusalem* is called 'A dark and unknown night, indefinite, unmeasurable, without end. / Abstract Philosophy warring in enmity against Imagination . . .' (5: 57–8). Again, we see the polysemous nature of Blake's symbolism, for Orc is not only a France hardened in the mould of empire, but also a portion of the being of every individual:

> . . . Orc incessant howls burning in fires of Eternal Youth,
> Within the vegetated mortal Nerves; for every Man born is joined
> Within into One mighty Polypus, and this Polypus is Orc.
>
> (29 : 29–31, E 126)

The Polypus is the erotic energy of every human being, coagulated by denial or incomplete fulfilment into a shapeless mass of suffering. Orc, guarded by the Shadowy Female as in *Vala*, is tortured by her alternative temptations and denials as she hovers over him in two forms, Oothoon and Leutha:[1] 'Orc in vain / Stretch'd out his hands of fire, & wooed: they triumph in his pain' (18 : 44–5, E 111). Finally, as in Night VIIb, he tears his tormentors to pieces, but he does not even achieve temporary freedom. His presence in the symbolism of *Milton* is vestigial, left over from an earlier plan of composition which could not, owing to the developments in Blake's thought which we have discussed at length, be realized.

5

After the famous lyric with which *Milton* begins and before the beginning of the epic itself, there appears the epigraph: '"Would to God that all the Lord's people were Prophets." Numbers, xi. ch., 29 v.' These words are spoken in the Bible by Moses in answer to Joshua's urging that Eldad and Medad be prevented from prophesying in the camp. Blake, having invoked the divine vision in the opening lyric, in this way expresses the hope that all men will join him in 'Mental

---

[1] Leutha is a symbol of veiled female sexuality, and as such she plays a highly mischievous role in the myth of Satan and Palamabron. See 11 : 27–13 : 11 and Damon's commentary, p. 409. Oothoon formerly represented female sexual expression (in *Visions of the Daughters of Albion*), but Blake has changed her meaning here: she, too, is a Female Will.

Fight', in building the prophetic community, Jerusalem, in England's green and pleasant land. This is the message, too, of the prose preface that precedes the lyric: Blake calls upon 'Young Men of the New Age' to renew the arts in Britain and to set their foreheads against those who would 'depress Mental & prolong Corporeal War' (E 94). This idea of the extension of prophetic vision to the whole human community is the major theme of Blake's last[1] and greatest epic poem, *Jerusalem*.

There are two important respects in which *Jerusalem* goes beyond *The Four Zoas* and *Milton* in its concepts of Energy and Imagination. One is that the struggle between Los and his Spectre is at the centre of the poem's symbolic action, the other Zoas having become relatively unimportant. The other is the theme which develops through this struggle, the idea of artistic creation as involving a synthesis of Energy and Imagination and fulfilling the vision of freedom which ideology had promised but betrayed.

In each of the four chapters of *Jerusalem*, there is an agon between Los and the Spectre (6:1–11:7; 33 (37):1–11; 74: 1–13; 91:3–58). The Spectre appears in several forms. Typically, he is Reason cut off from the rest of human identity:

> The Spectre is the Reasoning Power in Man; & when separated
> From Imagination, and closing itself as in steel, in a Ratio
> Of the Things of Memory. It thence frames Laws & Moralities
> To destroy Imagination! the Divine Body, by Martyrdoms &
> Wars   (74:10–13, E 227)

It is not, however, the human power to reason that Blake condemns, but an authoritarian attitude masking itself as

---

[1] Bentley, pp. 163–4, thinks a rough draft of *Jerusalem* was in existence by 1804. Erdman (*SB*, xvii. 8 n.) argues that 'Biographical and historical allusions in *J* . . . range in date from 1804 to 1814 or 1815 (the end of the war) and suggest a much later date of composition for most of that poem'. Publication, Erdman thinks, was delayed until 1818–20; no pages are watermarked earlier than this. In 1820 its imminent publication was announced in the *London Magazine* by Thomas Griffiths Wainright (Damon, *William Blake*, p. 184); Blake wrote to his friend George Cumberland in 1827 that he had as yet produced only one finished copy and did not expect to find a customer for it (K 878). Erdman (loc cit.) suggests that the date 1804 on the title-page of *Jerusalem* may refer to a division of this poem from *Milton*.

Reason. Such an attitude can as well have a religious manifestation, as in Plate 10, where the Spectre is the pathetic victim of a theology according to which man is never justified in God's sight.

For he is Righteous: he is not a Being of Pity & Compassion
He cannot feel Distress: he feeds on Sacrifice & Offering:
Delighting in cries & tears & clothed in holiness & solitude
But my griefs advance also, for ever & ever without end
O that I could cease to be! Despair! I am Despair
Created to be the great example of horror & agony: also my
Prayer is vain I called for compassion: compassion mockd[,]
Mercy & pity threw the grave stone over me & with lead
And iron, bound it over me for ever: Life lives on my
Consuming: & the Almighty hath made me his Contrary
To be all evil, all reversed & for ever dead: knowing
And seeing life, yet living not; how can I then behold
And not tremble; how can I be beheld & not abhorrd
(10 : 47–59, E 152)

It may be that the model for this suffering Spectre was the poet William Cowper, who had been 'mad' but, Blake thought, in the wrong sense:

. . . Cowper came to me & said. O that I were insane always I will never rest. Can you not make me truly insane. I will never rest till I am so. O that in the bosom of God I was hid. You retain health & yet are as mad as any of us all—over us all—mad as a refuge from unbelief—from Bacon Newton & Locke[1]

Here 'mad' is used in an ironical sense. Cowper's real madness lay, for Blake, in his belief in God as a punisher and judge. Blake, who believed in a God of infinite mercy, knew himself sane, but also knew he was considered mad by his detractors. ('It is very true what you have said for these thirty two Years I am Mad or Else you are so both of us cannot be in our right senses Posterity will judge by our Works' ('Public Address', E 562). Rationalism may seem the contrary

---

[1] Annotations to *Observations on the Deranged Manifestations of the Mind, or Insanity* by J. G. Spurzheim (London, 1817), E 652; see my 'Cowper as Blake's Spectre'.

of religious despair, but Blake sees underlying both attitudes
the same idolatry.

In Chapter 2 of *Jerusalem*. Albion's Spectre embodies both
Cartesian rationalism and the in-some-ways opposed associationist psychology:

> I am your Rational Power O Albion & that Human Form
> You call Divine, is but a Worm seventy inches long
> That creeps forth in a night & is dried in the morning sun
> In fortuitous concourse of memorys accumulated & lost
> It plows the Earth in its own conceit, it overwhelms the Hills
> Beneath its winding labyrinths, till a stone of the brook
> Stops it in midst of its pride among its hills & rivers[.]
> Battersea & Chelsea mourn, London & Canterbury tremble
> Their place shall not be found as the wind passes over[.]
> The ancient Cities of the Earth remove as a traveller
> And shall Albions Cities remain when I pass over them
> With my deluge of forgotten remembrances over the tablet
>
> (29 (33): 5–16, E 173)

'The tablet' is of course the mind as *tabula rasa*; nor, I think,
is the Spectre's use of 'fortuitous' fortuitous. 'Fortuitous' is
a word employed by both Cudworth and Berkeley against
just such views as this of the 'Spectrous Chaos.' Cudworth
considers that 'To suppose . . . that all things come to pass
fortuitously, by the unguided motion of matter, and without
the direction of any mind, [is] a thing altogether as irrational as
impious . . . That the mechanic Theists make God but an idle
spectator of the fortuitous motions of matter. . . .' Cudworth
considers it 'No more possible, that dead and senseless
matter, fortuitously moved, should at length be taught and
necessitated by itself to produce this artificial system of the
world; than that a dozen or more persons, unskilled in music,
and striking the strings as it happened, should at length be
taught and necessitated to fall into exquisite harmony. . . .'[1]
Berkeley's Philonous says:

Those miserable refuges, whether in an eternal succession of
unthinking causes and effects, or in a fortuitous concourse of
atoms; those wild imaginations of Vanini, Hobbes, and Spinosa;

[1] *True Intellectual System*, iv. 412, 491–2.

in a word, the whole system of Atheism, is it not entirely over-
thrown by this single reflection on the repugnancy included in
supposing the whole, or any part, even the most rude and shapeless
of the visible world, to exist without a mind? Let any one of those
abettors of impiety but look into his own thoughts, and there try
if he can conceive how so much as a rock, a desert, a chaos, or confused jumble of atoms . . . can exist independent of a mind. . . .[1]

This is, of course, what the Spectre does believe; it is why he
is a Spectre. In Chapter 3, as a parody of the Holy Ghost,
he spreads his wings over Albion and demands material
miracles as magical proof of Vision:

But the Spectre like a hoar frost & a Mildew rose over Albion
Saying, I am God O Sons of Men! I am your Rational Power!
Am I not Bacon & Newton & Locke who teach Humility to Man!
Who teach Doubt & Experiment & my two Wings Voltaire:
    Rousseau.
Where is that Friend of Sinners! that Rebel against my Laws!
Who teaches Belief to the Nations, & an unknown Eternal Life
Come hither into the Desart & turn these stones to bread.
Vain foolish Man! wilt thou believe without Experiment?
And build a World of Phantasy upon my Great Abyss!
A World of Shapes in craving lust & devouring appetite
                                    (54: 15-24, E 201-2)

To save the Spectre from his hellish vision of life as chaos and
love as appetency, Los must forge the dissociated analytical
function back into the whole human identity (as Milton
sculpted Urizen with red clay), where it will become intuitive Reason.

In *Jerusalem* the *activity* of Los is especially emphasized;
he is constantly depicted as working furiously with his imaginative tools—Hammer, Anvil, Furnaces—to break down
and smelt the political, moral, philosophical, and theological
systems men have made, reducing them all to raw material
for art. Apparent opposites ('Negations') must be forged into
unities, Contraries defined, the City of Imagination built.

Rational Philosophy and Mathematic Demonstration
Is divided in the intoxications of pleasure & affection

[1] 'Three Dialogues Between Hylas and Philonous', *Works* (London, 1820),
i. 161.

Two Contraries War against each other in fury & blood,
And Los fixes them on his Anvil, incessant his blows:
He fixes them with strong blows. placing the stones & timbers.
To Create a World of Generation from the World of Death . . .

(58 : 13–18, E 205)[1]

The blow of his Hammer is Justice. the swing of his Hammer:
  Mercy.
The force of Los's Hammer is eternal Forgiveness . . .

(88 : 49–50, E 245)

On Plate 75, his Hammer 'demolishes' Biblical tyrants and
kings and queens of England;[2] on Plate 91, he destroys
Leviathan and Behemoth, the 'pyramids of pride' which the
Spectre has built. Behind the figure of this Giant Form
swinging his Hammer and stoking his Furnaces, we glimpse
the prototypes Vulcan and Elijah as seen through the alchemical tradition. Paracelsus calls alchemy 'the work of Vulcan'.
'Vulcan is the fabricator and architect of all things, nor is his
habitation in heaven only . . . but equally in all the other
elements.' 'The artist working in metals and other minerals
transforms them into other colours, and in so doing his
operation is like that of the heaven itself. For as the artist
excocts by means of Vulcan, or the igneous element, so
heaven performs the work of coction through the Sun. The
Sun, therefore, is the Vulcan of heaven accomplishing coction
in the earth' (*Hermetic and Alchemical Writings*, i. 22 n.).

Paracelsus's 'artist' is the alchemist, but we have already
seen that Blake takes that Art as a metaphor of his own, both
involving the regeneration of life through the Imagination.
Los, it has been pointed out, is the alchemical Sol, at the same
time gold, the Sun, and Christ. He is also Elijah:

the Almighty gives therewith the understanding how to conceal
these and other like arts even to the coming of Elias the Artist, at

---

[1] Fisher (p. 86 n.) notes that when Blake transfers the demiurgic activity
from Urizen to Los, he also takes a more favourable view of it, indicating a more
favourable interpretation of the Platonic myth. In *Jerusalem* Blake–Los can
even say, 'O holy Generation [*Image*] of regeneration!' (7 : 65).

[2] The list originally went through 'Edward Henry Elizabeth James Charles
William George', but Blake on second thought deleted the line (l. 37, E 226;
see Erdman, *SB*, xvii. 28).

which time there shall be nothing so occult that it shall not be
revealed. (Ibid. i. 27)

. . . . they with once accord delegated Los
Conjuring him by the Highest that he should Watch over them
Till Jesus shall appear: & they gave their power to Los
Naming him the Spirit of Prophecy, calling him Elijah
(*Jerusalem*, 39 (44) : 28–31, E 185)

As we have seen, the Hammer as a symbol of psychic transformation is found in Boehme's *Threefold Life of Man*:

. . . there is a *Twofold* Longing or seeking in the soul: One is the
fire's greedy covetous fierce Longing, which always seeks after
Earthly Matters; and the other is from the Spirit, which is brought
forth out of the Fire, wherein the right Life of the soul in the Image
of God is understood, that is, God's Longing, which seeks the
Kingdom of Heaven.
And so when the right Hammer (viz. *the Spirit of God*) strikes in
it, then that Longing is so strong, that it overcomes the Fire-
source and Longing, and makes it meek, so that it desires the
Longing of Love, *viz.* the Longing of the Soul's Spirit . . . especially when the Hammer of the Holy Ghost sounds through the Ears
into the Heart, then the Tincture of the soul receives it *instantly*; and
there it goes forth through the whole soul. . . .
(Ch. 18, Secs. 48–9, in *Works*, ii. 194)

What Blake does in *Jerusalem* is to amalgamate these symbols
of psychic activity with his own philosophy of art. In *Milton*,
as we have seen, he avoided the problem of the fate of
Energy; but in *Jerusalem*, Energy returns (though not as
Orc)[1] as part of the synthesis of Art. We see this in the
imagery of both the beginning and the end of the poem.

In his address 'To the Public' on Plate 3 of *Jerusalem*,
Blake refers to the work as 'this energetic exertion of my
talent' (E 144). He expresses the hope that 'the Reader will
be with me, wholly One in Jesus our Lord, who is the God
[*of Fire*] and Lord [*of Love*] to whom the ancients look'd and
saw his day afar off, with trembling & amazement'. Here

---

[1] Orc is mentioned just once in *Jerusalem* (14 : 2–3), simply as part of a
description of the fallen Zoas. He is called 'the Serpent, Orc the first born coild
in the south' (E 156).

the two worlds of Fire and Light, Wrath and Love, so long
separated in Blake's work, have coalesced, struck by 'the
right Hammer' of Imagination. Again, in the introductory
verses to *Jerusalem*, the unitive theme of *The Marriage*
appears in a new form, as God speaks to Blake

> . . . . in thunder and in fire!
> Thunder of Thought, & flames of fierce desire:
> Even from the depths of Hell his voice I hear,
> Within the unfathomd caverns of my Ear.
> Therefore I print; nor vain my types shall be:
> Heaven, Earth & Hell, henceforth shall live in harmony
>
> (E 144)

Blake's 'types' are at the same time his etched plates and his
typological symbols, produced in the Furnaces of Imagination from which Los draws all created things, including those
contrary emblems of deity 'the tyger' and 'the wooly lamb'
(73 : 17, 18, E 226).

The Chariots which appear in Heaven at the end of *Jerusalem*
are symbols of the creative energies by which contraries are
reconciled:

> The innumerable Chariots of the Almighty appeard in Heaven
> And Bacon & Newton & Locke, & Milton & Shakespear &
> Chaucer[1]

Heaven, Earth, and Hell have met in harmony. These
Chariots, with the Chariots of Divine Humanity which appear
next, have analogues in Ezekiel, Dante, Milton, and Keats;[2]
but again, as symbols of the regeneration of life through the
free play of energy in art, they have a special meaning in
Jerusalem:

> The Four Living Creatures Chariots of Humanity Divine Incom-
> prehensible

---

[1] 98 : 8–9, E 254. Fisher comments: 'By the end of *Jerusalem*, he had brought
together the world of Los which was that of Chaucer, Shakespeare and Milton
and the world of Urizen which was that of Bacon, Newton and Locke into one
vision. The orbit of space and time was redeemed from its fixed condition,
and he saw it as a creation of the human imagination—as a part of Eternity'
(pp. 200–1).

[2] See Frye, *Fearful Symmetry*, pp. 272–4; and Blackstone, *The Consecrated
Urn*, p. 106 n.

In beautiful Paradises expand These are the Four Rivers of
Paradise
And the Four Faces of Humanity fronting the Four Cardinal
Points
Of Heaven going forward forward irresistible from Eternity to
Eternity   (98 : 24–7, E 255)

Another similar conception is found in Jewish Merkabah
mysticism, according to which the initiate ascends to the
hekhaloth, or halls of God, in the Chariot of Ezekiel (the
'Chariot of fire' that Blake calls for in the lyric introduction of
Milton). These *hekhaloth*, which Professor Scholem defines
as 'the heavenly halls or palaces through which the visionary
passes and in the seventh and last of which there rises the
throne of divine glory',[1] suggest the halls of Los in *Jerusalem*:

All things acted on Earth are seen in the bright Sculptures of
Los's Halls & every Age renews its powers from these Works
With every pathetic story possible to happen from Hate or
Wayward Love & every sorrow & distress is carved here
Every Affinity of Parents Marriages & Friendships are here
In all their various combinations wrought with wondrous Art
All that can happen to Man in his pilgrimage of seventy years
Such is the Divine Written Law of Horeb & Sinai:
And such the Holy Gospel of Mount Olivet & Calvary . . .

(16 : 61–9, E 159)

These 'bright Sculptures' are the fabulous originals which
Blake saw in vision and rendered into works of art, which in
turn are to be approached by the Spectator 'on the Fiery
Chariot of his Contemplative Thought'.[2] Coleridge, too,
uses the Chariot as a symbol of the synthesis of Energy and
the Imagination when he speaks of

that reconciling and mediatory power, which . . . organizing . . .
the flux of the senses by the permanence and self-circling energies
of the reason, gives birth to a system of symbols, harmonious
in themselves, and consubstantial with the truths of which they are

[1] *Major Trends in Jewish Mysticism*, p. 45.
[2] 'A Vision of the Last Judgment', E 550. Cf. on the same page: 'By the
side of Seth is Elijah he comprehends all the Prophetic Characters he is seen
on his fiery Chariot. . . .' Blake did a separate painting on this subject.

the conductors. These are the *wheels* which Ezekiel beheld . . . The truths and symbols that represent them move in conjunction and form the living chariot that bears up (for us) the throne of the Divine Humanity.[1]

* * *

'I know of no other Christianity', Blake wrote in his address 'To the Christians' on Plate 77 of *Jerusalem*, 'and of no other Gospel than the liberty of both body & mind to exercise the Divine Arts of Imagination.' Jerusalem, who is named Liberty, is the Emanation of the Giant Albion: she is a symbol of the community men and women could establish now if they were to practice the arts of life as 'sports of Imagination'. Art, to Blake, is the highest and most unitive activity of mind and body, but all life aspires to the condition of art. In *Jerusalem* Energy and Imagination meet in a new synthesis, the best exemplification of which is the great poem itself—a little world made cunningly, microcosm and object of art, painting, and prophecy—the Emanation of William Blake.

---

[1] 'The Statesman's Manual', in *Complete Works of Samuel Taylor Coleridge*, ed. W. G. T. Shedd (New York, 1853), i, 436–7.

APPENDIX A

The Argument to The Marriage

The Argument has been something of a puzzle for students of Blake. Some elements of it are clear, others obscure. Rintrah is wrath—but is he prophetic wrath or the counter-revolutionary wrath of Pitt as in *Europe*? Do his fires suggest the impending invasion of France by the allied powers or the Revolution itself? The 'sneaking serpent' must be, as usual, the priest, but what does Blake mean by saying *Now* he walks 'In mild humility' if the Revolution has already taken place? Or is he, as Erdman has suggested, the *émigré* priesthood in England (*Blake*, p. 176)? These problems involve the sequence of events; the meanings of the images are clear enough. I suggest that the Argument becomes understandable if we do not assume that the regained paradise of lines 9–13 is the Republic, or that the Argument was written later than the pages immediately following it.

If E 723 is correct in saying that in Blake's early lettering the serifs on the *g*'s point rightward, and that a leftward-pointing serif appears in the later parts of *The Marriage* to be maintained consistently until 1805, then the Argument is one of the earlier plates, along with the five plates immediately following it. Therefore there is no reason to believe that the Argument was written later than 1790, which is the year referred to on the following plate. These two pages are also closely connected thematically, the Argument drawing imagery from the two chapters of Isaiah which are cited on Plate 3. The meaning of the Argument must therefore concern the events leading up to and immediately following the Revolution, and not the formation of the coalition against France in 1792. Such a conclusion accords completely with the Argument's thematic function: *The Marriage* is a celebration of 'the return of Adam to Paradise', and the Argument leads up to this event.

The poem has four clear divisions, framed by a two-line refrain at the beginning and end. The divisions are indicated by the words 'Once', 'Then', 'Till', and 'Now'. If we understand what periods of time are meant by these divisions, we will understand the Argument itself. I suggest that these are: the period of the Old Testament, that of the New Testament, the 'night of Nature' or modern history, and the Revolution. *Once*—after the expulsion from Paradise and through the following age—man was a wanderer and an exile, walking the 'perilous path' that had been ordained for him. *Then* a new Adam, Christ, appeared in fulfilment of the messianic prophecies. Briefly there was a new Paradise on earth, *till* Christianity was subverted from within by 'the villain', who pretended to follow the perilous path only to found an institutional church. *Now* there exists a society calling itself Christian but with no place for the just man in it. The spirit of prophecy has been driven into the wilderness, to return appropriately in the form of a wild beast. The French Revolution will create another earthly paradise, but this time it will come about through God's Wrath.

APPENDIX B

Nights VIIa and VIIb of The Four Zoas

Two Nights of *The Four Zoas* manuscript are clearly headed 'Night the Seventh.' VIIb was at one time considered earlier than VIIa (see Sloss and Wallis, i. 137–8). However, there is considerable evidence to suggest that VIIb is the later of the two, before additions. One point is the stitch marks which show the manuscript to have been bound at one point, the sheets with elegant script (pp. 1–18, 23–42) in one group and the *Night Thoughts* proof-sheet pages in another (pp. 43–84, plus 111–12). The latter group includes Night VIIa and the three preceding ones. Thus Nights I through VIIa were stitched in two bundles, but VIIb was not stitched (see B 163). It is true (as E 737 argues) that this might mean VIIb was so early that by the time Blake stitched the manuscript, VIIa had already been written to replace it. However, there are two other unstitched Nights, VIII and IX, both unquestionably later than the stitched ones. It seems likely, then, that VIIb is later as well.

A second point is that Night VIIb in its original form took up exactly where VIIa left off (see M xiii). Later Blake inserted a direction changing the order of VIIb, and he also wrote a new ending for VIIa. This new ending connects VIIa directly with VIII (see E 758), which suggests that by the time he wrote it, Blake intended to set VIIb aside.

Index